EDWARD WRIGHT

INCIDENTS IN THE LIFE

OF

EDWARD WRIGHT

BY

EDWARD LEACH

AUTHOR OF "SKETCHES OF CHRISTIAN WORK AMONG THE LOWLY"

SCRIPTURE TESTIMONY EDITION

WALKING TOGETHER PRESS
ESTES PARK · JENTA MANGORO

© 2023 Walking Together Press

Published in 2023 by
Walking Together Press
Estes Park, Colorado USA
Jenta Mangoro, Jos, Plateau Nigeria
https://walkingtogether.press

ISBN: 978-1-961568-26-6

Incidents In The Life Of Edward Wright is in the public domain
Text and images from the 1871 edition published by McKinney and Martin, Philadelphia

Cover design by D. Thaine Norris
Typeset in Adobe Garamond Pro by Peter Kurdor and D. Thaine Norris

1

ABOUT THE SCRIPTURE TESTIMONY EDITION

IF VICE ever had a home, it was probably in the heart of Edward 'Ned' Wright. Born in 1836, Ned was so reckless that many believed he could never change from his life of drinking, smoking, wife-beating, stealing—even stealing from the dead. Yet, defying all expectations, Ned underwent a profound transformation. This narrative chronicles his journey from being an unwitting instrument for Satan in the abyss of sin, to the comforting embrace of Jesus, where he was able to lead hundreds like him to new life. This biography is a testament to the transforming power of the gospel of Jesus and how it can change even the most hardened of hearts. It is also a collection of stories that demonstrate the reality of God and the truth of His word.

The *Scripture Testimony Index* is an extensive research project by the story enthusiasts at Walking Together Press using artificial intelligence and data science to develop a New-Testament-driven subject index across a large body of missionary biographies and personal narratives. Data science reveals trends and patterns in information. In analyzing the database of these books programmatically; beautiful, bright threads emerge—threads of prayer, provision, deliverance, specific leading, healing, transformation, revival, and miraculous conversion. The end result is an index of short story excerpts organized by subject and Bible verse that empirically demonstrate the truth of the Scriptures, and which is freely available on our website at https://walkingtogether.life. Another result that bubbled to the surface of this research was the discovery of dozens of great books that are long out of print and in danger of being forgotten. The *Scripture Testimony Collection* is a set of these books that we so enthusiastically recommend, that we have made the effort to republish them.

Walking Together Press has enhanced this classic title, *Incidents in the Life of Edward Wright,* by adding forty-one *Scripture Testimony* boxes in the text identifying Biblical topics and verses that are demonstrated by a specific portion of the narrative. An extensive *Scripture Testimony Index* has been added at the end containing short summaries of how each Scriptural topic is illustrated, making it easier to locate specific stories.

CONTENTS

CHAPTER FOURTH

CHAPTER FIFTH

CHAPTER SIXTH

CHAPTER SEVENTH

CHAPTER EIGHTH

CHAPTER NINTH

CHAPTER TENTH

CHAPTER ELEVENTH

CHAPTER TWELFTH

CHAPTER THIRTEENTH

CHAPTER FOURTEENTH

CHAPTER FIRST

CHAPTER FIRST

I PROPOSE TO relate the story of the life of one who has been a criminal by profession, but is now a Christian and an evangelist.

The author shares too much the feeling which distrusts biographies of men written and published during their lifetime, to regard it as altogether unreasonable. Such memoirs are liable to be one-sided or highly coloured, and so unintentionally to deceive the public. They may even injure the Christian character of their subject, and either create an offensive pride which did not already exist, or fan a pride but too natural to humanity. Moreover, godly fear lest a subsequently blemished reputation should dishonour a previous profession, may well make a Christian author careful before undertaking a biography necessarily incomplete. This last objection must be left to Him who giveth the grace of perseverance to His saints. As to the others, the writer can only say,—

1. That this record of the life of a singularly earnest preacher of the gospel has been honestly and conscientiously written. Care has been scrupulously taken lest any statement of facts should have been in the slightest degree overdrawn; and to secure this each narrative has been subjected to revision by Mr. Wright, under whose sanction the work is issued; and the author has consulted many letters; the originals of which he has seen.

Some of the narratives, undoubtedly, are sufficiently startling to suggest to a few minds the question of their probability. As, however, they have nearly all been related by Mr. Wright himself, in the presence of those who

1

could readily have contradicted them if false or exaggerated, the reader may be assured of their truthfulness.

2. Those who know the subject of our sketch will cheerfully bear witness to his childlike spirit and general simplicity of character. If during his unconverted days he seemed to show much of the cunning of the serpent, the grace of God has given him since then much of the simplicity of the dove. The notoriety which he has already gained does not seem to have lessened his Christian humility, and the author therefore believes that the publication of this volume will not do it.

Many things are omitted which might have been related of Wright's career prior to conversion, but only those incidents are selected which fairly represent the kind of life he led when glorying in evil. Mr. Wright does not relate his most remarkable misdeeds as feats of which to be proud, but to illustrate the far-reaching energy of the grace of God. It is with this object that they are recorded here.

———

EDWARD WRIGHT was born in Lambeth on the 28th of July, 1836. His parents belonged to humble life, his father being a journeyman barge builder, amiable and honest, but until his conversion addicted to occasional intemperance. This event happened when Edward—or, as he is now familiarly called, Ned—was a child. The family lived in Pitt's Place, Bankside, where they occupied a small house, part of which they let. The banks of the Thames being much lower than at present, the high tides caused considerable inconvenience and dismay; and the cry of children announcing that "the tide was over" might frequently be heard in the alleys skirting the river. On one occasion the tide was very high, and Ned's mother sat at the window with her child, watching her neighbours stopping up the crevices of their doors with clay, and getting indoors by the windows to observe the progress of the tides. With the exception of a female lodger, who owed her twelve weeks' rent, the mother and child were in the house alone; and when the water ran in the doorway, and began to cover the floor, she cried for assistance to a man who came in a boat down the court. He, however, rowed on to the rescue of his own family, and Mrs. Wright was compelled to entreat the services of the lodger upstairs, and offered to forego all claims for rent if she would rescue her and her child. This was done, although the water in the room reached above the knees, and rose yet higher before the tide began to fall. Ned's father had endeavoured to make his way home by holding on to the railings of New Park Street Chapel, and walking along the brickwork. Suddenly, however, the top of the rails gave way, and he, falling into the water, had to wade through it, and so reach home. Soon after this occurrence, impelled by motives of curiosity, he ventured with his wife into the chapel where the late Rev. James Smith, the author of well-known devotional works, was preaching. Both were that evening converted to God, and immediately the home presented a different aspect The father ceased from his drunken habits; the Bible was read, and a blessing asked upon the provisions of the table.

As a child, Ned was noted for insensibility to danger, and although regarded as a favourite, he was permitted to play at the edge of the river. On one occasion he was nearly drowned, and being severely hurt, he was taken home insensible, and appeared to be dying. Having rallied, he was seized with the whooping-cough, which was cured in a singular way. His father, adopting the advice of friends who evidently believed in the rough-and-ready mode of cure, took him in a boat, and rowed him through the arch of Blackfriars Bridge against wind and tide; whilst passing through, he fell into a severe fit of coughing, during which his father compelled him to face the wind; and this method of treatment, which might have killed another boy, cured him. He soon showed a propensity for fighting; for he quarrelled with a neighbour's child, and brutally struck her who subsequently became his wife. From fighting he advanced to other feats of juvenile daring, and, craving money, he leagued himself with other boys to rob the till of a small shop. This was done one winter's evening, young Ned being the leader of the plot, and entering the shop upon his hands and knees. The stolen money was spent on baked potatoes, fried fish, and stewed eels. He thus acquired a taste for thieving, and no doubt the success of his first effort encouraged him to make a second venture. It was in vain his father, fearing he might fall into mischief through staying out late in the evening, watched his actions more narrowly. Though he was taken to chapel, and admitted into New Park Street Sunday School, accompanied his father on his rounds in the neighbourhood as a tract distributor, and often heard the simple utterances of his parent's devout heart at the prayermeetings held in his house, his disposition to pilfer increased. He could not be kept at school; every school into which he entered he was repeatedly reprimanded for bad conduct, and ultimately expelled. His father succeeded in getting him into the Blue School in Southwark; but before he had been there long enough to entitle him to the quaint costume of the school, he decamped, stealing several of the bright badges the boys then wore upon the breasts of their coats, and selling them for old brass. He was then sent to a school connected with York Road Congregational Chapel; but at the beginning of the second quarter, instead of taking the fees to his master as requested, he spent them with his companions upon curds and whey and cake. For this he was chastised; and while he was being punished, a neighbour expressed her satisfaction therewith. This aroused his ire, and, vowing vengeance against the woman, he resolved to throw a large knife at her; in attempting to carry out his designs, he fell with his head against a brick wall, making a deep gash in the top part, at least two inches long, the scars of which remain to this day. It was about this time that young Wright was treated for disease of the liver, and the doctors gave him up as incurable, believing that if he reached the age of fourteen, he would never see the year of his majority.

Ned's father finding employment in Battersea, the family removed thither; and the young pilferer found many opportunities, in passing some plots of garden ground on his way to and from school, to steal the produce grown by the labouring men. So incorrigible and hardened was he, that the schoolmaster found it impossible to keep him any longer, and once again he was expelled. His father thereupon resolved to find him a little employment at home, and send him to a night-school. Accordingly, an old barge was bought, broken up, and carted home, and Ned was left to chop it up, and dispose of it in penny and twopenny lots. The sight of the money proved too great a temptation, and he fell a victim to it. Again he was punished; but, undeterred, he continued his evil practices, until he was recognized by the neighbours as "a pest of a boy."

It must have been with no little anxiety that his parents put him to work. He was first employed to chop wood for a publican; he was then engaged at four shillings per week to frighten birds and follow the plough; and afterwards laboured in the yard where his father was employed, but so irregularly as to cause him great sorrow and perplexity. He was soon discharged, being accused of stealing half a sovereign which he had as change. Four days afterwards he met a "running man," who was then training to run a race, and Ned, with other lads, ran with him. The. man, evidently pleased with the lad's agility, gave him half a pint of ale, which intoxicated him. When he recovered, he found that someone had untied his handkerchief, and opened his waistcoat; and, as he was about to button the latter, he felt something like a piece of metal between the button-holes, which he discovered to be the half-sovereign he was supposed to have stolen. The youth was not so hardened in crime as to refuse to listen to the whisperings of conscience, and he was for some time undecided as to whether he should take the money to its rightful owner or not. He balanced the reasons for and against with much skill; but, alas! concluded in the debate between conscience and wrong-doing, that the "Noes" had it. The half-sovereign was spent in a few days, and shared with his evil associates. With the view to deliver his son from his bad companions, the father found work, and removed to Rotherhithe. Here Ned was sent to a Wesleyan Sundayschool, and was so impressed by witnessing the funeral of a scholar there, that hopes were entertained of a favourable change in the lad's feelings. The impression did not last long, and on the Thursday evening following, he took one of his mother's brass candlesticks, hid it in the yard, struck it with a large hammer against a stone, which doubled it up, and then he took it to a rag-shop, and obtained for it, as old brass, the sum of fourpence.

Like most boys, he had heard the story of "Jack Sheppard," or some one of the many versions of the story which has had such mischievous effects upon young lads. Many a thief has received his first education in his business at the penny gaff or theatre, where the play of "Jack Sheppard" arouses all the enthusiasm of the vitiated tastes of the boys of London. Ned only required a little stimulus to make him a skilful and habitual thief, and this he found one evening at a theatre in the south of London, where the play was being performed. It was his first visit to a theatre.

> "I was not a little startled at the glaring gas and scenery," says Ned; "and as I watched the performance, I well remember how often I fancied I could have got over the top of the walls of that house as well as 'Jack Sheppard' did, and I am sure I was taught that night a way to thieve, and escape without being caught, that I was not acquainted with before."

He did not leave the theatre until twelve o'clock, and it was not until one in the morning that he reached home, where he found his mother sorrowfully watching for him. Not being able to muster sufficient courage to meet his father at the breakfast-table on the following morning, he did not go to work all day; but before tea, and while suffering from hunger, he fell in with some lads who were known as "shore wreckers," and they invited him to go with them. He did so, and was appointed by the gang of five to act as sentry outside the door of a sweetstuff-shop, and to watch how cleverly the money was abstracted from the till. This was done without observation, and the amount, which was only twenty farthings, was divided among the five thieves. The money was soon spent, and half an hour afterwards, Ned was called upon to become the hero of the next adventure of a similar kind. Although trembling for fear of detection, he succeeded in his purpose, and not only abstracted from a till the sum of five shillings, but also stole a box of sweetmeats. Losing his situation through inattention to his duties, he ran from home, and spent three weeks in robbing summer-houses of spades and shovels and similar implements, and living upon the money realized by their sale. His anxious mother, who had indeed sought him sorrowing, was greatly rejoiced at finding and persuading him to return to the paternal roof. His father had concluded that he had gone to sea, and so had let his bed to a single young man, with whom it was now arranged that he should sleep. A fortnight, however, had scarcely elapsed before Ned sought his opportunity to effect a petty pilfer. This time he robbed his bed-fellow of a shilling, with which he bought an egg chest, which he rendered water-tight, and covering it with pitch, he put his extemporized boat into the river at the back of the garden, and found her capable of holding two and a half hundredweight. When the boat was finished, and it became dusk, the young voyager proceeded with it along the river, to some orchards, where he obtained a large quantity of apples and pears, and other fruit, part of which he ate, and the remainder sold to a greengrocer, who afterwards engaged the adventurer in his shop: this arrangement was soon broken in consequence of his thieving propensities. Again he ran from home, sustaining himself as before by committing petty thefts. It is unnecessary to detail each case, if that were possible. Some depredations were very ingenious, others were stupid in design, and ineffective in execution. Once he ventured into a ship's cabin, and stole a compass, which proved to be almost as awkward a possession as a white elephant. Not knowing, also, the value of the article, he broke in pieces the metal part of it, and sold it for old brass to a marine-store dealer, for fourpence a pound.

In all this he was not happy. Fear at times seized his buoyant spirit, and as he heard of the imprisonment for twenty-one days of a companion, he trembled lest such a fate might happen to him. Hungry and weary, he repented of his unfeeling conduct towards the parents who had made numberless efforts for his reformation. Without food the whole of one day he was glad to pick up a number of old nails from the shore to obtain one halfpenny, with which to purchase dry crusts. The baker filled his cap with pieces of bread, some of which were quite mouldy; and sitting down upon a doorstep, he ate with tears, but not with relish, the dry bread he had purchased. He resolved to wander to some spot where, in the dull light of the evening, his mother would be sure to pass; and when the poor woman met her ragged and deplorable son, she burst into tears of deepest grief. Not daring to take him home, she arranged for his staying all night at a neighbour's house; and in a few days his father prevailed upon a pilot to get his unruly son into a ship in the coal trade. As Ned had learned to row with some skill, the captain consented, and so he proceeded on board the *Ann of Hartlepool*, which place was to be her destination.

It was a beautiful day when he first stepped upon the vessel's deck, and the voyage promised to be pleasant and satisfactory. Up to the time of reaching Gravesend, Ned had been running about the ship's rigging like a wild cat, when a breeze suddenly setting in, the ship rolled heavily, and the young sailor fell sick, and began to curse his fate. Added to the pangs of a troubled conscience, he had to bear the reproaches of the captain and men, who likened him to Jonah, and offered to make some whale a present of him. This, it would seem, greatly disturbed him, for he clearly remembered the story of "Jonah in the whale's belly," which he had heard in the Sabbath-school; and when the ship reached its destination, one of the sailors terrified him by observing, "Now, old fellow, we mean to sell you and the ship together to the devil, and in a few days you may make up your mind to go down to Davy Jones's locker," which is supposed to be situated at the bottom of the sea. The captain and the men left the ship with a broom at her masthead, signifying that she was for sale, Ned remaining on board, eating the remains of "salt junk" and biscuits.

> "At the end of the week," he says, "having visited several ships, whose men very kindly gave me a little to eat, I was compelled from destitution to beg my way from door to door in the town of Hartlepool; this lasted for about ten days, when I at length persuaded the captain of a vessel, called the *Stokesley of Stockton*, to give me a passage to London; but we had only just fairly got out to sea when I again fell a victim to sea-sickness."

The ship being heavily laden, he had to lie about her decks both night and day, being cuffed and beaten by the sailors, who were anxious to get him out of the vessel altogether. When they had reached Gravesend, one of the sailors who thus desired to be rid of his company, seeing a "billy-buoy," or one-masted vessel, coming up the river, advised him to ask the captain to grant him a passage to London. This he did, and having gained permission, he was soon on board.

> "When I reached the deck of the 'billy-buoy,' her captain said that up to that very moment they had had a most beautiful passage; but it seemed to me that, from the day of my arrival on board, the ship was in constant trouble; for no sooner were we clear of one ship than we ran foul of another, and by high water,

instead of being near London Bridge, we were only opposite the town of Woolwich; and then, turning to me, the captain said, 'If we never had a Jonah on board before, we have certainly got one now; for we haven't had a bit of luck since you reached the ship: and so the sooner you get upon the shore, the better I shall like it.'"

Having picked up a small sailor's chest in the river, he resolved to take it ashore with him, to sell it at Woolwich; but before leaving the "billy-buoy," he put thirty of the captain's biscuits into it. At the arsenal gates he was stopped by several policemen, who demanded to know what he had inside the chest upon his shoulder; but ultimately he was allowed to pass, and after selling the box in the town, he walked on to London, puzzling his brains as to how he could account for his return home. After sundry efforts of the imagination, and failures in rendering his story harmonious, he concocted the following excuse:—

"We had a very fair passage to Hartlepool, where I joined another ship, agreeing with the captain for thirty shillings for the run home; we had not, however, been at sea more than two days and two nights, when I, being on the look-out, observed breakers ahead, and accordingly turned all the hands up; but before the ship could be brought about, she struck the rocks. The wind being at this time very fresh, she soon went to pieces, the captain and all the men were drowned, and I alone escaped to tell the tale."

A very likely story, indeed! And yet, strange to say, it was believed, and Ned was sympathised with by his relatives and neighbours. It so happened that Ned's uncle, who was an old sailor, heard the yarn, and disproved it to every one's satisfaction but the mother's, who gave credit to her son; and thus he was permitted to remain at home. Work was procured for him with his father, and for some few weeks he conducted himself properly, bringing home the money he earned, and resolving to labour honestly and with diligence. His weakness was not idleness, nor can it be said that he ever lacked in industrial enterprise, but his love of mischief was ever a prevailing passion.

CHAPTER SECOND

CHAPTER SECOND

THE GOOD resolutions which Ned had formed immediately upon his return from the unlucky voyage were soon forgotten. The taste he had acquired for pilfering grew upon him, until the temptation to steal became irresistible.

Unfortunately, he was surrounded by evil companions, who rejoiced in his daring spirit, and urged him to attempt bolder deeds than he had

SCRIPTURE TESTIMONY
Bad company corrupts good morals
I CORINTHIANS 15:33

yet committed. Among his friends was a young man, reputed to be one of the worst characters in Rotherhithe, who had been convicted before the magistrates thirty times for various offences, and Ned was now recognized in the neighbourhood in which he lived as an associate of thieves. His companion was known by the nickname "Witty," given him because of his ready and acute replies to the questions of his comrades. He was a professional thief, who was considered to be well qualified to train others in the calling he had chosen.

Passing one day along Swan Lane, Rotherhithe, Ned met an aged and infirm gentleman, known to possess a considerable independency, who, because of eccentric habits, was frequently the object of the insults and assaults of the boys of the district. From sheer love of mischievousness, Ned picked up the head of a fish, lying at his feet, and threw it with such force at the old gentleman as to knock off his hat. This act of wanton aggression was not resented at the time; but two days subsequently a policeman laid hold of Ned by the collar, and having charged him with the assault, led him to the station-house. The next day he was taken to Greenwich police-court, before the stipendiary magistrate, who sent him to Wandsworth prison for seven days, without the option of paying a fine. During his imprisonment, Ned determined to have his revenge upon the old man when he gained his discharge; and having solicited the advice of his friends, a plan was concerted among them to rob his premises. They had well surveyed the house, and made all necessary arrangements; but as the night came on, they learned that the owner had died. In the presence of death the hardiest of profligates have been cowed; and had not Ned and his associates been past all feeling, they would scarcely have ventured upon their heartless errand. Ned was still impelled by revenge, his companion by plunder, and death itself had no deterring power upon their hearts. The house was situated by the side of the Grand Surrey Canal and Docks, to which was attached a warehouse for the storage of the deceased man's goods. The two thieves perceived that an entrance to the warehouse could easily be effected from the towingpath of the canal; their plan, therefore, was to enter the Surrey Canal at a point where they could be unobserved by the night watchmen who patrolled the docks. They had noticed that, from the day of the old man's death, the warehouse had been closed, and they calculated that after the funeral an inventory of its contents would be taken, after which a robbery could be more easily traced, and the goods identified. They therefore resolved to commit the robbery on the night before the funeral; which they did, effecting an entrance into the building in the way described, and stealing therefrom several hundredweight of brass sheaves used for ships' blocks. The property was, of course, disposed of to a marine-store dealer who was in concert with the thieves of the district

Prior to this event, Ned's father had bound him apprentice as a waterman; and in order to secure the approval of the Waterman's Company, he was compelled to go for one month to a night-school, to learn to write. To him this was a difficult task, and although not succeeding very well, he managed to be able to write his name intelligibly. Had it not been for his association with "Witty," and with a worthless woman, he might have gone on for a time soberly and well. But the society of the latter was mostly, and money was needed to retain it; and his fellowthief so influenced Ned's mind that Ned could not resist the temptation of dishonesty. The consequence was that he again lost his employment, and so was thrown more hopelessly into the path of ruin. The restrictions of home became increasingly irksome: his father's admonitions and prayers made him wretched, and he longed to get away from those who sought so earnestly and persistently to restrain him in his evil courses. His mother's heart continually vibrated between hope and fear; at one time she was buoyed up with the hope that prayer would be answered; at another, she sank into despondency and sorrow. Often did she creep out of her bed room in the small hours of the morning to let her prodigal son in at the window, when his father had locked him out; and hour after hour, in the loneliness of her grief, would she lie awake, listening for the sound of the footstep she knew so well, and had yearned to hear so long. When he was out, she feared he would be locked up, and if he did not return during the night, she would make inquiries early in the morning at the police-station, in order that if he had got into mischief, she might be present at the court, should a fine be inflicted, to save him the humiliation of gaol-life.

It is not our intention to detail minutely the many heartless tricks perpetrated at this time. Many of Ned's robberies were cruel; here is one illustration, not the worst that might be cited. "Witty" planned a scheme to rob sailors as they arrived home after long voyages —not an uncommon practice, as every one conversant with life in the neighbourhood of the docks knows. Ned was engaged to assist "Witty" in robbing sailors of possessions which they had acquired while abroad. A "crimp," or man who decoys sailors so as to get them into his power, was sent to Gravesend to act in the character of a boarding-house keeper. His instructions were to get on board some large homeward-bound ships, and persuade as many sailors as he could to lodge with him during their stay in the great city. As soon as the ship was in dock and moored, "Witty" and Ned took a horse and cart to the place, and found that six of these poor fellows had arranged to live with the crimp in his boarding-house; and as soon as they were discharged from duty, the cart was ready at hand to receive their clothes and any valuables they may have had. Each man had a chest and a hammock, with bed and bedding, which "Witty" and Ned put in the cart, and with the six sailors drove off from the dock to a house of infamy in Ratcliffe Highway. Having entered the house, the poor sailors were treated with beer, and thus were fairly allured into the meshes—so much so, as to be delighted with the kind reception given by the keeper of the brothel. The crimp gave orders to put the horse into the stable, and the clothes into the warehouse, assuring the unfortunate seamen that his servants would see to the proper unloading of the cart; but no sooner was the door closed upon the sailors, than "Witty" and Ned drove off with the horse and cart containing the baggage; and when sufficiently out of sight, they broke open the chests, and sold their contents to the Jews in Petticoat Lane. The crimp subsequently followed, and, of course, participated in the booty.

These and similar acts of thieving occupied Ned and his companion for seven months, during which, being suspected by the police, they were strictly watched, but succeeded in eluding the iron grasp of the law. At times they escaped narrowly, and were compelled to hide themselves during the day, and to assume various disguises. This kind of life, so fraught with danger, did not teach them wisdom; it rather led them to resolve upon some more desperate act. Seeing that their old haunts were getting "too warm" for them, and that their footsteps were tracked, their opportunities for replenishing their exhausted funds became scanty. They therefore resolved to commit a burglary, which, if successful, might put them in easy circumstances for a little while. They gained information respecting a certain house in Rotherhithe, where it was well known that money was always kept on the premises. They were both well acquainted with the house, and were able to perfect a plan by which they might gain admittance at a suitable hour, and in an easy way. It was found that the sergeant of police invariably finished his rounds between two and three o'clock in the morning, after which time the police were less apprehensive of their services being required. It was necessary also to choose some convenient spot where the tools required for the burglary could be securely hid, and where they could watch the movements of the police unobserved. An empty house.

"A dwelling-place, and yet no habitation;
A house,—but under some prodigious ban
Of excommunication,"

happened to be close by, and the haunted house was chosen for their hiding-place, and for the concealment of their tools. The premises were taken possession of at ten o'clock in the evening, just at the time when the policemen were changing duty for the night. On entering the old deserted house, they found it to be in a very dilapidated condition, and the staircase was broken down and shaky. Failing to gain access to the upper floors, they reached the first floor, in the middle room of which they secreted themselves, lying down on the floor for more than three hours, watching a favourable opportunity to carry out their purpose. The dreary desolation of the place, the moanings of the wind, and the rattling of the windowpanes, such of them as remained, contributed to produce an unaccountable feeling of dread in the minds of the two thieves.

"O'er all there hung a shadow and a fear;
A sense of mystery the spirit daunted,
And said, as plain as whisper in the ear,
The place is haunted."

Neither of them would hesitate to face an opponent, or to commit a desperate crime, in case of detection; they were not to be thwarted in their designs by fear; and yet, as they crouched like pitiable objects on the floor, they were made cowards by thoughts they had never entertained before. Every sound was significant of a danger that was new to their experience; they grew alarmed at the rustling of their own clothes, and so great was their fear that they dared not speak to each other, lest the sound of their own voices should be prophetic of some fearful impending doom. It needed only the appearance of a ghostly spectre to make them quit in sheer fright the scene of their crime. This condition of dread was becoming unbearable after waiting two or three hours; when Ned was suddenly seized with such intense pain and cramp, that he cried out and rolled on the floor in agony. London at this time was visited with the cholera, and this pestilence had now fastened on Ned, as he lay upon the floor uneasy and trembling. All hope of carrying out their evil project seemed to be at an end; Ned told his companion that some invisible power had taken hold of him, and that he could not move from pain. "Witty" only replied by curses and oaths, calling him coward, fool, and other names of equal potency, at the same time urging him by numberless considerations not to give up the enterprise on which he was bent. It was in vain. Ned could not go on; the job, he said, must be given up for that night. Amid the jeers and curses of his companion, the suffering man dropped down from one floor to the other, which shook him severely, and added greatly to his suffering; and he managed to reach the street, and to crawl to the house where his mother resided. Though he felt himself to be an outcast and a vagabond, and unworthy to enter his mother's roof, yet where could he go, but to that home he should never have left? But what was his surprise and disappointment when he reached the house to find it unoccupied—no cheerful light to guide him to its welcome hospitality, no tender mother to succour him in his sufferings! He knew many of his neighbours, but none to give him shelter. Then he remembered having heard that his father had removed to Bankside, a fact of which he took no notice at the time, but which he gladly thought of now he was suffering from weakness and pain. The distance was considerable; but it must be walked, and that quickly, for fear the police, who knew him well, might arrest him upon some charge. Never did he feel his loneliness more than at that hour. His companion had forsaken him in the crisis of difficulty and distress, and there was no one to help the poor doubled-up man to crawl along the streets to his father's home. Stopping at a public-house, he knocked loudly, hoping to purchase brandy to give him some relief from his agony; but the landlord had retired to rest, and would not wait upon him. His agony was so great that he felt like a maniac; he would have given anything for a bed and shelter; but he must crawl yet farther, and farther still, or die like a dog in the street within the reach of the policemen whom he both feared and detested. At length he found a public-house open, and having swallowed sixpennyworth of brandy he resumed his journey. The brandy, however, gave him no ease; his pains seemed to increase, and he could scarcely walk upright He was afraid to take the main road, lest he should be observed by the police; and whenever he heard their footsteps in the distance he was compelled to seek shelter in some quiet alley. An hour and a half was spent in this way, and when he reached his mother's door he fell helplessly on the step. In vain he essayed to reach the knocker— all strength had departed; he could only groan. Those groans were loud enough to secure the attention of any one who might be awake; but apparently all were asleep. And yet the mother had a quick ear for her son's misery, and as she lay in bed she fancied the faint sounds that proceeded from the door were those of her child. She tapped at the window, but was only answered by a deeper groan; she opened it, and called out, but Ned could only respond with another groan. The poor fellow presented a pitiable appearance when found upon the doorstep, drawn up with cramp, and in awful torture. The doctor was summoned; every means adopted to give relief, and at last the malady yielded to the curative appliances. Throughout the time he was thus carefully tended by the whole family, no word of reproach was uttered by his parents, and he was so astonished at the kind treatment he received, that it led him to deep reflection, and for the time he seemed humbled. His manner of life had courted the severest reproof, and his want of affection had been so marked, that he was surprised not to receive some word of reproach. Such unexpected and undeserved consideration won his admiration, and he resolved that for the future he would behave differently. He kept his vows while he was sick, but broke them almost as soon as he recovered. He soon found his old habits to have a stronger hold upon him than his mother's affection. It happened unto him, as the apostle Peter said, "According to the old proverb, the dog is returned to his own vomit again; and the sow that was washed, to her wallowing in the mire."

This was not the only warning he received at this period of his life.

Having been brought up at the river-side, he not unnaturally took great delight in the Thames, and even at the early age of fifteen he was considered to be a most expert swimmer, and one of the best divers in Rotherhithe. Some of his companions were to him objects of envy for their daring. He had frequently watched, with high glee and with great envy, a courageous lad, who loved to climb up a ship's rigging with the agility of a monkey, then to sit on the truck of the masthead, strip off his clothes, throwing them down on the deck, and descending in a state of nudity, jump fearlessly from the rigging into the river, and, after swimming for a time, return to the vessel. Sometimes this lad would go to the masthead of a collier, and slide down some of the backstays head-foremost. Ned soon began to venture upon like feats, and in many instances he succeeded, while at times he placed himself in positions of extreme difficulty and danger. Not that he calculated upon danger, or was deterred in his acts of daring by fear; and the more others attempted to imitate him, the more anxious was he to excel. It was about this time that an event occurred which he has never forgotten, which, indeed, he has often related in public as illustrating the word of our Lord, "One shall be taken, and the other left"

One summer's day, while attending to some pitch that was being boiled on the shore of the river, several of his companions came down to bathe. The tide was fast ebbing out, and the shore was getting dry; however, fearing the police, they got into a coal-barge and undressed themselves. There was an artificial bed where this barge lay, and at the outside a campshear or kind of wooden quay, beyond which was deep water. One by one the lads got into the water, on the side where it was shallow; but one who was more venturesome than the rest, named Larney Holmes, an older lad than Ned, made for the stern, where a rope hung over the side of the barge. Larney was one of those fierce young spirits whom no discipline could tame, and had gained an unenviable notoriety in Rotherhithe as an incorrigible thief, liar, and blackguard; even his own associates both feared and disliked him, although he was regarded as their leader. Knowing he could not swim, they entreated him not to go outside the campshear; but he only answered with a volley of oaths, requesting them to leave him alone. They ran towards him as he lowered himself by the rope over the side of the barge, they persuaded and threatened, and warned him; but his only reply was, "I'll chance it; if I don't, I'll be..." Letting go the rope with one of his hands, he began to search for the campshear, but in vain; and while he was thus clinging to the rope with one hand he grew alarmed, and, endeavouring with both hands to haul himself up again, the rope slipped, and he fell into the water, and sank, to the bottom. The tide was running out very strong, and carried him into greater depths. Immediately the cry was raised, "A lad overboard!" The watermen at the stairs were lounging about, some sheltering themselves from the intense heat, while others were asleep in their boats. The cry for help aroused them all, including Ned, who, leaving his pitch pot, ran hurriedly to the scene. When he arrived there, he found that Lamey had sunk a second time; and as he perceived two fingers of a man's hand on the surface of the water, Ned would not wait to take off his clothes, but plunged into the river, and diving beneath, seized the drowning lad as he was again sinking. The moment Larney felt the touch of his rescuer's hand, he laid hold of him, placed his arms and legs around Ned's, leaving him powerless either to help himself or Larney. It was a critical moment, requiring great self-possession, determination, and skill, and a desperate effort, which only a strong man could make. But Ned was equal to it. He struggled to get his legs free, and having succeeded, though with great difficulty, he made another effort to disengage himself from the lad's death hug, and as he was losing his consciousness his body was seen to rise to the surface. The watermen seized him by his hair, and dragged him, in an insensible state, to a boat; but Larney was drowned.

The excitement of the crowd that had gathered on the shore was intense; every one admired and applauded the heroism of young Wright, and the anxiety for his recovery from insensibility was universal. His father felt proud of his son, and listened with no little satisfaction to the applause which greeted his bravery. As for Ned, even in the lowest state of debasement into which he descended, he sympathised with human suffering, and was always ready to display his skill and strength in rescuing any one from perilous positions. He is not the first daring sinner who has put all the better enthusiasm of his nature into the service of God when that service has been preferred to zeal for Satan. As a good soldier of Christ, he has learnt to "endure hardness," and to fight bravely for the good and the true.

Larney's body was not recovered until three days afterwards, and among the followers of his remains to the grave was he who, but for the merciful Providence that watched over his life, might have been buried by the side of the drowned man. His high spirits, however, were not tamed; and while others felt impressed with the solemnity of the occasion, Ned felt no fear.

When he was told by a companion that it was through God's mercy he had not been drowned as well as Larney, he replied with the utmost indifference,

> "If the fool had not let go the rope, he would have been here now."

A more "darkened understanding" no man, surely, ever had; alienated from the life of God, through the ignorance that was in him, because of the blindness of his heart, the man who had thus been brought into close proximity with death still continued to have no fear of God before his eyes. He was as resolute a sinner as ever.

CHAPTER THIRD

CHAPTER THIRD

ONE OF the commonest thefts in which Ned Wright indulged was that of stripping buildings of lead. One night he agreed with his companion thus to rob a large warehouse. The occasion was not favourable, for the moon shed its clear silver rays upon the earth, and rendered any attempts at burglary exceedingly hazardous. Nothing daunted, however, an entrance into the building was effected, and by one o'clock they had stripped the whole of the gutters of their lead. Meanwhile, their operations had been watched by a servant occupying a bedroom at the top of the house, who rang the bell, which was answered by the proprietor himself. A rattle was sprung, and some policemen appeared. This was just as the two thieves were about to lower the lead down below with cords they had brought for the purpose. In his perplexity, Ned asked "Witty" what he should do, and was told to be firm, and they would win yet. It was arranged that Ned should make his escape by the waterside, from which the entrance to the 'warehouse had been effected, and that "Witty" should escape by the half-opened window. The parting words of the latter were, "Don't let any one take you, Sarvo;" which being roughly interpreted meant, 'you had better kill him than let him take you;' "but if you are collar'd, plead guilty, and swear you were all alone; and if I'm taken, I'll do the same; but it will have to be more than one man that takes me tonight." Ned and his accomplice thus parted; and in a few seconds the former arrived at the lobby door by which he had gained admittance.

Here he put out his head, and looking down observed a man standing on the shore immediately under him, guarding the door. Having some of the. lead that had been stolen by his side, he took a piece weighing probably about twenty pounds, and remembering his associate's advice to be firm, he dropped it with the intention of striking the policeman with it on the head; fortunately, however, it glanced off from the glazed top of the helmet on to the poor man's shoulder, when he screamed out, "Oh, my poor arm's broken." The aggressor decamped as the wounded policeman ran up the passage for assistance; and hurrying along the shore, and wading up to his waist through the mud, he arrived at a granary, where he washed his clothes by walking into the water. Here he found a man with whom he was acquainted, watching a barge that was laden with indigo in bales; and Ned was able to dry his clothes by the fire in the cabin. In the morning he was conveyed over the river, where he met his accomplice, who related to him the story of a most terrible encounter he had had with two policemen in effecting his escape. As Ned had not been seen during the night's adventure sufficiently to be recognized, he did not fear detection, but his partner thought it prudent to leave the neighbourhood for a time.

Wright also deemed it wise to steer clear of difficulty by obtaining employment. He found work in the West India Docks, of a rough kind, viz., loading and carting deal; after which he did the same kind of labour for a few weeks at the Surrey Canal. Unfortunately, he again resumed acquaintance with the profligate woman with whom he had been previously associated; and lacking money, he ventured into the rope-house, and abstracted half a coil of rope that was used for the rafts. As this was bulky, and he was known to be an associate of thieves, he did not go far before he was detained and taken to the police-station, where his pockets were emptied, and he was formally charged with the robbery. We will tell the rest of the story in Ned's own words:

> "As I stood upon the stone steps of the police-court at Greenwich, handcuffed, and looking at my poor mother, my better feelings seemed to say, 'If you persist in this game, you will break that poor woman's heart!' but the thought had no sooner risen in my mind than Witty's words, 'Be firm, Sarvo,' and also the 'Jack

Sheppard' scene passed before my eyes; so with a grin upon my countenance I descended the steps, and with the rest marched along the Deptford Road, followed by my mother, who bitterly bewailed and lamented my most unhappy lot. On arriving at the court, we were brought one after another before Mr. Traill, and the drunken night charges having been dealt with, my turn came. In answer to the question, "Are you guilty, or not guilty?" I boldly asserted my innocence by swearing that I was only carrying the rope for a man whom I did not know. But the magistrate, not being credulous enough to believe the tale, soon sentenced me to twenty-one days in old Brixton prison. Accordingly, in the evening of that day, I was conducted, with half a dozen others who were convicted of similar offences, into one of Her Majesty's royal carriages, which contained about eight little compartments, just large enough for one person to sit down in; and when we had started upon our journey, some of the company, evidently intent upon making the most of their present opportunity, began to sing a song, the chorus of which I joined in with vigour."

When the prisoners were within ten minutes' ride of the old prison, the carriage stopped, and the policeman who had been sitting outside opened the door, and inquired what they were disposed to drink before entering the "palace," as it was denominated by the "company" within. Orders for certain stimulants were delivered to those who could pay for them; the driver and "footman" participating in the luxuries thus provided. Up to the time of his imprisonment Ned had been sustained by the advice of "Witty" to be firm; but now, shut up in a lonely cell for twenty-one days, and having to work every day very hard for small supplies of bread and soup, his courage failed him; and remembering the home and comforts he had left behind, he gave vent to tears, and indeed spent very restless nights.

The second day of his imprisonment he was introduced to the treadmill, which was known among the prisoners as "the stepper." Among the twenty or thirty men and boys who worked on this wheel were several noted pickpockets; and one day, one of these, more daring than the rest, offered to lay a wager that he could pick the turnkey's pocket of a portion of hard tobacco which he was in the habit of carrying in his waistcoat pocket.

> "The bet was made with a fellow-prisoner whilst we were performing our task; and the next day, about three o'clock in the afternoon, the old gentleman (the turnkey) sat down upon his seat, and had what he called 'forty winks,' during the enjoyment of which the pickpocket, taking his turn with the others from the seat to the wheel, had to pass the turnkey, and in doing so he politely drew from the left hand pocket of his waistcoat the coveted piece of tobacco. I need scarcely say that the men on the wheel at the time were in ecstasies; but the most curious part of the affair was, that although the turnkey upon waking felt for his tobacco, he never at any future period made reference to his loss."

The successful thief next day had, for some mysterious reason, a double allowance of soup; and since Ned regarded this as a reward for cleverness, he felt jealous, and was moved with a like ambition. He was not clever enough to pick pockets, but he was resolved to obtain two pannikins of soup as well as his companion.

> "Accordingly," he relates, " as we followed each other like soldiers down to the gate, where each one put his pot down till the warder filled it, and then passed on, I managed to be on this day about the third in number, and having secured an empty pot, I no sooner got behind the door than, although the soup was terribly hot, I managed to drink it off in two draughts; and following the last man with my empty pannikin, having left the other one behind the door, I thus obtained a double allowance."

This manoeuvre was repeated on two other occasions, and, much to Ned's delight, the prison servants did not seem to discover the cheat.

When his term of imprisonment had expired, Ned was met outside by his aunt, who took him to her house, gave him a good beefsteak, with bread and coffee; and earnestly urged him, as she had often done before, to forsake his evil ways, and to begin to serve another and a better Master.

He learnt that his father would not permit his mother to meet him outside the prison gates that day, lest his neighbours should conclude that he in any way approved of his son's conduct. Leaving his aunt, Ned joined himself again to his old associates in Rotherhithe, to whom he related his experiences in prison, not forgetting his manoeuvre in getting a double allowance of soup, which gained very hearty applause; and his companions tapping him on the shoulder, and crying out, " Well done, Ned," made him feel that he had done something worthy of high honour. As for regret or shame at his disgrace, he lost it all in the presence of those who persuaded him to believe he was a hero, who was as worthy of respect as though he had returned full of honours to his native home, after having fought bravely for his country. One is not surprised to find that, animated by such feelings, he should have been daring enough to apply to the station-house for the tobacco-box and penknife which he had left with the serjeant there, upon his committal to prison. The former article he obtained at once; but the serjeant not being able to find the penknife, he was asked to describe it. This confused the applicant somewhat; but having observed a buck-horn-handled knife among those that had been turned over by the serjeant, he coveted it as being greatly superior to his own. This he described and selected, and the tale, when told to his companions, raised Ned so much higher in their estimation, as to cause him to be regarded as an exceedingly acute fellow. These incidents in his career were not unimportant; they had, at least, an influence for evil upon his life, leading him to a more defiant attitude towards society, and to a stronger determination to continue his dishonest practices. He was stimulated in this course by the necessity of providing money for carrying on an unholy acquaintance with the young woman who had before led him into difficulties; and in a short time he was connected with so many robberies that, finding himself watched, he was compelled to quit the neighbourhood. He had been summoned several times for assaults before the magistrate at Greenwich, and was thus well known to the police as an incorrigible offender. His character was but too well known in the district where he resided: and he was everywhere dreaded and shunned. While hearing him preach, the Sabbath before these lines were written, before three thousand people at the Agricultural

Hall, in Islington, a neighbour volunteered to the writer this statement:
"I know his face very well, sir; I have seen him hundreds of times in South
London." "And did you know him as a thief?" I asked. "Not exactly," was
the reply, "but as an associate of the vilest characters; and one of those
low fellows that you wouldn't like to meet with alone in the dark." And
any one who has seen Ned Wright's face when fired with the passion of
earnest determination, will have judged him to have been once an object
of dread by all who knew him.

It is probable that had he not removed just then from the neighbourhood, he would have been apprehended on a charge of being concerned
in a silk robbery. He left Rotherhithe, and, in an assumed name, became
a soldier. Having accepted the bounty money, and obtained his clothing,
he was, of course, expected to attend and learn the drill. But from the first
he felt averse to the duties he had accepted, and became a source of great
trouble to the drill-serjeant, an amusing Irishman, who had no patience
with Ned's conduct. Observing the new recruit stooping one day on the
grounds, he went up to him, saying, "Arrah, sir, what's the matter wid ye
now?" "Oh, sir," replied the ever-ready Ned, "I've got the stomach-ache."
On which the shrewd Irishman observed, as he put his hand to Ned's chin,
and attempted to straighten him out of his double position, "Sure, C—,
you're one of the Queen's bad bargains;" and seizing him by the back of his
neck, and amidst the laughter of the soldiers, he was hurled on one side,
and bidden to join "the awkward squad." This kind of life and treatment
soon disgusted the raw recruit, who seized the first opportunity to return
to London, where he learnt that, during his absence, two men had been
convicted for the silk robbery.

To his parents he vowed that he would alter his course of living, and
settle down quietly and honourably; and on this condition he was permitted to return to his home. For a little time he seemed to abide faithfully
by this resolution; but the old spirit of lawless rebellion still remained
within him, and once again he courted some of his old companions. The
irresistible charms of a bonfire on the fifth of November won him fairly
into the enchanted circle he had for a time forsaken; and it was whilst
in the old society, witnessing the commemoration of "Guy Fawkes' Day,"

that a quarrel arose between him and a young man, which it was decided should be fairly fought out in true British fashion.

Both combatants were well acquainted with what is called "scientific pugilism;" and although Ned was never recognized as a professional prize-fighter by the society that is organized for the purpose of aiding and abetting this brutal pastime, yet, as we shall hereafter show, he subsequently fought a prize-fight. His encounter on the present occasion was, however, preliminary, and gave him a taste for the ring. The fight continued for an hour, during which the hitting was very savage; and at the close Wright was pronounced to be the victor. He was soon booked for an encounter with another adversary, who, however, failed to come forward at the last moment with the full deposit; in consequence of which the previous deposits were handed over to Wright.

Then followed his celebrated fight with Harry Cooper, who was known at that time to be "very clever with the gloves." The whole of the deposits being made for this fight, the combatants with their friends repaired to a field, where a ring was extemporized, and the fight commenced. It had not long proceeded before Ned received so severe a blow on his nose as to break it, a disfigurement which remains to this day, as will be seen by his photographs. Wright has described this encounter in many of his addresses to the lowest classes, as having continued for two hours and a quarter; at the end of which he says,

> "We had become so blind as not to be able to see out of our eyes; and my second, understanding his work, whispered in my ear, 'Take five paces into the middle of the ring, Ned, and then hit straight out from the shoulder' this I did for about ten minutes more, when the sponge was thrown up in my favour. On our arrival home, it was very much feared that I should lose my sight; my head being like a pumpkin, it was so very much swollen. I had hardly arrived, however, at the Ship public-house, when my poor mother, again coming to my rescue, fearful lest I should be hurried from such a dreadful scene into eternity, took me home, and bathed my eyes and face, contriving also to keep me without any work until I got better."

As soon as he had sufficiently recovered, he ventured upon similar encounters, and became familiar with those haunts of vice known as boxing and dancing rooms. This continued until he was again imprisoned for felony. It appears that one morning, having previously attempted to hide in the river at the bottom of his mother's garden some 68 lb. of metal he had purloined, but had found it difficult to dispose of quickly, he was watched by a custom-house officer's wife, who was well acquainted with his daring character. Supposing that he had murdered a child, and to evade detection was throwing it into the river, she raised an alarm. Ned did not suspect this, but went quietly into the house, and sat down to breakfast with his mother. That very morning the poor woman had watched for the arrival of her son, who had been out all night; and when he came home after one o'clock, she fell on her knees by the side of his couch, crying out in great agony of soul, "O God, rescue my boy from the dreadful life he is leading, which must end in death and destruction to both body and soul."

Ned had listened heartlessly to the words of his sorrowing parent; but he well remembered them after his conversion. It was clear that his mother had suspected him of wrong-doing again, but was hardly prepared, just as they had begun breakfast, to see a policeman looking in at the window. Immediately Ned left his swooning mother, hurried into the back garden, and hearing a crash, he supposed it was the policeman forcing open the door; and so, dashing into the river, he swam across, and fled. For three days he managed to escape detection, although policemen were hotly pursuing him, when he was met at the corner of Hanover Street, Rotherhithe, by the same policeman who had looked into his mother's window, and was made his prisoner. After an examination at Greenwich, he was fully committed to Newgate, to take his trial at the forthcoming Old Bailey sessions. His prison experiences we give in his own graphic words; for, although no writer, Ned has the gift of telling graphically his own story:—

> "On arriving at Newgate, the scene was quite different from what
> I had expected; for, although obliged to be bathed and searched,
> they did not take my own clothes from me; and on going to rest
> at night I was surprised to find that my bed was a large door-
> mat, laid in the rack, after the style of sailors' berths. Here I met

with a young man companion, who turned out to be one of the cleverest pickpockets in London; and he declared to me that he was innocent of the crime with which he was charged, that of attempting to pick a gentleman's pocket of his handkerchief. I shall never forget this poor fellow, who anticipated being found guilty at the sessions. His trial came on the same day as mine, and I remember we all proceeded along a narrow passage from our ward, near where all the executed criminals are buried, to a cell at the bottom of the stairs, leading up to the dock of the court. It was this poor fellow's turn to go up before me, and after about half an hour he returned down the steps, clasping his hands together as he did so, exclaiming 'Seven years! Seven years!! Seven years!!! and all for nothing!'

"My turn coming next, I, not forgetting Witty's words, 'Be firm, Sarvo,' proceeded up the stairs into the dock. This being my first appearance at the Central Criminal Court, I seemed for a moment confused, and as one witness after another appeared to give evidence against me, the chain of which was so firmly linked together, that when their testimony was completed, the jury returned a verdict of 'guilty,' without leaving their box; but the judge, considering my father and mother's respectability, passed, upon me the lenient sentence of three calendar months' imprisonment at Wandsworth Gaol. In proceeding back again, we passed a room where I saw that my new friend had changed his clothes for the prison dress, and had very evidently been weeping bitterly; and after I had passed this man, his sobs were so loud that I could distinctly hear them.

"Next day a carriage-load of us proceeded to the New Model Prison, at Wandsworth, and, on my alighting from the carriage, I confronted a gentleman that I first knew as a schoolmaster at old Brixton prison, who said, rather humorously, 'Hallo, Wright, what, come home again? How long for, pray, this time?' 'A drag' (i.e. three months), said I, when, after some good advice, I proceeded to the baths, and then to the scale-room, where, with my prison dress in my arms, I was weighed; after which, having dressed myself, I was directed to my cell, the number of which was 'D I—IO.'

"I had not been there very long when the turnkey came in, and showing me an apparatus that looked like a mangle in the cell, he remarked, 'There, that's what we call hundreds and thousands.' This, I found the next day, I had to turn with all my might in order to make the pendulum of the clock attached to it move, which would not do so until so many thousand turns were made. If this had been an ordinary clock, I should have smashed it to pieces a thousand times over. A portion of old rope was rolled into my cell shortly after, and I began to pick this into oakum, until my fingers were fairly sore; but no extra food did I receive for my hard work. Now came a fresh move. I had next morning to go out to what they call 'the pumps;' and when there, I found I had to take a little box to myself, and work alone; for these cranks were connected one with the other, and I found out very soon by bitter experience, that if I did not move round as quickly as the other prisoners, the warder on duty would hear a sort of clicking noise, and he would then report me for neglecting my task. For this we were mostly punished by having to spend two or three days in the dark cells, which is not the pleasantest part of the prison to live in; for you have to do without your bed until nine o'clock at night, and then it is taken away again at four o'clock in the morning. This was one of the most trying 'bouts I ever had, suffering as I did the greater part of the time from the toothache, and eventually being obliged to have some of the teeth taken out.

"Fancying one day by a man's walk that I knew him, I concocted a scheme by which I might really know, it being impossible to recognize any one, every man's clothes being alike, and each man wearing a mask. The prison waste paper is previously dipped in a chemical solution to prevent us from smoking it, thus depriving us of every chance of indulgence of any kind. But one morning, on going out to the pumps, I found a little corroded upon a portion of the machinery of the cranks, and on the work being over I brought a little of this away upon my fingers'-ends, and in passing along I picked up a small stick of wood about the size of a match, the end of which I bit until it became almost like a brush, and then dipping it into my patent ink, I wrote on a piece of waste paper these words: 'Ned Wright, next cell;' and on coming back to my cell next morning from chapel— we had to go there every morning—in passing my friend's domicile, I threw this funny note inside. The following day, on our way to chapel, a voice whispered in my ear, 'Are you Ned Wright from Rotherhithe?' 'Yes,' said I. 'Are you Mike S —?' Nodding his head, I understood that I was right in my conjecture, and said, 'How long have you got?' when he answered, 'Two years.'

"After this, until we were removed into different cells, we used every opportunity we could get of communicating with one another by signs, having no one to speak to being a great privation to us, and the chance of making yourself known to any one, and thus beguiling away the time, being a great relief to the mind in such a place.

"At length, after three calendar months, my clothes were again shifted, and I received my discharge."

Leaving prison, he was full of expectations, as most prisoners are, of being greeted by a few of his old companions. As he stood upon the stone steps of the dreary building which could never be associated with the pleasant memories of home, feeling an inexpressible relief at

> **SCRIPTURE TESTIMONY**
>
> *Forgive the repentant brother*
>
> MATTHEW 18:21-22 · LUKE 17:3-4
>
> *God, with great demonstration of love, forgives the truly repentant*
>
> LUKE 15:11-31

having left so dreary a world behind, he looked upon the world outside, wondering what there was in it which would minister to his joy. Were there any who cared for Ned Wright sufficiently to cheer him now in his loneliness? Was there not one solitary friend who had shared his gains, and had rejoiced in his prosperity, to shake his hand, and congratulate him upon the end of his imprisonment? At a little distance from the huge gate, under the frowning arch of which he now stood, were a group of men and women waiting for the appearance of some of their friends; but they were unknown to the one released prisoner who stood gazing wistfully upon them. "I wonder how it is," thought he pensively, "that none of my old pals have come to meet me?" Full of these thoughts, with empty pockets, meanly clad in clothes that had in them many a rent and many a patch, he started forth to walk—whither he knew not. So awful a feeling of isolation in the midst of life made him wretched and despairing.

He had not taken many steps before he espied an aged grey-headed man, with a bundle under his arm, walking steadily towards the prison. Ned's heart sank within him as he saw it was the same good old man who years before had placed his gentle hands upon his unruly boy's head, and prayed, "O God, help me to plead with Thee until this boy of mine becomes converted." Those were quick steps that the ragged prodigal son took to go to his father, and it was the instinct of a better conscience that led him to ask for his forgiveness. And the father had brought the best robe he could afford, that his son might not begin life again in the tattered clothing of crime. That wonderful parental affection which Scripture uses to illustrate the unquenchable love of God— "Like as a father pitieth his children, so the Lord pitieth them that fear Him"—was richly displayed to the erring son. "Yes, I forgive you," he tearfully exclaimed, after having heard the accents of penitence; "but don't do it again, or you will send me and your poor mother with our grey hairs sorrowing to the grave." And so they walked, silent and sorrowful, to a neighbouring coachhouse yard, where Ned speedily exchanged his old rags for the brand new clothes provided by a father's love.

Surely he will not transgress again!

CHAPTER FOURTH

CHAPTER FOURTH

ALL WENT on smoothly for a time, until Ned had renewed acquaintance with his old companion whom he promised marriage. The date of this forthcoming event was settled. The parties had been asked three times in church. Indeed, the appointed morning witnessed half a dozen persons proceeding orderly to the church, and they had reached the steps, when a few words of disagreement led to not a few high words of anger, and with an oath Ned turned upon his heels, and left his intended bride to mourn her loss of a bridegroom and a husband.

Subsequently he obtained employment as a pot-boy, but whilst thus engaged he connected himself with another robbery, and found it again necessary to quit the neighbourhood. This time he journeyed to Chatham without any money, destitute and hungry, having been compelled on one occasion even to beg for a piece of bread. Arriving at Chatham, weary and footsore, he went direct to the casual ward, and obtained a night's lodging, with some bread and a pint of "skilly" in the morning, for which he had to work nearly four hours in the stoneyard.

After a few applications at the ship yard, he succeeded in joining the *Wellesley* as a sailor. He found the sailors exceedingly kind and generous; seeing him hungry, they gave him some food, and finding him unusually lively, they complimented him upon being "a jolly spark," and themselves upon the happiness of having so cheerful an associate. He says that it was the custom for every man in the ship to be served with half a quartern of raw rum; but that the men, not deeming this a sufficient allowance, agreed that two should have the whole, viz., twenty-four half-quarterns of rum, with the portion of water served therewith.

> "These two are called the 'captain' and 'mate' of mess, and we all accordingly got a turn of office once in twelve days; of course, as may be supposed, unless in the case of those who sold a portion of their allowance, they were nearly mad drunk after imbibing this quantity of spirits, and their quarrels sometimes led to a court-martial."

In a few days he received his sailor's clothes, and then he began to learn how to knot and splice. It was soon found that he could row admirably, and he was therefore appointed stroke-oarsman in what was termed the captain's "gig."

> "Soon after this," he says, "I received my three months' allowance of 3 lb. of tobacco, with some serge, flannel, stockings, boots, etc. and it being my turn ashore, not having any money, I thought I would put on some extra clothing under my usual things, to leave at the pawnbroker's in the town, and thus procure some. Accordingly I did so, and then spent the money in drink; but this money going only a little way whilst I was at the public-house drinking and dancing to the strains of the fiddle, I became very desirous of obtaining more, and soon parted with my flannel. The next day I did not care to go on board until I could obtain a 'livener,' or glass of grog. So in company of a Londoner whom I had picked up the night before, I passed by the door of a pawnbroker in the town, and coolly cutting the string brought away a large bunch of silk handkerchiefs which we sold to a Jew at one-third of their real value."

He spent the afternoon in dissipation, took a boat with his evil companions, and rowed down to Sheerness, and then got drunk and was unable to row the boat back again. The next morning he was taken back to his ship; but this being his first offence, he was only punished by having his liberty restrained.

Some time after, he obtained leave to go on shore with the "liberty men." He had previously had a quarrel with one of the boatswain's mates, and was resolved to have his revenge. Filled with murderous designs, he hid him self in a by-path along which the unsuspecting man would have to pass; and as he came, the would-be assassin drew out his sailor's knife, and was about to attack him, when a woman's scream from behind the hedge providentially arrested him, and thus Ned was saved from being a murderer, and from a felon's doom. After this deliverance, aroused by jealousy, he resolved to drown a young man; but again did God graciously intervene. Indeed, the heart sickens as one learns the many deeds of violence committed at this time. His mother came from London to see him, and he first got drunk, and then demanded and obtained from her, under threats, all the money she had. He was soon after imprisoned in Maidstone Gaol for another offence,—a punishment, as he rightly deemed it, for his scandalous behaviour to his mother.

"Out in one ward," Ned relates, "there were, as a rule, forty prisoners taking their food together. In the corner of our ward there was a cupboard with two shelves, in which the men were in the habit of putting a portion of their day's allowance of bread which was always served out in the morning, first sticking in it a piece of wood with a certain number of notches upon its end. Into this box or cupboard some of the prisoners used, after eating very largely of their own bread, to look out for the biggest piece there was, and change the sticks by sleight-of-hand, so that scarcely a day passed without some poor fellow coming short of his allowance. One day, thinking my skilly was very cold, I walked from my seat over to the fire, and putting my pannikin over the coals, endeavoured to get it a little warmer. At this time there were a great number of the German Legion in that prison, undergoing punishment for various offences, and one of these was made warder over us. It being his duty to keep our pannikins clean, when he saw what I was doing, he flew into a passion, and threatened if I did not take my pot from off the fire, he would report me. To which I, closing my fist, replied, 'If you do, I'll break your jaw.' Clearly understanding what I meant, he challenged me to fight it out in the prison courtyard. Accordingly, with a few of the others, we adjourned there for that purpose; but about the middle of the second round I struck my opponent on the nose, blackening both of his eyes. This soon put an end to the fight, and we were all very anxious to blind the turnkeys as to what had taken place; and after some persuasion we succeeded in getting the German to tell the turnkey that, whilst he was walking along the front of the bed-cell, he had accidentally run his head against the iron part of the door, and striking his nose had given himself two black eyes. This yarn took admirably, and was the joke of all the prisoners up to the time that I left the place."

Upon Ned's discharge, he succeeded in getting a berth as stoker on board the *Alacrity*, which was ordered to take part in a grand review at Spithead. Having arrived there, he spent his first evening on shore. He had but little money, but he obtained more by selling his good clothes for old ones. He was absent when the men assembled as usual, and it was not until the end of three days that he returned in a most pitiable plight. His linen was mostly in ribbons, his blue canvas trousers had one leg off at the knee, and the other torn half-way up the calf, and he was minus shoes, stockings, hat, and comforter. In this state he was put down into the cock-pit, with both legs and hands in irons, where he remained for three days. He would have been flogged, but the captain was good-natured, and content to punish him by keeping him on board.

Instead of feeling grateful, the prisoner at large was dissatisfied, and wished he had been punished, so that it might all be over, and he be allowed to take his turn in going ashore. The consequence was, he grew grossly careless, until one morning, about a fortnight after his offence, the master-at-arms, looking down the ship's hatchway into the stoker's hole, beckoned the malcontent upstairs, and whispered to him, "Don't be alarmed, old chap. I'm very sorry, but I must tell you the worst of it —they are making arrangements for you to be flaked (or flogged) this morning." At first, Ned treated the information somewhat cavalierly; but on observing the pitiful looks with which some of the sailors regarded him, and the sight of the grating at the main rigging, and then the cat-o'-nine-tails, with its green-baize handle, his courage began to fail. Still he remembered the advice, "Be firm, Sarvo," and tried to maintain his wonted indifference.

"One of the marines drew near me, and whispering in my ears, said, 'Here's a lead button, Sarvo; keep this between your teeth whilst being flogged, and it will save you, from biting your tongue!' Ere I had got the button fairly in my mouth, a shrill whistle echoed fore and aft the ship, followed by a loud shout from the boatswain's mate,—'Hands, all hands, to witness punishment.' The momentary bustle brought about by this sound soon gave me to understand that I was on board a man-o'-war. The 'blue-jackets' were galloping up the stairs, the marines were rattling their firearms, and everybody going towards the quarter-deck. This all took the bravery out of me; yet I waited in silence, striving to muster up courage to play the man, when presently two marines with fixed bayonets marched me on to the quarter-deck. Here I found all the officers in full dress uniform, and the blue-jackets arranged in rear of the marines. I had scarcely taken my position against the mainmast when the commander proceeded to read the articles of war, after which, speaking to me, he said, 'Strip, sir.' Having previously been told what to do by the ship's corporal, I proceeded to tie the lanyard of my knife round my waist, and pulling off both my guernsey and flannel shirt—both of which had been lent me—I stood barebacked, ready for the dreadful work. My hands having been stretched out, and tied up to the grating, and my ankles fastened together, the boatswain's mate took the cat-o'-nine-tails, and having tucked up his sleeves, stood near to me, awaiting his orders. For upwards of a minute there was dead silence; then the commander called out in a loud voice, 'Boatswain's mate, do your duty.' Instantly the cat-o'-nine-tails was raised in the air, and like boiling lead fell upon my back.

"One dozen lashes having been given, the doctor drew near, and having looked at me, nodded his head to the commander, who gave orders to the boatswain's mate to continue his work. During the infliction of the second dozen, in my heart I said, 'Oh that I might die, and get clear of this dreadful punishment!' when all at once the veil seemed to be torn from my eyes, and I saw my once dear and happy home, with my godly father and mother, the open Bible, and the morning and evening acts of devotion, and seemed to hear the solemn warning of 'After death comes the Judgment,' spoken so often by my father."

For about the first time he felt really afraid of death, and trembled as he seemed to be on the verge of a dread eternity. The bystanders little knew the thoughts that flashed one after another, in quick succession, across his distressed mind, and Ned throughout was careful to conceal his feelings, since he was resolved not to appear as a coward. Having received the two dozen lashes, the doctor again examined him, and finding his lips feverish, ordered a quart pot of water to be brought, and, after drinking the water, the punishment proceeded. The three dozen lashes having been duly administered, he was untied, and kept under the charge of a sentry until sunset, when he was expected to return to his work as usual.

This awful scene in Ned's life has been to him, since he has become a preacher of the gospel, pregnant with illustrations. In describing the agonies of our Lord, and the treatment He received when dying for a lost world, Ned has made an effective contrast, in a most reverent spirit, between the Innocent Sufferer and himself, the guilty transgressor. Ordinarily, such a comparison would shock the sensitive ear of an intelligent hearer; but as Ned pictures it to his rough listeners, the semblance of blasphemy is avoided. Deprecating, as the writer would, all comparisons between human sufferings and that unique agony of the Unique Man, Christ Jesus, he cannot see the impropriety of the statement that our Lord suffered a punishment He did not deserve, while the preacher was punished for his own transgressions, and yet he was refreshed by a good draught of clean water, which was not proffered the sufferer on Calvary, when He cried out, "I thirst." No doubt, some of his comparisons would not bear the test of legitimate criticism; but to Ned's humble hearers they are very significant of a truth which no criticism can overturn.

Ned had no sooner taken his seat against the hatchway that led down to the mess, than he found that some of his messmates had procured him a quart pot of grog, three parts of which were rum; they also provided him with clean soft linen to cover his lacerated back. The grog stupefied him, and caused him to sleep until he was released from the sentry's charge. At four o'clock in the morning he was ready to assist in the operation known as "holy-stone decks," or, as the sailors irreverently call it, "reading the Bible." This is done by a number of sailors kneeling several in a row, and rubbing the stones along a quantity of sand previously laid down, to make the decks white and clean.

The lessons Ned had thus learnt, one would have thought would remain indelibly impressed upon his memory, and serve as warnings against further transgression. But fear could not teach where love failed to move. He had been entreated and besought by those who had not even yet given him up; but these entreaties had been despised and neglected. Punishment had been inflicted, sufficient to deter any ordinary sinner; but when the pains were forgotten, the lessons which had accompanied them disappeared also. "A rod for a fool's back;" but the rod still leaves the man a fool. Let sceptics say what they will, here was a sinner whom nothing but a miracle could ever change.

The first opportunity that presented itself was seized to transgress again. His past misdeeds having been atoned for by the punishment he had endured, he was placed among the liberty men, and privileged to spend one night on shore. By playing skilfully with dominoes and cards, he had succeeded in obtaining some pocket-money, to pay for a bed and two or three pots of liquor. But, instead of returning the next morning according to the regulations, he did not reach the ship until late at night. For this he was severely reprimanded, and ordered to be kept on the black list for three weeks. This consisted in the first place of turning out half an hour before the usual time in the morning to sand the decks, ready for the men to rub them with the stones; in the usual time for meals being curtailed by one half; in doing all the servile work of the ship, such as tarring the rigging, scraping and blacking cannon balls, and other humiliating services. Added to this, the black-list men were served with what was greatly dreaded, namely, "six-water grog," instead of three-water grog; a change so much for the worse, that the grog, in consequence of the over-abundance of water, tasted like nauseous medicine.

About this time Her Majesty was expected to proceed by water to Queenstown. Accordingly, five or six despatch boats, together with the *Forth* frigate, were ordered to sea for a ten days' Channel cruise.

> "Unfortunately for us," says Ned, "we had not got more than four days' provisions on board; but, depending upon our neighbours, the anchor was weighed, the sails unfurled, the steam got up, and we proceeded outside Plymouth Breakwater. After keeping company with the frigate a few days, we fell in with heavy and stormy weather, so stormy, indeed, that all thoughts of taking care of our neighbours vanished, and the motto of each man became, 'Each one for himself, and God for us all.' Several times during this fearful storm it was thought it would be necessary to cut away the ship's masts; some of the men even lashed themselves to the rigging."

Yet, in spite of their being on the very verge of eternity, they continued to swear and blaspheme. Ned did not think it necessary to lash himself to the rigging; he thought that he was sure of going to hell, and something seemed to say to him, "You may as well go there now, Ned, as go there a little farther on." After a very stormy night they found themselves safely housed in Plymouth Sound, and were ordered back again for not bringing the frigate in company. This they proceeded to do, uttering fearful oaths, and muttering blasphemous curses all the way. Afterwards they proceeded to Portsmouth, where the *Alacrity* was paid off, and a week's holiday given, when they were expected to join the *Agamemnon*, then a training ship at Portsmouth.

A week's liberty was of no moral benefit to the depraved sailor. However, he went with some of his companions to London, where he lodged with his mother. Here he formed an acquaintance with a respectable young woman, who subsequently became his wife, the same person, whom, when a young girl, he ill-treated. When the day arrived for his departure for Portsmouth, his mother managed to raise sufficient money to pay his fare down. On arriving at the railway station, half an hour before the departure of the train, he found some of the ship's company half drunk; and with them and some other depraved wretches he spent the night, and at four the next morning he awoke out of a drunken sleep in the streets of London, where he had been for more than three hours.

His career at Portsmouth was as wicked as ever; getting drunk, committing robberies, and neglecting his duty. At last he was put in irons on board ship.

"After I had been there twenty-four hours, I suddenly heard the shrill whistle of the boatswain's mate, followed by a loud shout of 'Hands, all hands to muster!' and instantly the clatter of the lads' feet was heard as they rushed up on to the deck. This made me think that the time had come for me to be flogged, that being the usual part of the day in which the punishments took place; but presently down came the master-at-arms, and unshackling my feet, bade me go immediately on to the quarter-deck. I had only just time to get on deck and see that all the officers were in uniform, when the captain said, as I was held fast, 'All you men who have joined Her Majesty's navy five years, go down to your messes.' This order being obeyed, I wondered what was coming next, when the captain, in a very kind manner, very different to the way in which he had before spoken, said, 'I take it for granted that all men present have joined Her Majesty's navy for ten years. I have just received intelligence from the Admiralty, that Sir Charles Napier has been successful in carrying a bill through Parliament to give every ten years' man his discharge, if applied for in any English port. Of course, I need not say that I purpose acting like a gentleman towards you, if you remain with me, giving you all the privileges that lie in my power to give, and doing everything to make you comfortable.' At this period of the proceedings I began to feel, I scarcely knew how; but when about to ask whether there was any chance for me, I was abruptly stopped by the commander saying, 'All you who desire to leave Her Majesty's navy, please signify the same by holding up your right arm;' and in case he might not happen to see my right arm raised, I held up both my arms. Of course this drew his attention, and he immediately said, 'Yes, you rascal, you can go; and I am glad to get rid of you. You may thank your lucky stars you did not stop long enough on board for your warrant to come from the admiral, since, if it had, I should certainly have flogged you.'

"However, now, with the rest, I felt myself at liberty to gather together my 'dunnage' (old clothes); and then all of us, tumbling over one another into the boats alongside the ship, some of us full of laughter, and others almost crying with joy, were rowed safely to the *Victory*, the ship in which Lord Nelson fought in the battle of Trafalgar. Here we found all to be bustle and confusion, the cook, for one thing, not being able to boil meat enough for us all."

However, for the next three days they continued to give the men their discharges, after paying them their wages, and then they were sent on shore, where there were hundreds of base women awaiting the arrival of each boat-load, more like bloodhounds than human beings, thirsting for Jack's money.

"Even whilst on board this ship, awaiting my discharge, I could not keep quiet; and, accordingly, on the second day after coming on board, I struck a man on the nose, which resulted in a stand-up fight for more than a quarter of an hour. For this, as a punishment, I was put on the black list the whole of the time I remained in the ship, during which time a portion of my work consisted of rubbing the plate which marks the place where Nelson fell, with brickdust and oil, until it became bright.

"At length, a quarter to one o'clock on the third day arrived, and my name was called out, upon which I proceeded to the gun-room to obtain my money and my discharge; but while there a dispute arose between me and the purser, who was not willing to pay me all that I thought myself entitled to, on the ground that nearly all my money had been spent in tobacco, clothes, soap, etc. The

question being asked me where I was going, I replied, 'To London.'
'Then,' said the captain, 'here's your discharge and a letter; and if
you go to the Admiralty, they will no doubt look over the books
there; and as they have more time than we have now, perhaps
they may be able to settle with you better than we can.' With
this I proceeded below for my bag of clothes, such as they were,
and was just coming on deck, after parting with some of my old
companions, when I heard a shrill whistle, and a voice calling
out, 'Hands, all hands to muster!' but a young fellow coming
on to the main deck said, quite loud enough for me to hear, 'Ah,
it's all up; they have got a counter order from the Admiralty, to
say that no more discharges are to be given to the men, for fear
they should lose all the navy.' Going near to him, I said, 'Is that
true, George?' 'Yes,' said he, 'it's too true, for I have just heard
the order given to let no one pass over the gangway, and also for
all the boats to be ordered away from the ship's side.'

"Of course I knew that while the ship was in commission, with
her pennon flying at the masthead, and I on board, my discharge
was perfectly useless; so I immediately proceeded to one of the
ship's port-holes, and found that all the boats had left its side,
with the exception of a very small foreign one, capable of holding
two or three persons."

Seeing no other way of escape, he threw his bundle of clothes into the
boat, and as quickly jumped into it, and soon applied the sculls to the
water, and so got free.

It was a hazardous attempt, and for it he might have been subjected to
severe discipline. But he was thoroughly tired of the restraints of a sailor's
life, and was determined to be freed of naval discipline. When all his
money was spent, he was obliged to part with some of his clothing to pay
his fare to London. On arriving home, he was treated by both parents and
relatives with great kindness, and ultimately his father obtained work for
him at a barge-building firm, where he received eighteen shillings a week.
He firmly resolved to keep to his work honourably, and to eschew all idle
habits and evil companions. For a time he kept true to his resolutions, but

gradually he fell into his old customs. Instead of bringing home his wages, he would frequent the public-house, drinking and playing at cards for money, and spending his evenings at the Victoria Theatre. For this he was sharply reproved by his father, who so aroused his temper as to cause him in a fit of fiery anger to hurl a chopper at the old man's head. Fortunately it missed aim, but for some time father and son were on unfriendly terms.

It may interest the reader to see (on the next page), a copy of Ned's certificate of service, which was granted him in lieu of the parchment certificate he had lost:

Granted in lieu of Parchment Certificate stated to be lost.

Certificate of Service of Edward Wright.

P.N.S.
——
62

Character.	SHIP.	Entry.	Rating.	Discharge.	Cause of Discharge.	Time of Service. Years.	Days
	Wellesley	12 Dec., '54	Ord. 2 cl.	21 Jan., '56	Prison		
	"	8 Feb, '56	"	29 March, '56	"		
Indifferent	"	16 April, '56	"	19 April, '56			
Indifferent	Alacrity.	20 April, '56	Stoker	3 Nov., '56			
	Blenheim	4 Nov., '56	"	30 Dec., '56	D.S.Q.		
Indifferent	"	10 April, '57	"	29 April, '57			
Indifferent	Assistance	30 April, '57	"	19 May, '57	Shore		

ADMIRALTY, SOMERSET HOUSE, 2nd July, 1870.

THIS is to Certify, that EDWARD WRIGHT was borne on the books of Her Majesty's Ships above mentioned, for the Time and in the Ratings expressed against each Ship.

G. C. HARRISON,

for Dep. Compt. of Pay Navy.

CHAPTER FIFTH

CHAPTER FIFTH

HOPES WERE entertained of Ned's reclamation by marriage. It was therefore with no regret that his mother heard of his attachment to Maria Beard. Indeed, she was resolved for his sake to facilitate matters as far as possible, and his mother and future mother-inlaw combined to furnish a two-roomed cottage for their use. The alliance, of course, became the object of conversation among the gossips of the neighbourhood, who solemnly assured themselves, then each other, and afterwards Ned's parents, that it was time the reign of courtship ended and the era of marriage commenced. Everything was therefore settled; but, just before the time appointed, Ned left his work as a barge builder, and again worked as a lighterman on the Thames. Here he had more frequent opportunities of obtaining drink and getting tipsy, and night after night was thus spent, including the evening before the marriage-day. The consequence was that the bridegroom did not put in an appearance until the morning, when he had not thoroughly recovered from the night's debauch.

But to church they went. One of the articles of agreement had been that none of the neighbours should be made acquainted with either the day, or hour, or place. Such a measure for self-protection was deemed to be absolutely necessary; for, with the poor, a wedding is a day not only for close staring, free criticisms, and obtrusive freedoms, but also for jollifications more or less ill-timed. But Ned had broken the covenant while under the influence of drink; and judge of the inexpressible disgust of the bride, when, on quitting church, she saw before her a row of nodding, and approving, and curious neighbours, some of whom had run hurriedly from the washing-tub, with their sleeves tucked up, and their masculine arms perfumed with soapsuds! Not having sufficient courage to faint, she complained to her husband, and charged him with violating his promise, and wilfully annoying her. Ned answered her sharply, and when the party had left the churchyard gate, he vowed he would have no more to say to her, and leaving her walked towards home.

An inauspicious beginning, certainly, of what proved for a time an inauspicious union. However, an arrangement was effected during the afternoon, which satisfied the little that was left of the husband's honour, and brought peace of mind to the distracted bride.

Ned was now resolved to work hard, and to make money. A policeman called him up early in the morning, and he continued his labours until late at night. He soon began, however, to ill-use his wife, and one morning he so far forgot every manly feeling as to turn her out of doors, *en chemise,* where she remained, sitting in the doorway, under the drenching rain, for a little time, until a neighbour hospitably invited her inside her house. A week after this disgraceful occurrence he went down in a barge to St. Catharine's Dock, to bring a cargo of Ostend rabbits up the river; and on his way he coveted some of the goods, and breaking open one of the flats took out a few rabbits, fastening it up again so cleverly as to defy detection. One or two were cooked in a pie; but because the wife did not care for the dish, her husband, deeming her excuse to be a pretence, in a fit of passion put his foot under the table, and, raising it up, sent the whole of its contents to the other end of the room. This kind of treatment naturally frightened his wife, who so soon had cause bitterly to repent her marriage with so furious and brutal a husband. Added to this, she had to endure hunger, and on one occasion was thankful to satisfy her wants by roasting and eating three old onions that were scarcely fit for human food.

Finding himself out of work, and unable to obtain any, Ned took again to thieving, and in half-frantic desperation stole some of the lead from off the roof of the house in which he then lodged. In a few weeks, however, he succeeded in obtaining employment; but his poor wife suffered still more from his ferocious and ungovernable temper, until, fearing that he would murder her, she left the house, and remained for three days with her friends. This so exasperated him that he sent word that if she did not return he would blow her brains out. The landlord of the house, fearing that Ned would carry out his purpose, entreated him to leave at once; offering, if he would consent, to forego a claim for seven weeks' rent. This delighted Ned, who speedily removed his furniture; and obtaining an excellent situation, and receiving much encouragement from his employers, he conducted himself more creditably than before. In the course of time, however, he was dismissed for inattention to his duties, and then he gave himself up to drink, selling all the furniture which he had recently acquired; and pawning his wife's clothes. Although she had only just been confined, he made attempts, on three separate occasions, to cut her throat; then he deserted her for two days, leaving her to such attentions as she might receive in her weak condition from neighbours and casual visitors. Money was occasionally obtained from playing at cards, bagatelle, and dominoes; but he soon got deeply into debt, and the landlord sent upstairs a broker, with instructions to sell the goods. How the intruder was received will be best told by Ned:

> "At twelve o'clock that day a man came upstairs, and, entering our room, sat himself down, saying, 'I'm very sorry to have to come at all; but you see I must do my duty.' I was standing near the window at the time, and so I said to him, 'Come here, old chap;' and the man unsuspectingly came up to me; whereupon, throwing up the window, I said, 'It's a long distance to the ground, old fellow; but you must get there in less than half a minute, either through the door or this window.'"

Not being prepared for such summary treatment, nor for the fierce looks with which the threat was accompanied, the poor man was startled, and hesitating he was caught hold of, and would have been thrown out of the window, but for the interference of Ned's uncle, who happened to be in the room. The broker speedily took to his heels, evidently thankful for his release from a grip that portended such mischief. Ned afterwards obtained a cart, put all his furniture into it, and was about to remove, when the landlord made his appearance with a policeman, and a compromise was effected, which spoke well for the generosity of the landlord and ill enough for the meanness of his lodger.

Other lodgings were found—a small room in a house near to his mother's, where he began again to ill-treat his wife. One evening, having succeeded during the day in committing, with others, a robbery which happened to be more than ordinarily lucrative, he proceeded towards home, when, on passing a public-house, he was attracted by the sound of a violin. Not being able to resist the temptation, he went inside with the intention merely of "wetting his whistle," as he called it. This does not appear to have been so simple an act as it would seem at first thought; at least, it required the swallowing of so large a quantity of liquor that his thirst increased by what it fed on, and ended in his staying in the public-house all night, and finding next morning when he awoke from his drunken stupor that he had been relieved of all his ill-gotten gains. The consequence was what frequently occurs in the drunkard's home, a scene of furious temper, the wife being kicked and bruised, her eyes blackened, and her face disfigured. To this day, Ned shudders as he calls to mind his brutal conduct towards the woman whose amiability and patience should have won his esteem and tender care. But a drunkard is an insensate brute, wreaking his vengeance upon the weak, and cruelly punishing the innocent. Such a life as his wife was now living could only lead to one issue; human patience and powers of endurance are not unlimited, and although she had patiently borne much suffering caused by her husband's wanton cruelty, she determined to quit her home, taking her child and some of the furniture with her.

> "Sitting one morning, miserable," says Ned, "not knowing where my wife and child were, the drink previously received into my system now becoming dead, and having no means to revive it by feeding the thirst it created with a fresh supply, I determined upon calling in a broker, and selling the few things that remained. But just as I was about to do so I heard a loud gruff voice calling out 'Edward Wright,' and descending the stairs a little way I saw that my visitor was none other than a policeman from a neighbouring

police-court, who handed me a summons. Not being a good scholar, I asked him if he would read it for me, which he did, saying at the conclusion, 'You'll get a sixer for this job, Ned!' Laughingly I turned my back upon him, and proceeded upstairs, swearing vengeance against the police, my wife and family, and cursing mankind everywhere.

"The morning arrived on which I was expected to appear in answer to the summons; but having previously been compelled to attend at the court, not only for felony, but also on three following Saturdays for being drunk and disorderly, I made up my mind not to go into the court, and accordingly I conceived a plan to render such an appearance unnecessary.

"On arriving at the waiting-room of the police-court, I soon discerned some of my wife's relatives, who held the baby, and surrounded my wife for fear of my violence. I knew that the man who kept the door of the police-court was friendly towards me, so making him acquainted with my purpose he fell in with it; and the doors being opened, the persons to whom summonses had been issued went inside, but I took care to remain without.

"My wife's mother went in first, my wife followed, and then my wife's sister, who carried the baby; and this being what I desired, I made a sign, and, as was agreed upon, the policeman said to the young girl, 'Have you got a summons here?' Of course she replied, 'No, sir.' 'Then,' said he, 'you must take that baby outside, for we cannot have him screaming here;' to which my mother in-law, of whom I was most afraid, said, 'It's all right, Betsy, you can keep the baby outside.' Expecting my case would be about the third on the list, I lost but very little time, and went to the policeman, saying, 'Mrs. Wright wanted outside, here's her baby crying.' To this the policeman, winking at me, called out, Mrs. Wright;' and on her drawing near to him, he whispered, 'Your baby is crying outside; you had better go to it.' Of course, her mother wanted to go too; but the policeman, knowing his work, said, as he pushed my wife outside and shut the door, 'This isn't a beer-shop that you can go in and out of just as you like.' I knew that if I could only get my wife alone, I could gain power over her, and this I did by asking her whether she was willing to come home and forget all the past. For a moment she seemed to hesitate, and knowing that the time was passing quickly, and that our case would soon be called on, I said, 'Well, if you won't come, the baby shall.' Accordingly I ran into the next room, and snatching the child from my wife's sister's arms, I rushed out of the place, and into the public-house which was next door; so my wife, seeing me determined, said, 'Well, if you will promise not to beat me again, I'll come home.' Back we went, to the disgust of my wife's relatives, who declared they would never help her again."

Mrs. Wright relates that when she applied to the magistrate, her appearance was so deplorable that he asked whether she was in a position to pay for the summons. She replied that she was exceedingly poor, as her husband had not given her any money for a long time past, and the little she had to maintain herself and child was allowed her by friends. The magistrate judged that, as in many similar cases, she would refuse to appear against her husband when the day for hearing the case arrived; but seeing her terribly disfigured face, he granted the summons without cost, on her solemn promise to appear against her husband, and not to permit him to gain an ascendancy over her in the meantime. This unexpected kindness made her firmly resolve not to forgive the defendant, as she had overlooked his conduct so many times. But he must be a poor student of human nature who would be greatly surprised at the triumph of cunning and plausible professions over a yielding and affectionate, though ill-used woman.

> "Men have marble, women waxen minds
> And therefore are they formed as marble will;
> The weak oppressed, the impression of strange kinds
> Is formed in them by force, by fraud, or skill."

After this event, Ned was engaged at a gun and shot wharf, and earned respectable wages. During this time he associated with some of the most expert thieves in London, some of whom were pickpockets, others cracksmen, and he grew more desperate than ever. Of course, this kind of life had its dangers; and his employers eventually discharged him. He was then reduced to deep poverty, his children suffered from hunger, his wife was on the eve of confinement, and had not even sufficient linen in which to wrap the new-born babe. That evening, moved by his wife's condition, he ran into a beershop, and played at "crib," in the hope of gaining money. But the society of card-sharpers was so infatuating, and the games so exciting, that he remained with them until the next morning, when he found, on reaching home, that his wife had been safely delivered of a girl. The doctor was in the room, and directing Ned's attention to a red herring that was lying on the table, said, "Is that what you feed your wife upon, sir, during her confinement? Were I you, I should be ashamed of myself." But Ned began so to curse and swear, that the doctor in disgust took his departure, and refused to enter the house unless he was assured that the husband was away. Only two days after this he threw a piece of bread-crust at his wife, which, in warding off from her child, severely bruised her arm. Maddened by drink, he frequently committed other acts of violence; on one occasion striking his own mother on the head, and breaking the furniture, and smashing the windows, for which he was bound over to keep the peace for twelve months. On another occasion he ill-treated his wife, and turned her and children outside the room, where they remained huddled up on the stairs until the morning, whilst he was lying snugly down before the fire. For this inhuman conduct he was remonstrated with by the landlord of the house, who, fearing his violence, gave him notice to quit.

About a quarter to three o'clock one Sunday afternoon, Ned, with a few boon companions, was standing at the bar of a public-house at Bankside, drinking beer and spirits as quickly as possible before the house closed, when he observed a tall young minister, with a band of ten followers, take his stand upon a vacant piece of ground in front of the public-house, and close to the railings which protect persons from falling into the Thames. In many of the low parts of London, it is considered by the "roughs" to be excellent sport to worry, if not ill-treat, an open-air preacher, and such an one must expect to encounter much opposition if he would seek to labour among the rude and vulgar. Ned was soon tempted by his companions to upset the open air preacher, and he resolved to throw him over the rails that he might enjoy the privilege of a soft bed in the water. As he was on the point of carrying out his purpose, the preacher, guessing the nature of the plot formed against him, gave utterance solemnly to some of the most-powerful warnings of Scripture, in the hope that they might arrest his assailant. Ned was compelled, involuntarily, to listen, and paid deep attention to all that followed; and could not find it in his heart to molest any further the man who had thus mastered him.

Not long ago, Ned was preaching the gospel at Southampton, and a number of the ministers of the town were seated on the platform, when he observed one whose features he recognized as an old acquaintance. He whispered in his ear, "Did you ever preach at Bankside?" "Oh, yes," was the reply, "I was at one time the minister of — Chapel, and often used to preach in the place you mention; by the way, I once had a very narrow escape of being thrown into the river in that very place." The result was a mutual recognition; and the reader may judge of the powerful impression made that evening by the recital of this story to the audience when it came to be the minister's turn to speak.

As an illustration of the daring disposition of Ned, the following story may be here given: Although a reputed thief, he was determined to accept a wager laid by some of his companions that he could get into the Thames police. He therefore went one day to Scotland Yard, and was one of about thirty men, most of whom had apparently come from the country, who that morning made application for the Metropolitan Police. He was examined by the doctor, who did not seem to notice the scars on his back, received when in the navy, and was thus far approved of, and ordered to attend the next day at the Thames Police Station, situated at the lower side of the London Docks. Here he feared failure in putting forth his claims; but two things were in his favour—he had succeeded in obtaining a written character from an old employer, very carefully worded as most testimonials are, omitting all that was essential, and dealing in such commonplaces as are deemed sufficient passports to respectable positions; and one of the Thames police, who had to test his skill in rowing a boat, was as afraid of

Ned as Ned was afraid of him, and both could tell stories of each other which would be damaging to each. The result was that the application proved to be successful, and Ned resolved, having gone so far, to join the force, knowing that eighteen shillings or a guinea a week was not all the money a shrewd and dishonest Thames policeman could secure. It was about this period, however, he joined, as we have already stated, one of Her Majesty's regiments of the line, in order to escape the consequences of complicity in a large robbery.

Ned's adventures in tap-rooms might alone form an interesting, if not amusing, chapter. One occurrence had so serious a lesson for him, that it must not be omitted here. Generally spending all his spare evenings in a public-house, drinking and gambling, and rarely leaving until he was compelled, his wife was sure of being able to find him whenever he neglected his home in the evening. One Friday evening he sauntered into his favourite public-house, with his wages in his pockets, entirely oblivious of his starving wife and children who had counted upon a meal that day, resolved upon winning more money. But he found, as he had done on many prior occasions, that it was easier to lose all that he had than to gain more; and so he went on playing until he had lost every penny, and staggered home at twelve o'clock at night, ashamed for once of himself, as he met the accusing glances of his hungry wife. The next morning he procured a small advance from his master, and leaving a shilling at home for his wife's use during the day, he again tried his fortune with the rest of the money in the public-house, after work. Again he lost, and attempting to outwit his opponents he was embroiled in a row, during which there was a fearful fight, the chairs being broken, and everything at hand being hurled at each other: when, in the middle of the fray, a bull-dog belonging to Ned's antagonist rushed into the room, and commenced biting him savagely about the legs and arms. At last he managed to seize the animal round the neck with both hands, pressing his windpipe so hard as to leave it on the floor almost dead. The fight was then resumed; and although both men were turned out of the taproom, they fought as they went out, and continued the combat outside until the police made an appearance, which was of course not before both parties had become tired of the conflict. Ned was so severely injured, both from the biting of the dog and the blows of its master, that it was not until four months had elapsed that he recovered fully from its effects—a just punishment, as he rightly deemed it, for his cruelty to his wife in keeping her without money and food.

One Monday afternoon, five men, one of whom was Wright, went on board the *Mary Ann* barge, with white bags resembling pillow-cases across their shoulders, each of which contained breasts of mutton, coffee, sugar, bread, and other necessaries, which were to supply their wants during a three or four days' journey down the Thames, to a place where a certain description of sharp sand could be obtained from the bottom of the river. They arrived at Gray's Village about nine o'clock at night; but the wind being against them, they found it impossible to "drudge" up the sand, and for four days they were unable to proceed with their labours. At the end of this time they got the barge loaded, but, as they found their provisions eaten, they applied to the master builder, for whom the sand had been provided, to give them the job of unloading the barge with his carts, for which they were paid thirty shillings in advance.

During their stay in this village they frequented a public-house kept by an aged widow, who treated them with much consideration, but who was treated by them with less than she evidently deserved. They got drunk, fought among themselves, had pitched battles with the villagers, and became a pest to the place. One of the men was even more vicious than Ned, who regarded him with dread: They could not agree, and prepared to fight each other. The fight took place, and at last Ned's adversary tried to strike him over the head with his shovel; but, luckily for him, the blow was evaded, by his raising his hand, but not without receiving so severe a wound in his thumb as to disable him—the scar of which is to be seen to this day. Finding this fail, the man took out his knife, and would probably have killed Ned, had he not jumped overboard, and so got clear of his opponent, who became helpless through drink, and was punished by the men for using the knife, by being lowered into a well which contained two feet of water, in the presence of many of the villagers, who were highly delighted in witnessing this curious punishment.

Failing to get drink upon trust, the men sold their jackets, Ned received for his the sum of three shillings with an old labourer's cow gown, which he describes as reaching nearly to his heels. Ned then suggested that they "should do a bit of cadging," and so he proceeded to a quiet street, where, having left his companions at the corner, he put his old hat under his arm, and assuming a very beggar-like look, he sang, in mournful tones, the following ballad:—

> "One summer's eve, when work was o'er.
>   And the birds were sweetly singing,
> A poor old tar, worn out with age.
>   Through the village came a-begging.
>
> As thus he sung his mournful tale,
>   A female gazed upon him;
> And bursting into tears of joy,
>   She sank upon his bosom.
>
> Then as she smiled, 'twas his only child.
>   Whose duty ne'er had failed her,
> 'Come, old man, live and die with me,
>   You poor old worn-out sailor.'"

Either this doggerel was more affecting than it can be to the reader, or the singer's condition was so pitiable as to awake sympathy, for the success was all that the sham mendicant desired. Whilst singing it he was stopped half a dozen times to pick up coppers that were thrown from the windows. At one of the open windows stood an aged woman, who, resting upon a young man's shoulder, said to the lad, quite loud enough for Ned to hear, "Ah, my boy, there's better days in store for that poor man; but may God keep thee from ever falling into the condition in which he is placed."

A few years after Ned's conversion he was relating to a large assembly in Victoria Theatre one Sunday evening the story of God's goodness in plucking him from shame and misery and eternal woe, when, at the close of the meeting, a young man who had been sitting in the gallery made his way to him, and exclaimed, "O sir, I remember hearing you sing the 'Poor Old Worn-out Sailor' opposite my mother's door at Gray's Village, some few years ago. I came here to laugh and scoff; but you have just reminded me of some of my poor dear old mother's words, and I'm very wretched; how can I be saved? " Ned told him of the Saviour, of His finished work, of His power and willingness to save, and subsequently had the gratification of hearing that the young man had made an open avowal of his faith in Christ, and had joined a Christian Church.

"I will bring the blind by a way that they knew not; I will lead them in paths that they have not known."

CHAPTER SIXTH

CHAPTER SIXTH

O F ROWING matches Ned was specially fond, and he engaged in
several with great zest. At Bankside there lived a freeman of the
river Thames, who made it his pleasure to collect money from
the public-houses of the district to purchase the freedom of the water every
year for one apprentice. The freedom was arranged to be contended for
by six apprentices, who were elected to row in wager boats from London
Bridge to Westminster and back. Ned succeeded in getting his name put
down as a candidate that year for the prize, and so ably did he row, that,
amid the plaudits of the excited throng on the shores, he was hailed the
winner of his freedom of the Thames. This race having made him somewhat
known in the aquatic world, he was soon backed by some persons to row
"Young Woody," an expert hand. Money was collected to send him into
the country for training, and he was forbidden the use of all spirituous
liquors. About this time he became a teetotaller, and by those who were
total abstainers he was lionized, and the race announced as "water against
beer." During the time of his training, however, he sought the aid of "a
glass of old ale and a biscuit;" and either the biscuit was very dry, or the
old ale very inspiring, for he demanded more, and succeeded in getting
enough to make him intoxicated. On the morning of the race they started,
in the midst of pouring rain, in outrigger boats, from Putney to Mortlake,
the stakes being £10 : £5 a side. In the course of half a mile, such was the
speed with which Ned's boat went, his opponent was left quite a hundred

yards behind. Pleasing pictures of a convivial festival that would be held that night with the £10 that would certainly be his, filled his mind with unusual delight, and spurred him still onwards, when suddenly the scull on the off-side broke right across the blade, and the hapless rower sat madly watching "Young Woody" row by, winning with ease. Soon after this engagement he became a member of the South London Rowing Club, and an acknowledged stroke-oarsman, and served in that capacity in the winning-boat of the club's annual race, said to have been the best race ever rowed over that course. He also rowed for the Leander Coat and Badge, said to have been a splendid race, in which Wright came in second; and competed for similar honours and possessions at Putney, but without success.

A few months before the change that turned the whole current of Ned's life into another channel, he was a candidate for a prize for a coat and badge, which was the object of many a young waterman's ambition. All young men who had finished their apprenticeship, and obtained a license to work as watermen on the Thames, were entitled to draw lots for the privilege; only six men could row, but this year upwards of ninety were privileged to take part in this preliminary test. Ten days before the race these ninety men and their friends assembled at Fishmongers' Hall to cast lots for the competitors for Doggett's Coat and Badge. Ned was there to watch his chance, and the first five names drawn out were prizes, amongst whom was a favourite rower named Short, of Bermondsey, who had the confidence of the betting fraternity, the other four being regarded as of meaner ability as prize rowers. One name remained yet to be called to make up the required number, and there were eighty-five names left in the ballot-box. Seventy of these proved to be blanks, and the excitement increased and became quite feverish as name after name was announced as "blank." Only one name remained, and the Bankside party were aroused to the highest pitch of enthusiasm when it was known that Edward Wright was their champion.

Ned was at this period in deep poverty, and it was agreed that he should prepare for the race at home, his friends making arrangements for a due supply of bitter beer and beefsteaks and mutton chops, which are considered to be essential for a man in training. The confidence of those who belong to the betting world in Ned's condition and skill seemed to be almost unlimited, and competent critics were so satisfied with him that he was regarded almost universally as the best man. Carefully were his movements watched by those who were interested in the race, and large sums of money were laid on his winning. He had been sober and careful in his diet, since the rowing would be all against the tide from the beginning to the end, and he would therefore require great physical endurance.

Two days before the contest, an event occurred which brought Ned into still greater notoriety. He had performed his usual morning exercise on the river, and had just brought his boat to the shore at Lambeth pier, where a number of his admirers had assembled to witness one of his trial trips, and many persons had put forth their hands to pull him out of the boat, when, as he was dressing, the cry, "A boy overboard," greeted his ears. The whole assembly hastened to the steam-boat pier, which was crowded, and Ned accompanied the crowd. It seems that two steamers had just arrived at the pier, one an up and the other a down boat; and every eye was fixed upon the spot in the river where the boy had gone down; but there were no signs of him, and scarcely a ripple was observed on the surface of the water.

Looking carefully upon the water, Ned observed bubbles close beside the inside steamer; and in a moment the thought occurred to him that these bubbles were probably caused by the last breathings of the drowning lad. Instantly, with the quickness of an apparition, he plunged into the river, dived beneath the surface, and while the crowd on the shore and pier were awaiting in breathless suspense his reappearance, he dived to the bottom, and there lay the body, as if dead. Passing one arm under the lad, and with the other raising himself and his burden to the surface, Ned was seen with his prize above the water, and was greeted with a simultaneous shout from the spectators, such as a British crowd of admirers know how to give. A boat was meanwhile sent to his assistance, the boy put in it, and conveyed to a public-house, and Ned, amid such plaudits as nearly bewildered him, swam safely to the pier.

As he was going away, the captain of one of the steamboats cried out, "Hold on! we are going to make a collection for you." "All right," was Ned's response; "while you are doing so, I'll just run up and see how the lad is getting on." The boy had been so long under water that he appeared as one dead; and although stimulants were freely given, and every appliance obtained for restoring animation, it was feared for some time that the case was hopeless. The means were at last successful, and the frantic mother, whose wild shrieks of sorrow had been heard from outside, pushed her way into the room, clasped her child fondly to her bosom, and having relieved herself by a flood of tears, inquired, "Where is the man who saved my child?" The brave rescuer was pointed out, and falling at his feet she thanked him repeatedly, asking what she could do to reward him for his bravery. Ned laid his hand on her head, and said, "All right, mother; I've a little one of my own."

Returning to the pier, he found that the collection had been made by the captains of the two steamers and the man in charge of the pier, and his jacket pockets were filled with coppers, and his trousers pockets with small silver. Of course, he could not resist the temptation to drink too much rum, and the consequence was that he spent all he had that night in the public-house, going home drunk and penniless! He could expose his life to danger, to rescue a drowning child; but he could not be brave enough to resist the temptations of drink. He could sympathise with a mother's sorrow and a child's suffering; but in the midst of these allurements to drink he could forget his young and hungry wife, and neglect the wants of his infant child. It was in vain that he knew that he endangered his success on the coming race-day by over-drink; neither ambition nor health held him back. With his wet clothes still on, he remained at the bar of the public-house, drinking until he was almost incapable of journeying home.

Inured to this horrid kind of life, he did not suffer as others less accustomed to dissipation might have done; and on the morning of the contest he presented himself at London Bridge, the starting-point, in fair condition, determined to win. This race for Doggett's Coat and Badge, contrary to all others except that for the championship, is rowed for in "the bare buff," no special dress or colour distinguishes the men, and each of the competitors has a representative or seconder, who arranges all the preliminaries, including that of drawing lots for the starting stations of their respective men. The last lot drawn takes the first or best station—the Surrey side of London Bridge, and the last lot but one takes the next station, and so on. Ned's seconder was fortunate in securing him the best place, and as it happened that Short was his next neighbour, the two favourites were side by side. Each race boat was attended by an eight-oared galley, to pilot them over their course, and several steamers were crowded with spectators to witness the result.

Ned was confident of victory. He had set his heart on the prize. He had in his way asked God to give him the coat and badge, although in other things he had not recognized His existence. He imagined himself already dressed in the livery, fancied how he would look with it on him, and pictured the proud position he would then occupy. The thought of failure seemed so distasteful that it was regarded as impossible.

After three false starts, the company got away; but before Ned had rowed three boats' length, his neighbour Short and he fouled each other; Ned, being slightly in advance, managed to get the blade of his scull against Short's back, and held him fast. The other four men were rowing ahead, while Short and Ned were wrangling and swearing at each other. At length, Ned begged Short to let his boat go out into the stream, so that they might clear one another, as they had to row against the tide. His opponent did so, but Ned at once, with the assistance of his attending galley, so manoeuvred as to get clean away from Short. By this time, of course, the other four were considerably ahead, and by dint of the utmost exertion, and the most skilful rowing, he took the third place at Blackfriars Bridge, and after a severe struggle he shot ahead of the second boat The excitement on the side of the river, and among the Irish coal porters of Bankside, to whom Ned was well known, and also among the passengers on board the steamers, was indescribable. Wagers of £12 to £1 were freely made in favour of Ned's winning, and he was encouraged by the cheers he heard on all sides. As he neared the first man, an untoward event occurred, which decided the race as far as Ned was concerned. Shooting out round the point on the south shore between Waterloo and Hungerford bridges, the tide caught the bow of Ned's boat, and carried her out in spite of all his skill; and although he used his left hand with double power, whilst his right hand scull was in abeyance, yet he failed; his boat came athwart a buoy, and his scull became locked between it and a barge, and before he could get himself freed he had the mortification of seeing his five opponents pass him. Short was fast beating the rest, and eventually the race resulted in his winning the coveted coat and badge. Ned subsequently rowed leisurely after the others, over the whole distance, that he might obtain the sovereign given to every one who rowed; and was sufficiently near to hear the band strike up, "See the conquering hero comes," as Short came in first. He had no sooner reached the shore, than, in a fit of jealous anger, he offered to fight anyone of his competitors, when some man answered by saying, "You might be beaten at that, as well as at rowing," and for this he was felled by Ned to the ground. Fortunately, Mrs. Wright was present, and a publican having advanced the sovereign, she persuaded him to take a cab, and drive over to Bankside. In the evening, according to announcement, a "grand extra performance" was given in Victoria Theatre, at which the six competitors for Doggett's Coat and Badge appeared on the stage. The theatre was crowded; and when the curtain rose, the six men stood before the audience and received a perfect ovation, and although Ned Wright had not been successful in the race, he received no small share of the applause.

This was Ned's first appearance on the boards of Victoria Theatre. It was in the character of a defeated, chagrined man—his first and happily last appearance in that character. Very different indeed was the occasion which brought him the second time, some eighteen months after, to stand in the same position. Again were the walls placarded with his name, but it was as a successful man, having won a greater prize—the salvation of his soul. Not this time as a mere object of curiosity, to take part in a dumb-show; but as a preacher of the gospel, an illustrious instance of the power of Divine grace in rescuing from sin one of the most zealous adherents of the cause of impiety and rebellion.

For a long time Ned rebelled against his fate in failing to win the coat and badge, and could not understand why he should have been so unfortunate. On two other occasions he had rowed for coats and prizes, and this was the last opportunity he could have of gaining Doggett's much-coveted honour, and he had put forth all his skill, and had even used trickeries, but without success! His pride was deeply wounded, and he felt his position keenly. It was twelve months after this event that he saw his opponent strutting proudly down Tooley Street, wearing the full dress of a waterman—scarlet breeches, silk stockings, red cap, coat, and silver badge. The sight awoke painful recollections of his defeat and disgrace, and Ned felt humiliated for the moment. But he was not annoyed. A great change had come over his life in the meantime, and the ambition that once aroused his whole nature had ceased to stir him into action. He was better prepared for the taunt, "Well, Ned, you did not get the coat and badge after all," as his adversary pointed with vanity to his silver plate. "No," said Ned, "I certainly did not; you got it. But I've a garment, for all that, and it is in the shape of a robe;"

and before the crowd he stood and told in simple words, and in an unaffected manner, the wondrous story of the revelation of Divine love to his poor heart, and concluded by setting before his hearers the higher ambition of winning Christ, and being found in Him.

On the 9th of November following, Ned again encountered the wearer of the uniform and badge, carrying the banner of the Waterman's Company in the Lord Mayor's show, going first, according to privilege. Ned that day carried a banner too,—the banner, as he called it, of a King, and on it was written, "Be sure your sins will find you out" and beneath was the inscription of the covenant of mercy, "The blood of Jesus Christ, God's Son, cleanseth us from all sin." No man was happier, not even the Lord Mayor himself, than Ned that day, as with the flag in one hand he distributed tracts with the other; and, as he looked at his old friend so gaily decked in the procession, he shouted, "Look at this—these are the colours to fight under; none but Jesus can do helpless sinners good."

Most of Ned's robberies were committed on the water, and they were generally characterized by great ingenuity and hardihood. His story of the stolen pump is illustrative of his audacity. Walking one morning into a wharf on the Thames, his eye was captivated with a new galvanized iron pump, lying on the deck of a barge over which he had been scores of times. Throughout the rest of that day his mind was occupied with schemes for stealing and disposing of this new pump. He went from wharf to wharf, carefully looking over every barge that might probably need such a pump; and at length, near Waterloo Bridge, he saw a vessel that would be likely to require it. About ten o'clock that night he went on board this barge, and informed the captain that he had for sale a first-rate pump, six feet long, five-and-a-half-inch bore, in good order, already in use; but, as he was not in want of it just then, he would sell it for thirty shillings, although it had cost him three guineas. This was said in so business-like a manner that the captain was deceived, and after a few inquiries gave him fifteen shillings for it; and Ned proceeded at once to the stairs, and observing the coast pretty clear he rowed on board the barge, and seizing the pump lifted it into the boat, and delivered it to the captain, who handed him at once the sum agreed upon. Ned observed that its new owner put the pump into the forecastle, pulled the hatch over it, and left it there. "Oh," said Ned to himself as he rowed to the shore, "no hatch-bar, no lock; hum! I must have that pump again." Away he sped to his old haunt, the public-house, where he joined in the wild carousals of his pot-companions, who were treated by him with drink, and by closing-time, which was two o'clock, Ned was so intoxicated that he dropped down on the steps of Southwark Bridge, and fell asleep. Early in the morning he awoke, shivering with cold, parched with thirst, and wretched in body and mind, only possessed of twopence-halfpenny out of the money he had gained by the sale of the pump.

Having spent that small sum at a coffee-shop, he walked down to the wharf from which he had stolen the pump, and having heard the gossip about the robbery he strolled away, and had just reached Blackfriars Bridge when he met his old employer, the owner of the pump. Finding it impossible to avoid him, he boldly accosted him with "Good morning, guv'nor;" adding, "Unless you put some one on board your barges all night, its no use for you to think of keeping things safe; there's been thieves on board the *Mary Ann*, and stole the new pump either last night or this morning."

"How do you know that?" asked the owner, as he looked curiously upon Ned.

"Oh," was the reply, "I've just been down to the wharf, and they're all talking about it."

"Well," said he, "come on, let us go and see about it;" and Ned was reluctantly compelled to return with him to the wharf.

Arriving there, he found he was not suspected, and so he offered to assist in the discovery of the thief. It was suggested that bills should be printed, offering a reward of ten shillings for the conviction of the thief; but Ned hinted that it should be for the recovery of the missing article, as he was anxious it should be found. "Oh," said Ned to himself, "ten shillings reward! I must have that." The bills were printed and circulated in due course.

Ned was now fully engaged in scheming for the recovery of the pump, and with it securing the reward. The difficulty was how to accomplish his purpose without suspicion. The chance of gaining ten shillings so easily quickened his wits, and he soon hit upon an ingenious method of securing the reward. The second day after the robbery he found the barge which had the pump in her forecastle still in the same place, not having completed her loading. That night he seized another boat, rowed off to a number of coal barges lying close to Waterloo Bridge, and at high water he sheared one of the empty barges in shore, so that she came alongside the barge that contained the pump. No one would notice a lighterman stepping on board the strange barge, and taking a turn with a rope to check his own lighter in passing; and, although the persons in charge of the strange barge looked up out of the cabin as Ned's barge bumped against them, they soon retired, thinking that it was only due to a passing coal barge. Ned at once, lightly and quickly, removed the hatch of the forecastle, laid hold of the pump, placed it in the side of his own barge, which he stopped at the roadstead abreast the wharf, and making her fast he took his boat, and rowed on shore.

Early, next morning Ned made diligent inquiries at the wharf as to whether the pump was found. On receiving a reply in the negative, he said to the owner of the wharf, "Let me have a try to find this pump; depend upon it, it has not gone far, and I may as well have the ten shillings as any one else, if I can earn it."

"To be sure you may," was the reply. "Go, Ned, and have a try; which way will you take? "

"Why," said Ned, "if you will lend me one of your labourers and a boat, we'll begin to search every barge round about."

This was done, and Ned, leaving the labourer in the boat, pretended to search each barge, until he had visited every one in the roadstead. As if in despair of success, he left the barge which he had removed during the night until the last; and when he came to it, he shouted, "Here it is!" and lifted the pump up to the gaze of those who were watching the movements of the searchers.

"I see through it all," cried Ned, as he reached the shore with the pump, "it hasn't been stolen at all; a little thought and common sense would have saved us all this bother and trouble. Some barge has been going off the ways in the night, and has borrowed the pump to get rid of her water, and not being able to put it back again, has left it in one of the barges in the roadstead."

It was an ingenious story, and could not have been fully believed; enough, however, for Wright that he received ten shillings reward, and five more for his trouble, making altogether thirty shillings which he got out of his theft of the pump. Not that it was worth the scheming, and lying, and anxiety,—none of his evil deeds were,—for he spent the whole of the money, as usual, at the bar of the public-house. Poor hapless wretch.

Ned's conduct with Regard to the pump troubled him frequently afterwards. He had wronged an old employer, whose visage seemed to follow him wherever he went. One day, after his conversion, he was addressing people in the neighbourhood where the man he had injured resided; and accidentally meeting him, he felt ashamed as he remembered his past villany and all its accompanying misery. He would have spoken, but trembled to do so; when his old employer accosted him, asking whether his name was Wright. He replied in the affirmative.

"I believe you owe me the sum of ten shillings. Say, did you not steal that pump of mIne, four years ago?"

"Well, sir," said the ashamed Ned, "as regards the ten shillings, I admit I had it; and you are perfectly right in your suspicions, for I did steal the pump. But, sir, since then I wandered, in the providence of God, into Astley's Theatre, and there the Lord Jesus met with me, pardoned all my sins, and saved my soul; and now I am working for Jesus, and telling other sinners what a dear Saviour I have found; indeed, sir, I have been preaching here for several days."

"I know it," was the response. "I have heard of it, and know all about it. I forgive you."

And kindly he gave his hand to Ned, and, shaking it, bade him good-day; but Ned detained him, and begged that he might for a moment have the privilege of telling him something about the Saviour of all classes of men. Simply, unaffectedly, did Ned speak of the leading verities of our evangelical faith, laying out with much plainness—perhaps ruggedness of speech—the way of salvation through the Cross of Jesus Christ.

CHAPTER SEVENTH

"Dog rob dog."—Ned grows wild in wickedness.—A challenge to fight.—Preaching in Astley's Theatre.—NED AND HIS WIFE CONVERTED.—The happy home.—The sequel to the projected prize-fight.—Ned tells the story of his conversion.—No employment.

CHAPTER SEVENTH

J UST BEFORE Ned's conversion he was involved in many robberies, and was regarded as the boldest spirit among the fraternity that rejoiced in his fellowship. Running foot and boat races, and getting drunk on the proceeds, fighting with friends and foes, ill-treating his wife, and starving his children, and committing thefts either of a petty character or on a large scale, he was not the man to be controlled or changed by human power. As a sample of some of his minor robberies, the following may be given:—

Being acquainted with an iron-moulder in a small way of business, who was a receiver of stolen goods, Ned, with two companions, frequently took him a truck-load of pig-iron, weighing about a quarter of a ton, obtained from the barges. To avoid creating suspicion of being concerned in the proceedings, the three thieves had to put the pig-iron on his premises before the receiver was up in the morning. As soon as they arrived inside his gates with their load, they would not only put their own five hundred-weight of iron into the scales, which would weigh half a ton, but took the same quantity from one of the stacks in the yard, so as to make their weight double what it would otherwise have been. It would seem that this system of deceiving the receivers of stolen goods is commonly carried on among practised thieves, by whom it is called, not inappropriately, "Dog rob dog." The receivers of stolen plate are frequently duped in this way. In most cases the plate is presented without being weighed, and is put, without a moment's delay, into the crucible, that it may be melted. The molten mass runs into sand moulds in the shape of long bars. It is then weighed, and booked to the thieves' account, at so much per ounce. The receivers are compelled, to avoid detection, to keep a good stock of these bars upon the premises; and the thieves seize upon what they would call "half a chance" to steal a few of these silver bars, and throw them into the crucible to add to their "swag."

At this period of his life, Ned's uncontrollable nature became even more wild, and he spent his days in committing most aggravated offences, such as making his way through the city sewers, and tempting servants to drop silver spoons down the gully-holes. On one occasion, while in the sewers, he was nearly drowned, and this seemed to alarm him sufficiently to lead to the discontinuance of these wild adventures. He was deeply in debt, was shunned by all respectable honest people; and found it exceedingly difficult to procure a suitable cottage for his family. The house in which he lived at the time of his conversion was obtained under false pretences, and the landlord was abused by the neighbours for permitting such a low-life man to occupy one of his cottages. He was, however, determined not to quit it, as it presented peculiar facilities for carrying on his nefarious practices; and the landlord was afraid to give him notice to quit, lest he might offer violence.

One day he met an old gentleman, who inquired the way to the Thames Tunnel. Having told him, he unblushingly asked for something to drink. This was agreed to; a pint of the best old ale was obtained at the Waterman's Arms; and this led to successive calls for a like quantity, and in Ned and his companion, with some friends, becoming drunk. The man who had thus treated them was robbed of all his money; and a quarrel ensued in sharing the booty, which quarrel led to a fight Ned was declared winner, and, as a reward, he was expected to fight "Jack Connelly" on a subsequent day. After the encounter he wandered home with some pieces of the clinkers sticking in his back, which had been laid on the road on which he had fallen. These having been removed, and his wounds dressed, he went to Bankside, found out a man who, he believed, had not shown him fair play during the fight, and began at once to attack him with his fists.

This, of course, led to a row, and the row led to something beyond, and terminated in the use, by assailants and defenders, of pokers, sticks, and stones, and in Ned's being carried into his mother's house, when the shutters and doors had to be closed and blocked up, lest the opposing forces without should gain admittance.

The challenge which Ned had received to fight Jack Connelly was now regarded as a stepping-stone to some high position in the sporting

SCRIPTURE TESTIMONY
Holy Spirit convicts people of their sin
JOHN 16:8

world. Unsuccessful in four different attempts at robbery, through the vigilance of the police, and being without money, he fixed his hopes upon a victory in this prize-fight. An arrangement was therefore made, which was duly recorded in the sporting papers, and Ned put himself in training for the encounter. At length Easter-day—the most memorable day in his life—arrived. After tea he informed his wife of the projected prize-fight, and invited her to accompany him to Pimlico, so that if any of his companions should call that night, with a view of persuading him to drink, he might escape a temptation that would materially interfere with his prospects of success in the approaching prize-fight. The two children were thereupon put to a bed composed of cane cuttings, and covered with a thin patchwork quilt, and the parents commenced their walk. A more meanly clad couple could not have been seen. Ned was dressed in a threadbare pea-jacket and waistcoat, and his limbs were encased in a shabby well-patched (or ill-patched) pair of trousers that ought to have been long ago consigned to the dustheap. His wife was but thinly attired—indeed, barely clad. Husband and wife had not proceeded far towards Westminster Bridge, when they were accosted by a young boy who, handing him a small bill, informed them that a working man was announced to speak at Astley's Theatre that evening, the particulars of which he could read for himself. "But," said Ned, "though I can read a little, I can't manage such small type as that." The lad was not willing to be put off, and so he read aloud the bill; and when he got to the words, "All seats free, no collections," Ned, nudging his wife, whispered, "That will do for us, mate; the seats are free, and there's nothing to pay."

If it were a subject for his neighbours' astonishment to see Ned and his wife out together—of which they did not fail to inform him—it must have been still stranger to witness them walking into a building where a religious service was about to be held. Ned was one of the rather numerous class of the poor who never see the inside of a place of worship excepting at their wedding, and perhaps at the christening of their children. Had it been a church or chapel, he would not have accepted the boy's invitation; but curiosity, and the fact that Astley's Theatre had been a favoured place of resort on the week-day, induced him to spend an hour there. On an ordinary day, when a performance was going on, he would not have hesitated about occupying the most prominent seat in the building; but, through fear of being observed at a preaching service, he took his place behind a pillar under the boxes. Stooping down towards his wife, he whispered, "Do you ever remember coming here before, mate?" Alas, she remembered it quite well—remembered his protestations of love, and his professions of hatred of the man who would strike a woman. And yet, as a commentary, there were two blackened eyes and a sorrowing heart! He was a little pained by his wife's reply, and it made him wretched as he thought of the past seven years of cruelty and crime. The singing of one of the lively so-called revivalistic hymns, common at most theatre services, soon dispelled all melancholy, and by the time the working-man preacher commenced his address Ned had forgotten his remorse.

SCRIPTURE TESTIMONY
God using a vision to communicate
ACTS 10:3 · ACTS 10:9-16 · ACTS 11:5 · ACTS 18:9-10

The address was an impassioned appeal, full of references to the sublimities of heaven, the terrors of hell, the nearness of death, and the certainty of a judgment-day.

To Ned it was but an idle tale. He thought more of the glaring attractions of the theatre, and the uses to which it was ordinarily put; and, rather wearied by the sermon, he resolved to leave the building, when his attention was suddenly arrested by the preacher falling upon his knees, and praying so earnestly, that Ned was constrained to listen.

"Whilst praying," he says, "for all runaway children, I could not help believing that he meant me; and here came an urgent appeal that God would save the young men who were sending their father and mother's grey hairs with sorrow to the grave, after this prayer, he cried with a loud voice, 'Young man, where will you spend eternity?' This he repeated six times, causing an interval of solemn quiet to pervade the meeting between each cry of 'Eternity.'

"During these awful moments all my past history rose up before my mind, even from my very boyhood. Then came the thought as to whether I was prepared to die, and I remember what the preacher had been saying, 'The wicked shall be turned into hell, with all the nations that forget God.' This all tended to harrow my feelings, until at last I swooned."

It was while in this partly unconscious state that a vision seemed to bring to him all the lessons of truth he had heard during his life. Ned has often described his feelings in so thrilling a way as to create a deep impression upon his listeners:

"I felt carried away," he says, "and found myself arraigned before the most awful tribunal I ever witnessed. There sat the Judge of high heaven, upon His throne of glory, surrounded by angels and archangels and the ransomed saints. The brightness of these beings dazzled my eyes, and made me feel as if I would give ten thousand worlds to crumble into dust But no! I was there! The books were opened, and without a word being spoken, I felt myself to be the only unhappy being there. Sins that had been committed and forgotten seemed to appear before my eyes, caused me to hang down my head with shame, and in my heart to exclaim, 'Oh that I had never been born!' Then the devil dared to intrude, and suggested the words to me by way of temptation, 'Be a man, Ned; curse God, and die.' At this moment a voice echoed through the vaults of heaven, saying, 'Prisoner at the bar, you are charged with an enormous number of great offences; do you plead guilty?' Shivering like an aspen leaf, not daring to raise my head, I felt this to be ten thousand times worse than being tried at the Old Bailey—that was nothing compared with this; indeed, when the jury returned a verdict of 'guilty,' I have stood unmoved, and apparently the most unconcerned of all in the court; but here I felt the case to be entirely altered. There was no deceiving the Judge of all the earth, no bringing false witnesses to swear one clear: His eyes were as flames of fire, searching me through. I would fain have sunk into dust, or even into hell, rather than stand before that great assembly. My hands refused their office; I could not upraise them to cover my eyes. Oh, what a dreadful feeling was that! I knew I was guilty; I felt condemned; and I stood a wretched sinner before the Judge. Then, too, in all that vast assembly, there was no voice raised in my favour—my case was hopeless. I stood in breathless suspense awaiting my sentence; and while trembling and quaking with fear, the scalding tears running down my cheeks, and my heart bursting within me, I heard a voice softly and gently whispering in my ear, 'Look to Jesus; there is pardon and life, through looking to Jesus.' Then I cried in agony of soul, 'Where, oh, where is Jesus?'"

All this seemed to be the work of a few moments. The sin-stricken man, whose soul was feeling its own guilt, and earnestly desiring pardon, was amazed, and yet more heart-broken, as he saw by faith a vision of Christ crucified. He looked and believed. The Judge rose, and pronounced his acquittal. "Prisoner," He seemed to say, "you have been accused of many, very many, heinous crimes, and have pleaded guilty to them all; not a witness could say a word in your favour; you have not one redeeming point in your character. You have incurred the extreme penalty of the law, which you have so repeatedly broken; you are absolutely without excuse; but this is now the award of love,—solely because of the merits of my dear Son to whom you have looked; I ordain that you be taken from the kingdom of Satan, and be translated into the kingdom of my Son, and that you be made an heir of God, and joint-heir with Christ Jesus."

It was at this moment that "poor Ned," as he pathetically designates himself in relating this remarkable story, came back to consciousness. He was then sitting upon a back seat, the perspiration streaming from his brow, and tears were channelling his cheeks. So full of amazement was he, that he knew not what to do. The thought came to him, that if his old companions saw him in tears, they would ridicule him, and to escape observation he started to his feet, and hastened to the door with the intention of leaving the theatre. But so strong a hold had the scene upon his mind, that he returned to his wife. The service was then over; the preacher had left the stage, and was speaking to those who had accepted his call to remain for religious conversation.

"Coming to my wife, he said, 'Well, my friend, and how do matters stand between your soul and God?' Trembling, she answered, 'I am very unhappy, sir.' Of course I thought she was alluding to my past unkindness. I could not suppose it to be possible for her to be unhappy in her soul because of sin, for I believed she had none. Here again I attempted to leave the place, feeling quite overpowered by what I had heard; but no! God would not allow me to pass that door, and so I was forced back, almost unconsciously, to the same spot I had started from; and just as I did so the preacher, rising up from his seat beside my wife, clasped together his hands, exclaiming with joy, 'Thank God, the woman's saved.' With the bright picture before my eyes of the Judge in heaven, and the precious words of pardon that had fallen from His lips, I felt almost ready to say, 'And I'm saved too,' but was deterred by the fear that after all I might be lost. Here my wife arose from her seat, and turning to me said, with tears in her eyes, 'Oh, Ned, do trust in Jesus.' All I seemed able to say was, 'Come on;' and turning sharply on my heel, I tried to leave the building again. But I was abruptly accosted by a young man who, putting his hand upon my shoulder, said, 'Young man, I have a message for you from the eternal world;' and as he so said, he opened his Bible, and drew my attention to the 16th verse of the 3rd chapter of St John's Gospel. When he had read the words, 'For God so loved the world, that He gave His only begotten Son, that whosoever believeth in Him should not perish, but have eternal life," he turned to me, and said, 'Can you read, sir?' 'A little,' I replied; when, holding the Bible close up to my face, he rejoined, 'Can you see your name there, my friend?' 'No,' said I; 'I haven't heard it, nor can I see it.' 'Now, you know,' said the young man, 'if you were walking along the country road, and if you saw a board up in the corner of a field, and upon it written, 'Whosoever trespasseth upon these premises will be prosecuted,' you would know very well that *whosoever* would mean you as well as anyone else; and so in this verse God says, 'Whosoever believeth on Him shall not perish.' 'Well' said I, 'I believe in Jesus—that is, that He died for me.' 'Then,' said he, 'if that's true, God says you shall never perish; let God be true, and every man a liar.'"

Ned, with his wife, then left the theatre, and wended his way home, full of thought as to what had passed, and wondering greatly at the surprising change that had come over his entire nature. He was staggered, and could not realize what it all meant. He had entered upon a new and to him perfectly strange experience, and whither it tended, and what it involved, was beyond his ken. His wife's mind was filled with similar thoughts, and she could find no heart to speak a word. Upon their arrival home she led the way into the cottage, and, lighting a candle, proceeded to the bedroom.

> SCRIPTURE TESTIMONY
>
> *Salvation transforms*
>
> 2 CORINTHIANS 5:16-17 · GALATIANS 6:15

"From the time we left the theatre," says Ned, "we had not spoken a word to each other. Watching my wife's actions narrowly, I became full of wonder as to what should be the next step, when, to my surprise, she fell down beside the bedstead, and began to pour out her soul before God in thankfulness for His wondrous love made known to her in Christ Jesus that night. Looking at her as I stood beside the doorpost, I felt something of a desire to pray also. It having been a long time since I had heard prayers of any kind, save those heard that evening in the theatre, I felt at a loss as to what I should say. By this time my poor wife's utterance was choked by the sobs that seemed to proceed from her very heart. Although Satan fought very hard with me to prevent me bending my knees, still Jesus gained the victory, and I fell down beside my poor broken-hearted wife, purposing to say that simple prayer, 'Our Father which art in heaven;' but as I was about to do so, I seemed to forget the words, and became wholly occupied with the sublime scene I had witnessed whilst in Astley's Theatre. One particular part of this scene interested me more especially—which was Jesus appearing on my behalf as a good and gracious intercessor; and here I became so absorbed with the love I felt towards Him, that I could only exclaim, 'Blessed Jesus, blessed Jesus, I thank Thee from my heart for saving my soul.'"

Ned's simple evangelical faith was very clear. As he often remarks in public, he had cause to be thankful that he was able to believe his sins to be already forgiven, and his salvation to have been already accomplished, instead of hesitating and doubting, and looking at certainties as if they were probabilities. Ned's confidence was solely the result of taking God at His word. He believed that Christ had died that he might not perish; and so, instead of asking God to reveal this to him, and so to save his soul, he praised Him that the work had been done. In humility he bowed himself, and said,

> "'Tis done! the great transaction's done!
> I am the Lord's, and He is mine;
> He drew me, and I followed on,
> Glad to obey the voice Divine.
> High heaven, that heard my solemn vow,
> That vow renewed shall daily hear,
> Till in life's latest hour I bow,
> And bless in death a bond so dear."

His wife heartily joined with him in prayer and thanksgiving, in which they continued for some time. When they arose, Ned observed at the other end of the bedroom, on the couch of cane cuttings, his little boy and girl sitting as if full of wonder and fear, not knowing what to make of the scene. Ned had hitherto felt but little, if any, love for his offspring; but at this moment he understood the refined, inexpressible joy of fatherhood. This was to him a new revelation, which filled his eyes with tears, and his heart with an emotion better understood than described. He had ill-treated them with a severity which was painful to contemplate. How he could have been so savage a brute, seemed now to him strange. How he could have permitted them almost to starve while he was drinking and rioting, passed all comprehension, now he had his heart filled with the generous impulses of affection. But he knew that it had been so; and there were the poor little creatures, huddled up in the corner, the victims of his ill-humours and resentment! His first feeling was to weep; his next to take them up in his arms and kiss them. There and then he made a solemn vow that, with the help of Him who had awakened such gentle emotions of love in his breast, he would ill-use them no more, but act the part of a Christian parent.

Ned and his wife then adjourned to the other room, for his cottage only contained two apartments, for "a bit of supper." It was but a small portion, but never meal seemed better. "We were about to partake of it," he says in his simple way, "but both of our hands seemed to refuse to touch it. I remember that my feelings at this moment were, that I must ask God's blessing upon the food now; and although I had not said grace for years—indeed, from the time of my boyhood—still I thought I would put my hands together, and open my mouth, and ask God, in words that I had often heard from my godly father, to bless the food He had given us."

When he had done so, Mrs. Wright felt too broken-down to partake of anything. "O God," she cried, with a heart full of joy, "this is too much for me." It was an occasion for weeping; and so instead of eating they wept and talked of all that the Lord had that night done for them. What a change! What a salvation!

SCRIPTURE TESTIMONY
Strengthening and encouraging new disciples
ACTS 14:22-23

The door was opened, and in came a Christian man who had lodged in Ned's house, before his conversion. "Whatever has led you here?" inquired Ned, surprised at the abrupt appearance of the visitor. "Oh," said he, "Ned, my boy, as soon as I got home to-night I heard of what had taken place with you;

and although I was a bit sceptical about its reality, I thought I would come and see."

It was just such a visitor as they needed at this juncture in their life. He was able to give wise counsel; and although a man in humble circumstances, and of no intellectual acquirements, he was competent to show the new converts "the way of God more perfectly." With the Word of God before him, he directed their attention to its precepts, urged upon them an open, frank avowal of their faith in Christ, that the brethren might rejoice, and sinners be convinced of the power of the gospel. With this he urged the necessity of communicating to Ned's old associates the good tidings of what God had done for him, at every favourable opportunity, believing that when they knew what a change had been wrought in his character, they would be impressed with the importance of religion. It was wise counsel. "To him that knoweth to do good, and doeth it not, to him it is sin." If every Christian really believed, and consequently acted upon, this precept of inspiration, the world would, in a Christian and moral sense, be very different from what it is now.

The next morning brought with it some peculiar difficulties which Ned had never before confronted, and in meeting which his piety must, he knew, be put to the test. He had arranged to fight Jack Connelly; but this engagement could not, of course, be fulfilled. The first thing after breakfast he went to the friend by whom the matter had been arranged, and announced his intention. Of course he was met with many bitter reproaches; called a cur, and a fool; and one remarked, "Poor Ned, he's gone off his chump (i.e. mind) at last." "I thought it would come to that before long," remarked his companion; "you see, the loss of Doggett's coat did him no good." Ned overheard these free criticisms, and observed, "No, Jerry, I never was in my right mind before; but I am now, thanks be to God." And with many more words did he converse with them of the new feelings which filled his breast. But in vain. They could not understand "the babbler." Convinced that he was mad, they resolved to quit his company; but one of them, who was more kind-hearted than the rest, saw him home; and when he reached the humble cottage, was convinced that Ned's madness was not altogether unenviable.

Instead of spending the evening, as he would probably have done but for his conversion, in the public-house, among ungodly associates, he accepted an invitation to attend a place "where prayer was wont to be made." The preacher of the preceding evening was there, and gave Ned such advice as he thought suitable, and furnished him with a little help in his poverty. But his great desire now was honourably to gain his livelihood. He spent some time in seeking employment, and at last he succeeded in getting a job of digging up a gentleman's garden; but, after working with great zest for the whole day, he was much disheartened by receiving only one shilling, with some stale crusts and a piece of mouldy cheese. Next Sabbath evening, Astley's Theatre was closed, in consequence of the disappearance during the week of the lessee; and the writer well remembers seeing the crowd of working people that assembled at the foot of Westminster Bridge to hear some speakers address them from a window in the corner house; but little knew that Ned was one of them, and that he had startled every one by the remarkable story of his life and new birth.

Not unnaturally, he was asked why he could not return to his old occupation as lighterman. The fact was, however, that before his conversion he worked without a license, but this he would not do now, as it would not be honest or fair. The cost of such a document was between two and three pounds, and through the goodness of some Christian friends the money was raised, and Ned soon found employment. Unfortunately, however, a man who had long known him as a rogue, informed his employer, and although Ned had been by that time, through sobriety, ability, and general good conduct, promoted to the post of foreman lighterman, he was thrown once more upon the world. It was a hard trial, but Ned felt called upon to bear it cheerfully. By doing odd jobs he succeeded in gaining bread for himself and family; and in the evening he and his wife went to a night school to pick up a little of the three neglected "r's." Meanwhile, he sought constant employment, but was discouraged by frequent refusal. One person whom he asked, shouted out, "No, you vagabond, certainly not; but if you're not out of that gate in double-quick time, I'll have you locked up; for we know now who it was that stole our bales of indigo and barrels of tobacco."

Poor Ned ran away as quickly as possible, conscious that he had been guilty of the robbery, crying out as he went along, with his heart full of grief, "Guilty, Ned, guilty." God had forgiven him, but society would not. Yet he did not murmur. After so dishonest a career he did not expect better treatment.

CHAPTER EIGHTH

"Mother, give us some bread."—Prayer answered.—Ned selling bibles.—The pipe.—Ned's first temptation.— Ned learns humility at Victoria Dock.—Ned learns the power of prayer.

CHAPTER EIGHTH

OR MORE than thirteen weeks poor Ned tramped the A streets of London, seeking work, and finding none. During this time some Christian friends gave a little assistance, and Mrs. Wright laboured day and night at the washing-tub, until she fell ill through over-work.

Ned describes this as one of the most trying seasons in the whole course of his life; for, having parted with nearly everything in the house that would realize a halfpenny, he

SCRIPTURE TESTIMONY
God answers prayer
LUKE 18:7 · JOHN 15:7 · ACTS 12:5 · JAMES 5:15

and his wife sat one evening gazing at the few embers in the firegrate, without any articles that could be pawned, when in came the little ones from the street, in which they had been playing, crying out, both at once, "Mother, give us some bread; I am so very hungry."

The saddened parents were unable to answer, and, after looking at one another for a few minutes, Ned broke the silence by asking, "Isn't there any bread in the house, mate?" When, walking to the cupboard, she produced a piece about the size of a penny loaf from the shelf, and having asked the Divine blessing upon the frugal meal, she divided the bread between the two children.

Ned very touchingly describes his emotions:

"At this moment there began a most terrible struggle between my soul and Satan; the Enemy suggesting that I should get bread

99

for my children anyhow, either by fair means or foul, since even an infidel would do that. Here I buried my face in my hands, and cried bitterly; at which my dear wife exclaimed, as she fell down upon her knees and tried to comfort me, 'Oh, Ned, don't cry, but cheer up; remember that a crust with Christ is better than all the world without Him.' Feeling a little encouraged by these words of comfort, I knelt down by the side of my wife, and asked God to help me; and within an hour after this prayer we received the intelligence that a Christian man was prepared to give me twenty-five shillings per week to sell Bibles and Testaments among my old companions; and although this appeared too good to be true, yet we had faith in God to believe that He had thought fit to answer our prayers; and, indeed, that very day, I received a sovereign to enable me to redeem my clothes from the pawnbroker's, and to procure some substantial food."

Here it may be said, that from the time of this offer being made to the present, though Ned has sometimes been brought so low in poverty as to have only a few halfpence in his pocket, yet he has never known what it is to be wholly without the means of supplying the absolute necessaries of life. For three years he sold Bibles in the streets, and with his small salary he managed to save enough to pay off the debts he had contracted in his unconverted days.

SCRIPTURE TESTIMONY
God answers prayer
LUKE 18:7 · JOHN 15:7 · ACTS 12:5 · JAMES 5:15

The Christian reader will readily understand that, in so great a change as Ned Wright's conversion, all his evil and questionable habits were not conquered without stern conflicts. Drink was a giant power that had been dethroned on the night of his conversion. Since that memorable occasion he has never tasted intoxicating liquors. The cause of so much of his poverty and wretchedness was, therefore, summarily removed without a pang of regret. This was no small moral triumph, and in conquering this infatuating habit he displayed the courage of a hero. But there was the pipe; what was to be done with that? All his life he had been a terrible smoker. Early in the morning, before and after all his meals, going to and returning from his work, in the evening and at night, Ned might have been seen with his pipe. He took it to bed, and sometimes fell asleep with it in his mouth, and if he awoke during the night he would at once relight his pipe. And after his conversion he still felt the fascinating power of the pipe, and remained for a while a slave to his old propensity. Even on the Sabbath, after leaving God's house, he would indulge in this habit.

An American divine has recently given the following concise hints to smokers: "1. Never smoke when ladies are present 2. Never smoke in the presence of gentle-men. 3. Never smoke when alone." Several godly brethren endeavoured to enforce the propriety of following this recommendation. Ned listened with respect, and tried again and again to adopt their advice. But the roots of the habit were deep; and although he abstained on one occasion for a whole week from his practice, he resumed it again. At another time he abandoned it for a month, but again he was overpowered. Determined, however, to succeed, and remembering the proverb relating to the ultimate issues of trying again, he denied himself for about six weeks, when, coming home one night from a meeting that had been held in North London, the temptation once more assailed him with its wonted force. As he was crossing Blackfriars Bridge he passed a gentleman who was smoking a Havannah cigar. The smell was delightful; poor Ned was enchained by the fascination; the old appetite was stronger than ever.

> "Well," reasoned Ned, "there is no harm in smoking, after all. It has a soothing influence, it comforts me, and perhaps God would have me smoke; and, indeed, there is nothing in His word to prohibit smoking. Many good and pious men have been great smokers."

The result of his reasoning was a determination to have a smoke if he could find a tobacco shop open between the bridge and his house; but if he could not find one, he would regard it as an intimation from God that it was His will he should leave off smoking. Not a very satisfactory way, certainly, of ascertaining the Divine will; and the fact was—and we need not conceal it—he set about securing a settlement most pleasing to himself. He saw many shops, but found them all closed, and passed by the last on the road home, and found that also to be shut. The Divine will seemed against his desires; and, on the plea that he had not reached home, he went through the New Cut, where he knew there would be plenty of tobacco shops open, and soon he found the longed-for tobacco and the charming long pipe with its sealing-wax end.

Instead of retiring to rest, he sat in his humble garden summer-house, smoking his pipe, and surveying the star-bespangled heavens. But his wife was filled with apprehensions lest this habit, however harmless when not immoderate, should become to Ned a temptation to return to other and worse habits. She concluded that it was safer for her husband to abstain altogether from tobacco, and, in her anxiety for his welfare, she earnestly prayed that God would cause the pipe to turn his stomach, that he might be disgusted with it. Ned was meanwhile enjoying his rest, but at length he turned indoors, complaining that he was inclined to vomit. "Thank God for that," replied his wife; "for I have been praying to God this last hour to cause that pipe to turn your stomach. Oh, Ned, you are surely taking a wrong step in resuming that pipe. You have given up all for Jesus, and now you have gone back to one of your old habits, so connected with our past unhappiness and misery. I'm sure you have not asked God to bless the pipe to your benefit and His glory." Ned made the matter a subject for prayer, and abandoned the pipe altogether. Since that time his wife has had no cause to fear consequences which might follow smoking.

SCRIPTURE TESTIMONY
True disciples forsake the old self and put on the new self
EPHESIANS 4:20-27 · EPHESIANS 4:28-5:9 · EPHESIANS 5:10-20 · COLOSSIANS 3:5-17

If this story illustrates the simplicity and genuineness of Ned's piety, so also does the following, the first temptation that presented itself after conversion. It occurred at the time when Ned was in great poverty through not obtaining employment. He wandered down to the waterside between Blackfriars and Waterloo bridges, and observing several vessels waiting the tide to go up through the bridges, the thought struck him that if he could get off to some of these craft, he might obtain the job of navigating some of them up the river. A waterman who knew Ned, and who was rejoiced to hear from him that he had given up all his dishonest practices, lent him one of his boats to endeavour to get a job. Ned thereupon rowed towards Waterloo Bridge, and as it was nearly low water, he saw, just above the bridge, something black, lying half-concealed in the mud, and having the appearance of a dead body. Rowing his boat aground, and stripping off his shoes and stockings, he waded through the mud, and found the black substance to be a large tarpauling, used for protecting the cargoes of barges navigating the river. Having washed the mud off his prize, and hauled it into his boat, he found the tarpauling to be new and valuable.

While thus occupied, he was observed by the captain of a billy-buoy lying close at hand, who seemed somewhat vexed that he had not picked up the prize, as he had seen it before Ned had arrived. The captain called out, "Don't take that away, young man; I'll give you ten shillings for it." Ned was confounded; he looked first at the prize, then at the man; he had found the article, he wanted his breakfast, and so did his children, and ten shillings were worth having in his poverty-stricken condition. What was he to do? Something seemed to say to him, "Ned, it is not yours to sell." So he washed off the mire, and discovering the name, "J. Hasler, Paul's Wharf," he resolved at once to return it to its proper owner. The enraged captain, when told by Ned that he "was converted the other day," and could not sell the article, all the more as the owner's name was upon it, remonstrated with Ned for being a fool; but he insisted that the word of God said, "Let him that stole, steal no more," and rowed away from the tempter, only, however, to be troubled by another, who seemed to say to Ned, "What a fool you are to refuse that half-sovereign! If you return the tarpauling to the owner, perhaps he will only give you the price of a pot of beer, or a glass of grog, for all your trouble, and yet your wife and little ones are starving at home. You have been asking God to supply your wants, and now He has put this thing in your way, and you refuse the gift. If God had not intended you to benefit by it to the amount of ten shillings, you would never have seen it." To Ned, unaccustomed as he was to specious reasoning, these injections of Satan seemed very plausible. He rowed a little reluctantly down the river;

"Satan," as he puts it, "seemed to clog the sculls," and the boat appeared as disinclined as himself to leave the ten shillings behind. And yet Ned felt convinced he was only acting rightly in refusing the captain's offer, and was glad that he had had sufficient courage to resist the temptation. Having reached the shore opposite Paul's Wharf pier, he went at once to the owner of the tarpauling, and informed him of the recovery of the lost article. Mr. Hasler was glad, looked over his purse as if searching for some small coin; and Ned, fearing that a sixpence might be offered him, was surprised to hear the gentleman say, "Young man, I have no smaller change than half a sovereign; I dare say you have had a deal of trouble with the tarpauling, so take that, and I'm much obliged."

Was it possible! He looked first at Mr. Hasler, and then at the gold coin, in blank astonishment. Half a sovereign—honestly obtained—the very same sum the captain had offered him! "Glory be to God!" shouted Ned, as he ran down with frantic delight to the boat; "My Jesus does all things well!" He rowed with speed to the other side of the river, and hurried home, and showed his wife the half-sovereign, and told her how God had enabled him to resist the temptation, and had rewarded him with His goodness. And they both knelt together in prayer, with hearts full of gratitude, for "grace to help in time of need."

"Blessed is the man that endureth temptation; for when he is tried, he shall receive a crown of life, which the Lord hath promised to them that love Him."

SCRIPTURE TESTIMONY
Salvation transforms
2 CORINTHIANS 5:16-17 · GALATIANS 6:15

Ned had not long entered upon his "new life " before he was surrounded by temptations of still greater potency than the one we have just described. His old companions sought by cunning devices to bring him again under subjection to evil. While he was seeking their best welfare, they laid traps to undermine his integrity. His little sermons to them about the love of Jesus Christ were ridiculed, although their power was really felt. The bargemen with whom he had so frequently been intoxicated, tempted him with drink, and laughed with scorn when he told them that, although not a pledged teetotaller, he had given up all alcoholic drinks.

"No more of that for me," he cried, as they offered him a full pot to drink; "I've had my share of it, and now I have turned it all up; for God has pardoned my sins, and I am a different man now. 'Old things have passed away, and all things have become new.' I have given up my old ways, and am happy in my Saviour."

And so he told them at the bar of the public-house how sinners were saved and brought into the fold of Christ. The men were silenced; they could not understand the matter. As his employer's son said, Ned was regarded as the last person in the world to turn from his drinking habits.

During the first week of his foremanship, Ned sent five barges to Victoria Dock at high water, with two men in each, while he followed in his barge alone. Having arrived

> **SCRIPTURE TESTIMONY**
>
> *Be reconciled to your brother*
> *before going to the altar*
>
> MATTHEW 5:23-24

at the dock in due course, he made his barge fast to the floating pier. The tide was just then running out very hard, and before he could get his oars put in, and prepare to drop his barge clear of the pier, to allow the passenger steamboat to approach, the pierman cast off the rope which held Ned's barge, and sent him adrift, although the passenger boat was then at Blackwall. This was a malicious act, and Ned's anger was so aroused that the consequences might have been serious, had the pierman been at hand. Away went the barge, the tide taking her still farther and farther from the shore, and drifting her right over to the other side. Ned was at a loss to know what to do, having no anchor to let go, and nothing on which, to lay hold to check her course. At last a Christian man, master of a small tug, observed Ned's dilemma, and steaming after the barge he took the headfast, and towed the barge back to the pier, and laid her athwart the lighter.

Ned at once remonstrated with the pierman for his unkind action, upon which he became abusive, and made use of the disgusting language so common among low men when provoked. Whenever Ned was on the pier he was irritated by similar abusive words, and at last was so angered, that he seized the man by his coat collar, ran him violently along the pier to the extreme edge, and threatened to throw him overboard. Never was man held in a more powerful grasp, and it would have been easy for Ned to carry out his intention. But just as he was about to let go, he remembered God, and was troubled. Immediately he dragged the man back, and walked off the pier.

The wretchedness that filled his soul at that moment Ned has not forgotten. The peace of mind which had once filled his heart with joy had departed. He had permitted Satan to master him, and had pained his Saviour. During the whole of the day his remorse was great, and when he got home he sought his heavenly Father, and confessed with bitterness of soul his sin. His old feelings, however, were not restored; as he wended his way to the Gospel Hall he felt self-condemned and unhappy. He was not the same joyous believer of yesterday, but a backslider.

One of the working men who addressed the meeting that evening observed Ned's dejected look, and Ned thought he knew all that had occurred. At the conclusion of the service the preacher addressed him, and inquired the reason of his dejection. Ned frankly told him all "You must," said the preacher, "go to that man and confess your fault before you can get peace."

"But," said Ned, "I've confessed it to God; is not that sufficient?"

"No," was the reply, "it is evidently not sufficient, or your peace would have returned. You must go to the man himself, and confess your sin, and tell him how much you have grieved God by it. For the Scripture saith, 'Therefore, if thou bring thy gift to the altar, and there remember that thy brother hath aught against thee, leave there thy gift before the altar, and go thy way; first be reconciled to thy brother, and then come and offer thy gift.'[1]

You must indeed do it, Ned, before you can have peace with God."

"But," was Ned's rejoinder, "he is an unconverted man."

"No matter," was the reply; "it must be done."

This was perhaps the severest trial of all. Ned's natural pride and feelings of self-respect rose against such a humiliation of himself before an adversary who had wronged him so maliciously. "I can't humble myself before him," he said to himself. "It's no use, I can't do it. The man was the first aggressor, he cast off the rope; had it not been for the owner of the steam tug, a whole

---

1   Matthew 5:23, 24.

tide's work would have been lost. How can I submit to this man, of all others? He would tell it out to all his mates and acquaintances that Ned Wright had begged his pardon." Ned felt he would rather submit to a heavy thrashing than to the humiliation of begging his enemy's forgiveness.

And yet he could not bear the intolerable load of misery which weighed upon his spirits. He sought refuge in sleep, but nature's kind restorer could not bring him relief. He endeavoured to pray, but found something clogging his utterance. Next morning he went as usual to his work, but his mind was occupied with thoughts that distressed him. He knew that he must go through the trial. He pictured himself going on to the pier, begging his enemy's pardon, and hearing in return the sneer, and bitter taunt, and jeering laugh. He had been unaccustomed to such a scene. Before his conversion he would have disdained the thought of submission, and for ever dispelled it from his mind; but now he could not shake off these feelings. Every sound he heard had for its echo "Victoria Dock," and at every step he took he seemed to confront "Victoria Dock." At the close of the day he found himself at Fenchurch Street station. How he got there he scarcely knew; but being there, he took a ticket for Blackwall. Leaving the train, he walked on the pier. The boat was there waiting to convey passengers to Victoria Dock, and Ned half wished she would start before he could reach her. The struggle between the flesh and the spirit here reached its climax. He had fought bravely with members of the "ring," and had not been troubled with misgivings and fears; but this conflict vexed him more than any other. Standing undecided as to what he should do, with one foot on the bulwark rail of the boat and the other on the edge of the pier, the boat at last moved off, and a voice cried, "Look out, governor, or you'll be overboard." Now was the decisive moment. He must either jump one way or the other, or fall into the river; and just as he was about to spring on to the pier, a hand behind seized and pulled him on board the boat. He had no alternative now; he must go to Victoria Dock. On his arrival there he saw the very man he so much dreaded stationed to collect the passengers' tickets as they landed. Ned's heart began again to quake. He walked round the boat several times, allowing every passenger to land but himself. His turn, however, came; and so, giving up his ticket, he said to the man: "George, I want to see you."

"I should think you did," was the reply, "after the manner you served me yesterday. Why, you might have drowned me."

"Well," said Ned, "the fact is, George, I was converted a little while ago, and I now confess to you how very wrong I was to act toward you as I did yesterday. It has made me very miserable and unhappy ever since, and I am compelled to come and acknowledge myself in fault, and beg of you to forgive me. It is a wonder, George, that I did not throw you overboard; for you know what a character I have been in times past, before God, in the greatness of His mercy, converted me. Ah, George, I would have thrown you into the river then; but now God's preventing mercy restrained me. I shall be contented and happy now that I have told you, and I am sure you won't take further notice of it, or be offended. The Lord, I know, has pardoned all my sins, and saved my soul; and I feel deeply grieved that I should so soon offend Him who has done so much for me. You will forgive me, George, won't you?"

Ned had touched the pierman's heart, and he burst into tears. They both went into the cabin, at George's request, and the latter, addressing Ned, said that he had a praying mother, but he was still a wicked man, without God, unsaved, and sure of being eternally lost. Weeping like a child, he inquired of Ned what he should do.

"Shall I pray for you?" asked Ned.

"Yes do," was the reply, "pray God to save me now— at once."

The two burly men knelt down in the cabin, and Ned besought God's mercy for his companion. While they were thus engaged, three or four lightermen came and stood over the hatchway, and hearing Ned's fervent supplications, they sought to interrupt him by throwing in their midst a "bollard," or large piece of wood. It scarcely touched Ned's leg, and did not hinder him.

When they arose, the lightermen laughed at them, and mocked their prayers; and so they moved farther away from the hatchway, out of sight, and Ned produced his Testament, which he always carried in his pocket; but, not being a good reader, he asked his friend to read the well-known

verse which Martin Luther once happily designated "the gospel in minia-
ture,"—the 16th of the 3rd chapter of John's Gospel. Ned expounded as well
as he could the meaning of the message, and in simple language entreated
George to believe on Jesus Christ whom God had sent for his salvation.

George's eyes were opened to see the spiritual significance of the words
Ned had chosen for his text. He realized the forgiveness of sins, and by
the simple act of faith in Christ he found the peace which passeth all
understanding. They rejoiced together, and praised God for the mercy
He had shown them both.

Now was Ned light-hearted and happy. He had humbled himself, and
God had highly exalted him. His troubles had vanished; his soul was filled
once again with the joys of "first love;" and God had enabled him to be
useful in the conversion of the man whom he had dreaded. Heartily did
he sing—

> "Ye fearful saints, fresh courage take;
> The clouds ye so much dread
> Are big with mercy, and shall break
> With blessings on your head."

The extreme simplicity of Ned's
religious life cannot be better illustrated than by the following story.
Shortly after the occurrence at the
Victoria Dock, he was engaged in

SCRIPTURE TESTIMONY
Ask Me anything in My name
MATTHEW 18:19 · JOHN 14:13-14 · JOHN 16:23-24

obtaining gravel from a dredging machine in the Thames. He had under-
taken the work of his employer by contract, and therefore endeavoured
to economise, by taking up the empty barge himself; but it was necessary
to have two men on board when the barge was laden with the gravel, to
guide it safely through the arches of the various bridges, especially those at
Chelsea and Battersea. On one occasion Ned went up the river as usual with
a large empty barge, capable of carrying seventy tons, giving strict orders
to one of his men to join him at high water when the barge was loaded.
High water came, but no assistant; and, no casual helper being at hand,
Ned was alarmed, knowing that it would be the height of imprudence to

attempt single-handed to pilot the barge through so dangerous a bridge as that at Chelsea. If it struck against the pier, instead of taking the arch in the centre, it would be sure to sink. While thus perplexed, he was aroused by a man on board the dredger, asking him if he did not think the barge was deep enough loaded. Ned at once sprang to his feet, and found that she was already overloaded. The dredger was thereupon stopped, the fastened ropes were cast off, and another empty barge let in to load. The ebb tide drifted the full barge down the river, and before him was the dreaded bridge. He was now at his wits' ends, being certain of striking against the piers.

In his extremity he sought the Lord. He ran down into the cabin, thinking that a retired spot was essential to prayer, crept up aft right under the deck, and entreated God to help him out of his difficulty, telling Him that it was impossible to guide the barge through the bridge alone without help, and it was not his fault the man had not kept his word. He forgot for the moment that he ought to be on deck, working as well as praying; and so, leaving his retirement, he went above, and, to his great astonishment, he saw the heavily laden barge driving straight through the centre of the arch, not needing any guidance. The best skilled lightermen could not have done better. And so, when he had cleared the bridge, he shouted with joy, and sang so loudly as to surprise the people on the bridge, one of the revival hymns which he knew so well—

> "Glory, glory everlasting,
>   Be to Him who bore the cross."

From that time Ned believed intensely in the power of prayer.

CHAPTER NINTH

CHAPTER NINTH

AT THE time of his conversion, Ned's firstborn son was six years of age. From his birth he had been an extremely delicate child, and little indeed able to bear the brutal treatment he received when his father was in a drunken fit. Ned's sudden change of conduct seemed to produce a shock to his little boy's system, and now that the excitement in which the child was constantly living had subsided, his delicate state of health was more manifest.

The children attended the house of God as regularly as their parents, and it was more than once observed how marked was the attention which little Edward paid to the

SCRIPTURE TESTIMONY
There is no sting in death for the believer
I CORINTHIANS 15:54-57

services. He evidently understood much of what the preachers said, and he appeared lost in thought when in simple words the story of Jesus' love and His death on the cross for sinners was related. It was feared by some neighbours, that his close attention to these topics might affect his mind, and cause him to be subject to melancholy, and his mother was advised not to bring him so often to the place of worship. The little fellow, however, soon gave evidence by his conversation and inquiries that he had emotions in his heart which were the fruit of the indwelling Spirit of God. He would take some of his father's tracts, and put them under the doors of the neighbours' houses; and those who probably would have repelled a grown-up person, received with interest a tract from the little missionary. At last, however, he grew very weak, and was compelled to keep his bed. It was a sad trial to his parents, who had taken even a deeper interest in him since what they believed to be his conversion, but they were persuaded that the Lord was calling little Edward to his heavenly home. He received every attention possible, but his case was hopeless. His mother was about to put on him a mustard plaster, but he begged she would not, as it would not do him any good. "I'm going," said he, in such pathetic tones as sank into his mother's heart, "to be with Jesus, it is far better, and it won't be long, mother." The father came home just as he was entreating his mother not to weep since he was going to live with Jesus in heaven. "Teddy," said his father, "are you sure your sins are all forgiven? Because, you know, only such can enter the kingdom of heaven." "Oh, yes, father," was the reply, "they are all washed away in the blood of Jesus." While his parents were weeping bitterly, he gasped out, "O Jesus! O Jesus! And, as he uttered the words the third time, his spirit took its flight to the Saviour whom he so fondly and so simply loved.

Deeply grieved as Ned was, he resolved not to follow his child to the grave with the usual mourning habiliments, for he regarded many of these appendages of grief as suitable only for a masquerade. Attired therefore in their every-day clothes, father and mother entered the carriage with their little girl, who carried in her hand a bunch of flowers, and at the grave, after the ceremony, Ned gave an address.

The death of her brother caused a great change in the deportment of Louisa, Ned's eldest daughter. Her brother had frequently talked to her of the Saviour, and her parents made her the special object of earnest prayer. Their prayers were answered, and little Louisa was only six years old when, at a large meeting of Sunday-school children, she ventured to ask the teacher who conducted the service, whether she might be allowed to tell her little friends how she was converted. Every one was surprised, Ned most of all; and her simple story, so unaffectedly told, brought tears into many eyes, and caused some to exclaim, "Out of the mouths of babes and sucklings God hath perfected praise." Since then she has manifested by her daily conduct the reality of the work of God in her young heart;

and, although only between ten and eleven years of age, she is a great help and comfort to her parents.

These facts may well put to shame those Christians who either do not believe in, or are indifferent to, the conversion of little children. Thank God, the cases of these two children are not exceptional. But they greatly encouraged Ned in his work as an evangelist and a salesman of Bibles.

Among the lightermen of the Thames the news of his conversion quickly spread, and Ned was for some time the subject of their conversation. He had hitherto been shunned by them as a reprobate character, unworthy of their society and confidence. And now that he was a changed man, and was engaged in Christian labour, they suspected him of being a hypocrite. For some time they refused to be convinced of his sincerity, declaring it to be utterly impossible that such a vagabond should be converted. One of their number, however, was more open to reason, and he resolved to hear Ned speak at the first opportunity. A lighterman's tea meeting was soon afterwards given, and this man, with his wife, attended it out of curiosity. Two or three Christian men addressed the lightermen, and among them was Ned, who seemed to produce quite an impression upon his old companion. At the close of the meeting Ned went to him, and said, "Well, old chap, have you a desire to be saved?" The inquiry was felt to be very direct, and he replied, "I'm convinced there is something in this, but I cannot stay to talk about it now; it's more than mere excitement. I believe there is a reality about the matter that I have not yet understood. It is perfectly true what you have said tonight; no man could by any means act the part you have taken tonight of himself. No, Ned, there must be something here that I have not got. I see I am in a dangerous position, and need a Saviour as well as you."

Ned was delighted with his friend's answer; and at once he invited him and his wife into an adjoining room, where he might still further converse with them. There they knelt down in prayer, Ned pleading with the Lord on their behalf; and after conversing with them about the gospel of the grace of God, light dawned upon their minds, and with joy they left the room, believing that God had, for the sake of Christ, forgiven them their sins.

The news of this man's conversion spread rapidly among his associates, and they were surprised to find him telling the story to all within his reach. This led to another lighterman, who was bitterly prejudiced against Ned, and would believe anything of him but that he was a reformed man, listening to Ned's addresses. Taking his wife with him, he went into the hall where Ned was announced to speak, and heard with much interest the earnest address given to the unconverted. The service also powerfully touched the hearts of this man and his wife, and both eventually became exemplary Christians. One man is now the deacon of a church, and the other a leading speaker at a "gospel hall"—the latter being greatly useful in promoting the knowledge of Jesus Christ among the men stationed on board the fire-brigade floats.

Ned gives us an instance of the kind of treatment he received as an open-air preacher about this time. He says:

> SCRIPTURE TESTIMONY
>
> *Holy Spirit convicts people of their sin*
> JOHN 16:8

"Not long after my conversion, I felt a desire to stand at the corner of the streets, and tell of the love of Jesus to poor sinners. I got a board for this purpose, upon which I had some texts of Scripture, and also a light for the purpose of showing them more plainly to the people. One Saturday night I had a very large company, and, in the midst of my speaking, a man at the back of the crowd, who was one of my old companions, threw a stone weighing nearly half a pound, which whizzed by my ears like the sound of a child crying, and made a dent on my board, which was on a level with my head, quite a half-inch in depth. This man was a Romanist of the most bitter kind. He was caught, but promising not to do it again, I told them to release him; but he had scarcely left the place when I felt it my duty solemnly to warn the people of the anger of God. I announced in a loud tone of voice several passages of Scripture, especially dwelling upon this one: 'The eyes of the Lord are in every place, beholding the evil and the good.' This had the desired effect upon a young man in the crowd, who had only that morning returned from Wandsworth prison, after six months' hard labour for felony. He now began his evil practices again, and in his first attempt he succeeded in getting 'a solicitor' (i.e. a white handkerchief). He made another attempt in the hope of getting a silk one this time; but while his hand was in the gentleman's pocket he heard the Scripture, which came like a thunderbolt to his conscience; and so, dropping down upon his knees, he screamed out to God to have mercy upon him. Here the gentleman was advised by several of the bystanders to give him in charge, and prosecute him; but as a Christian he declined doing so, preferring to leave the man in the hands of God, praying that He would save his precious soul, which we have every reason to believe was acccmplished that night. Providing him with lodging and food till Monday, he was taken to a home, where he conducted himself in a proper manner, and was eventually got into a situation, and I believe he is employed there at the present time."

From the first, Ned was not only useful among his old workmen, and the class of dishonest men to which he had belonged, but also among the policemen. In former days they were but too well acquainted with him, courting his company, and asking after his welfare too freely;

"For," says Ned, "if I were not in prison, seldom a day passed, but what one of them inquired for me, either to know what I was doing, or where I was situated; indeed, they looked after me carefully, and liked nothing better than to have an eye on me." After his conversion, when it had become known that he was really living a different life, those of the police who had watched him so long, ceased to feel any further interest in him. Indeed, they shunned Him not unfrequently; for he would approach them in the character of an "informer," and having awakened their interest, would "inform" them of the love of God, and "the manslaughter of Jesus" on the cross, and would tell them that the Lord's murderers were named "sinners," and that they were of that class too.

"Several times," says Ned, "did I have the opportunity of address-ing the police in a body, and then I would pick out the men who at various times had me in their custody, and would tell them what a character I was, as they well knew, and also what God had graciously done for my soul; and at the same time I would urge them to believe on that Saviour who had changed me, and made me a new creature in Christ Jesus.

SCRIPTURE TESTIMONY
The blood of Jesus cleanses us from all sin
I JOHN I:7

"At one of these meetings an elderly man, a detective, belonging to the South of London, sat listening to me.

"On several occasions he had sought me before my conversion, and although he was considered to be one of the cleverest men in his division, yet he never had the luck to find me out. Eagerly did he listen, as if riveted to the seat, to all that was said; and after the meeting I went to him in the hope of saying something personally to him of the Saviour; but he declined to hear, and abruptly left the place.

"Some time after this I was with the Bible carriage near the 'Elephant and Castle' and gathering a few people around me, I read portions of God's word to them, telling them also of the love of Christ; and, far outside the crowd, who should I spy but my friend the detective! And as I waxed rather warm in my work, I observed him take out his handkerchief, and wipe away a tear from his eye, though at the same time he professed to be wiping his face; but my eye was upon him now, and I saw that his emotions were very strong. He tried to conceal his feelings; but it was only too plain that he was brokenhearted, and went away because he could not listen any further.

"A short time after, whilst preaching at the hall, a tall lady-like-looking person came in, and at the close of the service, addressing me, said, 'You will perhaps excuse me, sir, but are you "Ned Wright, the converted burglar"?' 'I am,' said I. 'Then, sir,' said she, 'you are the person my husband talks so much about. He has been an infidel all his life; but he is now very ill, and says that you haunt him day and night, asleep or awake, and that he is continually thinking of you. I know he is not on the right road, but he wants to see you; will you come?' She spoke so earnestly, and so like a child of God, that I took her to be a Christian, and so I promised to call at once upon her husband. What was my surprise, on arriving at the house, to find that it was my old friend, the detective, on his dying bed! I shook hands with him, and then came direct to the point about the salvation of his soul, and the greatness of the love of Christ for all poor sinners, and the way by which sinners could be saved. But the dying man cried out, 'O Ned, O Ned, say no more—say no more; I cannot bear it, it will break my heart.' 'Would to God it may!' I replied; 'for then there will be two broken hearts together. Reproach broke the heart of Jesus; let the word break your heart, and then Jesus will heal it for you; for it is His delight to heal the broken-hearted.' 'Oh, but, Ned,' said the poor fellow, 'I've been such a sinner; my sins, too, are of a more peculiar kind than those of other people; if policemen will aspire to be sergeants, they will sometimes seek their ends by unfair means; and I, like many others, did not attain my position in the force in the most honourable way, and I feel it bitterly to-day.' 'But,' said I, soothingly, 'the blood of Jesus Christ, God's Son, cleanseth us from all sin, and whosoever believeth on Him shall be saved.' This led the poor man to see that there was 'life for a look at the crucified One,' and looking he lived. Shortly after he fell asleep in Jesus, rejoicing in His name. His wife and daughter both became Christians, and are glorifying God by consistent walk and conversation."

As a Bible agent, Ned had many opportunities of serving the Lord in unexpected and unlooked-for ways. To have confined him to the observance of certain rules would have crippled his efforts and spoiled his work. He was not content with selling Bibles and Testaments to those who made application for them. He as frequently read or recited portions to the passers by, and was always ready to expound, so far as he could, the meaning of those passages which referred more directly to the work of Christ in the redemption of man. His experiences in this department of Christian labour were greatly useful in awakening the careless. One day, whilst standing opposite Christ's Church in the Blackfriars Road, he was asked the price of a Bible by a man who told him that he had been very ungodly, but he would like to know how God could righteously pardon such a sinner as he. Ned told him in a few simple words, and the poor man was much comforted, and went away believing that there was mercy even for him. There was a group of persons around, to whom Ned gave suitable tracts, and spoke of the love of his Master. For some time he was with his Bible carriage in the New Cut, a low and crowded market street in South London, and each evening he had congregations varying from one hundred to several hundreds of persons, to whom he preached Jesus Christ.

SCRIPTURE TESTIMONY

Jesus will never send away those who come to Him

JOHN 6:37

"On one occasion, when I had finished speaking," he reports in the chronicle of the work done by the mission with which he was then connected, "and while some of the brethren were singing a hymn, I went amongst the crowd, and distributed tracts. A gentleman extended his hand for one, and said that he had been a Sunday-school teacher, and had prayed very much; still he could not say as I could, that he had everlasting life, nor could he realize peace. I explained that peace was the result of pardon, and pardon was the result of faith in the precious blood of Jesus which cleanseth from all sin.

"Some time afterwards, when in Stamford Street, several persons, after I had been speaking, bought Bibles and Testaments. One young man, who lingered about the carriage, I felt constrained to speak to; so I told him simply of the great love of Christ in dying for lost sinners, and asked him if he had not proved it. He said that he had just left home, being out of work; his mother and sisters were believers, and were continually asking God to show him the error of his way, and he wished he had not spoken to me, as he felt truly miserable, and the whole of his sins seemed to come up before him. 'Thank God for that' said I, 'and now is your time to take them to Jesus; He casts out none who come to Him.' With this the young man went away broken-hearted, and a deeply convicted sinner.

"Some short time after this, the same young man came up to me when I was standing at the corner of Trinity Street, Borough, and said, 'I have been looking for you, sir, to thank you for your kindness to me, in telling me that day in Stamford Street the way in which I could be saved. Thank God, sir, I can now say that Jesus is mine. I am rejoicing in Him as a redeemed sinner, pardoned through His blood, which He shed on Calvary.'"

For this work, great aptitude is required. While being careful lest he should be drawn into controversy, the Bible agent should be quick-witted and conclusive in his replies. When a man is spoken to about the importance of his soul's salvation, if he enters upon controversy, it is invariably with the motive of shelving the real question at issue. He must be shut up to the one all-important subject before a personal appeal is likely to be successful with him. That little insinuating, active, versatile, nimble-fingered, and swift-footed friend known as Tact, is the servant to employ. By using tact, a man will be patient under rebuke and reproach, and will meet them, not by repelling frowns, but by the kindly smile and the brotherly word. Ned seems to have been in this respect well adapted for his peculiar and difficult work. One man, whose mind was filled with pretentious nonsense which he ventured to call science, asked Ned what was the use of the book he offered him. "Use," said Ned, "it contains the blessed promises of God to lost sinners, and the only way in which you can be saved is described within its covers." The man's watchword, however, was declared to be "science"—it was "science" that was wanted now-a-days. But Ned only answered that *his* fancied science would perish in the using; while the only enduring science was the science which saves. Many objections to Christianity were so palpably foolish, that Ned very easily disposed of them. Sometimes he was met by the most absurd arguments. The replies of ignorance, however, as a rule, worked favourably to Ned's mission; for their absurdity, and sometimes the interest which they created, led to good results—crowds assembling to hear what the Bible-man had to say in defence of the word of God. Many persons, too, passing to and from the City, heard Ned's voice and the texts of Scripture which he quoted, and thus something was given them upon which to meditate. The majority of the police were not opposers of Ned's missionary efforts; indeed, some, being Christians, highly approved of them, and saw that he was not molested.

"What do you call yourself?" asked a young man, in a sneering manner.

"A poor sinner," was the quick response, "saved by the blood of Jesus."

"You have never seen Jesus," was the rejoinder, "and so what do you know about Him? "

Ned replied, "It does not matter about my seeing Him; for God's word says, 'To as many as received Him, to them gave He power to become the sons of God, even to as many as believe on His name 'Whom not having seen we love: in whom, though now we see Him not, yet believing, we rejoice with joy unspeakable and full of glory,' for we have redemption through His blood, even the forgiveness of our sins; we have peace with God, through our Lord Jesus Christ." The young fellow turned away, silenced.

> SCRIPTURE TESTIMONY
>
> *Preach the word, in season*
> *and out of season*
>
> 2 TIMOTHY 4:2

Naturally of a restless disposition, Ned could not be inactive when the slightest opportunity for service presented itself. One day, while in Tooley Street, he had to seek shelter from the rain under a railway arch, where a number of persons were standing for the same purpose. So he took advantage of their presence by reading to them the Scriptures, and speaking of their value. The consequence was that some Bibles were purchased, and a young woman who had lived a reckless life, although her mother thought she was still in service, was rescued from her shame, and is now in respectable circumstances. Ned also managed to take his stand with his Bible carriage where he might meet workmen as they emerged from the warehouses and factories at dinnertime and in the evening; and at night he went to some unusually busy thoroughfare, lit his lamp, set out his books, and discoursed respecting the Saviour. The result of these efforts was that many were influenced for good, who never, or very rarely, attended any place of worship, while some were taken from the depths of infamy and vice, and made respectable members of society.

Occasionally poor Ned was outwitted by objectors, and not having so full an acquaintance with the word of God as he has now, and not being accustomed to the tricks of professed disbelievers in Christianity, he was occasionally sorely put to it for an answer to their quibbles. On one occasion, while endeavouring to arrest the attention of some workmen who were leaving their factory in the Blackfriars Road, by reading portions of Scripture, he was interrupted by a man who inquired, "What are you reading there, guv'nor?"

"I am reading the Bible, sir, as well as I can," replied Ned, eagerly and gladly, hoping to secure the attention of the inquirer.

"Well," was the cynical reply, "but you don't believe what you read, do you?"

"Oh, yes," ejaculated Ned; "I believe every word in this most precious book."

"But," replied the man,, "that cannot be surely; and if you'll lend me your book for a moment, I'll show you that you don't believe it.'"

Accordingly, Ned handed him the book, when, turning to Ecclesiastes, the third chapter, the nineteenth and twentieth verses, the man read: "For that which befalleth the sons of men befalleth beasts; even one thing befalleth them, as the one dieth, so dieth the other; yea, they have all one breath; so that a man hath no pre-eminence above a beast: for all is vanity. All go unto one place; all are of the dust, and all turn to dust again."

"There now, do you mean to say you believe that?"

"Oh, no, my friend," was the too eager response; "for that is not in the Bible."

"Well," said his opponent, "it is in the book that you sell for Bibles;" and so pointing Ned to the passage, he left him to read it at his leisure.

The Bible-seller was confounded as he read the words, and was greatly surprised that they should be found in the book he so much loved. The bystanders laughed at his confusion, and he had not a word to say. Fearing lest he should not have enough grace to endure their taunts, and afraid of being subjected to still further ridicule, he put his Bible into his pocket, and wended his way home.

In the evening he attended the usual service, depressed and burdened in spirit. The preacher was keen enough to observe that something was wrong with Ned; his responses, for which he was perhaps somewhat famous, were not so hearty, and his devotion not so great. At the close of the service he inquired what was on his mind that made him sad. He was told what had taken place.

"Ah," said the preacher, "my dear brother, but you should have asked the man to read the next verse, which says, 'Who knoweth the spirit of man that goeth upward, and the spirit of the beast that goeth downward to the earth?'"

Ned's mind saw it at once, and wondered that he had been so stupid as to forget to read on, that he might understand what the passage meant "I learnt such a lesson through this," he said, "as I trust I have never forgotten; viz., to take care for the future to look at a scripture's connection before I come to a conclusion."

SCRIPTURE TESTIMONY
Salvation transforms
2 CORINTHIANS 5:16-17 · GALATIANS 6:15

Sometimes Ned's appearance in the neighbourhoods where he was so well known, and the novel modes to which he resorted for securing an audience, produced quite a sensation. Thus, he took his Bible-barrow into a street in Rotherhithe, in which there was a large dayschool, and planted himself opposite the building just before twelve o'clock. At this hour the little ones, he knew, would leave the school, and a number of workmen would be flocking past on their way home to dinner. After patiently waiting a little time, the children came running from school, and seeing Ned with his barrow, not unnaturally flocked around him. Holding three or four attractive "picture-books" in his hand, he invited the little ones to come to him; and when they did so, he said, "I want you to sing me that pretty hymn beginning,

'I think when I read that sweet story of old'

and if you will, I'll give one of these pretty books to the three best singers." The children were of course delighted, and the competition for prizes began.

Their musical voices soon charmed up the windows, and brought out the neighbours. The workmen stayed and listened to the sweet songsters. When they had finished, Ned spoke for a few minutes; then they resumed singing, and preaching followed. It was a pleasing sight, and all were delighted, the children gaining more prizes than had been offered in the first instance.

"Having been away from this neighbourhood for some years," says Ned, "I imagined that the people would not recognize me, but I found the reverse to be the case; for in less than a quarter of an hour an old woman who remembered me made it her special business to run up and down from door to door, bearing the intelligence that I was Ned Wright. And never shall I forget the delightful scene that took place as soon as the men came back from their dinner on their way to their work, some of them evidently filled with surprise, and others, who were Christians, glorifying God for the marvellous change. For in this street alone I had for several years kept the inhabitants in constant fear, lest at the dead hour of the night their bolts and bars might yield to my exertions, and I might offer them violence. I should think that for upwards of twelve months I indulged in the gathering of children in the streets, until at last my voice gave way, and I was' compelled to discontinue the practice."

CHAPTER TENTH

CHAPTER TENTH

THE STREET market in the New Cut affords a sight once witnessed never to be forgotten. The poorest classes of South London purchase here most of the necessaries of life in smaller quantities, and perhaps at a cheaper rate, than in any other district. The road is lined on each side with costermongers' barrows, sellers of staylaces, trinkets, stationery, herbs, and common wares. Whether such a street is the best in which to preach may be debatable; the fact, however, that there were so many persons passing who might be disposed to listen, was too tempting to Ned; and, notwithstanding the possibility of inconveniences arising from a crowd, he resolved to make the street the scene of some of his evangelistic labours.

The inconvenience could not have been at any time greater than that ordinarily arising from the interest excited by the fervid eloquence of "Cheap Jack," and the police did not at first interfere with Ned's open-air efforts. Some, indeed, were Christian men; and while the speaker chose a suitable corner, they approved of his mission. One day, however, witnessed a complete change in the district police; for it happened that a somewhat officious Roman Catholic sergeant had been put upon the New Cut beat. In the evening Ned took his barrow into a quiet by-street, and began to offer his Bibles for sale, and to speak to those who had collected around him. In the course of time he gathered a crowd of nearly a thousand people, who listened attentively to the speaker's story. In the midst of his address the police sergeant pushed his way through the crowd, and in a rude and ungentle-manly manner peremptorily ordered Ned to dismount.

"Come down, sir; we don't want any of your claptrap here."

"Ay, sergeant," said Ned, smiling, "that's just what I'm trying my best to do—to keep these poor people out of your trap."

Pleasantries and expostulations however failed to change the sergeant's purpose, and although the people entreated him to let the preacher alone, he threatened Ned that if he did not speedily remove he would lock him up. Of course the books were gathered together, and Ned began to move. Meanwhile about forty persons standing by struck up a tune:

> "Happy day, happy day,
> When Jesus took my sins away."

Ned, however, was not to be beaten. He had not given the sergeant any provocation, and he believed that if the man had not exceeded, he had at least gone to the extreme boundary-line of his duty. "Cheap John" was permitted to shout with the voice of a basoon; why should not Ned "testify" with not inferior lungs to the virtues of his superior wares? Knowing that the police could not interfere with him if he only kept moving on, with a steady and tantalizing step he proceeded along the New Cut, wheeling his own barrow, preceded by a Christian man carrying the naptha lamp, and followed by a company of sympathising brethren singing most lustily.

It was Saturday evening, at an hour when the New Cut was more than ordinarily crowded; and as the singers marched along, preceded by Ned—who, we dare say, sang as lustily as any—the crowd became so great, that the street was rendered impassable, and "Cabby" could not make headway. Ned was by no means desirous of causing so great an inconvenience, and was purposing to leave the street, when the sergeant pressed his way to Ned, and urged him to "move on."

"Why, you see, my friend," replied Ned, "that is impossible; there are so many people here, however, we'll just show you a little of that commodity that you would not grant us just now—namely, grace;" and so saying, he exhorted the people to move away on their own respective business, adding that he intended occupying the same spot from which he had been ejected, on the following Saturday evening. This he did without any interference on the part of the sergeant, who evidently gave him up as incorrigible; and from eight o'clock in the evening until ten minutes to twelve at night he spoke to the large crowds that assembled, amidst the occasional interruptions of a persistent organ grinder, who smiled, as only an organ grinder can smile, as if delighted with the annoyance he was creating, and at the same time unconscious of the meaning of all remonstrances that were not backed up by money. Then Mr. Cheap John would vary the monotone of the wretched music by his coarse but not always ungenial sallies; and he in turn would be drowned by the blasts of a trumpet that affected the tympanum of the bystanders, whilst Ned was seeking to affect their consciences. However, notwithstanding all these and other difficulties, the preaching went on, and at the close five persons remained behind to thank the speaker for his appeals to their hearts, and to testify that they had been moved by the power of God's grace. It is now four years ago since this scene occurred, and meeting quite recently with two of these converts, Ned was rejoiced to find that they were still walking in the light of Divine truth and fellowship.

Ned sought other equally lively places in which to bear testimony to the worth of religion. In the company of two or three of his brethren, he went to Lambeth fair, a scene of much conviviality and dissipation. On their arrival they found that it would be imprudent to venture inside; they therefore sought to arrest the attention of the people as they were going in and coming out. Ned spoke first, and in an effective way he shouted, "The way to the fair is the way to hell, but the way to Jesus is the way to heaven. 'Repent ye, therefore, and be converted, that your sins may be blotted out.'" This was repeated frequently, and seemed to excite considerable feeling among those who were standing by. While Ned was speaking, he observed a man in a cart driving along very rapidly, evidently maddened with drink; for when he saw the speaker on his stand in the road, he shouted out to the crowd as he whipped up his horse, "Out of the way! Just see how I'll upset his old applecart for him!" What would have been the consequence of his infuriated rage, had not Ned dismounted and stood aside, it is impossible to tell; but as the drunken fellow passed by, his whip whistled over Ned's head, and his oaths filled the ear with dread. After the addresses had been delivered, and the people began to disperse, Ned, speaking to a man and woman who lingered behind, asked what they thought of the message they had heard. "Well," said the man, "to tell you the truth, I dunno what to think on it; I know this much, how sumever, I've come a long way to this 'ere fair, and now, I dunno how it is, but I haven't pluck enough to go in." "But how is that, my friend?" asked Ned. "Well, to tell the plain truth, measter," said the poor fellow, with tears in his eyes, "you've been saying to me this very night just what my poor old mother said to me twenty year ago." Finding that he had sold the Bible his mother had given him upon her dying bed, Ned gave one to the poor man, who parted with him in a different state of mind from that he was in when he came to the fair.

SCRIPTURE TESTIMONY
Hopeful, patient and prayerful
ROMANS 12:12

Perhaps, however, the worst place Ned ever attended with the view of preaching the gospel was Billingsgate Market. Many descriptions have been published of the scene to be witnessed early in the morning at this resort of the costermongers of the metropolis; but no words could exaggerate the wickedness of the place. Even Ned, who had been accustomed to use the foulest language, confessed that the oaths and curses used at Billingsgate exceeded anything he had heard in his life. Having prayed for guidance, he left home early one morning, and proceeded to this scene of iniquity. Arriving there, he occupied a suitable position, and began quoting several passages of Scripture in his usual rough-and-ready mode.

He had not been speaking for more than three minutes, when some one responded by throwing with great force a very large cod's head, accompanied by the not very complimentary assertion, "There's two of you!" Undaunted, he continued his address, when a young mischievous fellow came behind him, and putting his basket over Ned's head, shouted in high glee, "Hallo, boys! Here's another guy!" Ned soon extricated himself from his ludicrous position, when another man, who had observed the insults that had been offered the speaker, and whose hands were smothered with fishes' fins, came in front of him, and opening a book, began to read:

"Behold, ye despisers, and wonder, and perish; for I work a work in your days, a work which ye shall in nowise believe, though a man declare it unto you."[1] This poor but brave Christian man, who has recently gone to his eternal reward, turned the current in favour of poor Ned, and the addresses which followed were listened to respectfully, some of the costermongers being affected even to tears.

Unpleasant opposition to his work most frequently proceeded from drunken men. One Saturday evening, at Shad-Thames, whilst endeavouring to dispose of his Bibles, Ned was greatly annoyed by a wretched sot. In his trouble he sought in silent prayer help from heaven; and the prayer was speedily answered in a way that created some surprise in his breast, for in a short time he sold all the books on his barrow. He then commenced preaching the gospel, and continued doing so, in spite of the continued interruptions of the poor drunkard, for half an hour, at the close of which Ned invited the disturber to attend a meeting at which he was to speak in a few minutes in Dockhead. The man accepted the invitation, and with an oath warned the speaker not to attempt to deceive him. Accordingly, with the greater part of the company who were present, he adjourned to the hall, and after spending an hour in proclaiming the good tidings of salvation, the service ended. During the hour, Ned had been frequently interrupted by the man, who by this time was getting sober; and at the close he invited him to have some private talk in an adjoining room. The two were thus closeted together, when Ned questioned him as to his motive for disturbing the meetings both in the hall and without. The man, who had grown half-ashamed of his foolish conduct, acknowledged his fault, and attributed it to the drink. "Yes," rejoined Ned, "that may be true, my friend; but you must not blame the drink for what you're guilty of yourself, you know." Here the man felt still more confused, and after a pause he said, "I see now what I didn't think of before: it's me that's the fool; for if I wasn't to take the drink, I couldn't get tipsy; but you must know, sir, that I've signed the pledge nearly a hundred times over, and I can never keep it for more than a week." Ned confessed that it had once been so with him; for he had both signed and broken the pledge many times; but that

---

1 Acts 13:41.

he needed God to help him to abstain, and that it was not until he knew the Son of God as his Saviour that he was able to abstain from the sin of drunkenness. The result of the conversation which followed—and it was prolonged until eleven o'clock—was that the poor man repented of his sins; and to this day he has been enabled, through Divine mercy, not only to abstain from the sin which did so easily beset him, but also to "let his light shine" as a consistent Christian and member of a religious community. Furthermore, he is no longer a mere labourer, but is a respectable contractor in the building trade.

The enmity evinced by some to the gospel which Ned had thought, in his simplicity, would either be welcomed or at least respectfully listened to, wherever earnestly proclaimed, sorely taxed his patience and spiritual ingenuity. One incident that occurred on a Derby day is amusingly characteristic of the man.

> "Taking my place one day," says Ned, "with a band of open-air preachers, I went down to Epsom on the Derby day, in order to give away tracts, and speak a word to the careless and gay. After working very hard all the day, a few of us took our stand at the bottom of a hill, for the purpose of distributing tracts. We had not, however, been there very long before an old kettle was shied at the head of one of the brethren, who, however, bore the malice of our assailants very patiently; but presently there came up two drunken rough-looking fellows, who took their stand opposite me, while one of them, spinning a penny in the air, said to his companion, 'I'll toss you who is to carry this fellow down to the corner.' Accordingly he cried 'head' but as it came down 'a woman' it resulted in the taller of the two having to carry me, and the lesser one having the office of putting me on his companion's back. Not caring for this treatment, and feeling that no time should be lost, I proceeded to take this man by the stem of his breeches, and thus I slung him three parts of the way across the road, where, lying in the mud on his stomach, he looked perfectly bewildered and unable to speak, and he and his companion slunk away crestfallen."

Ned gravely observes that "this was the right kind of gospel to give these fellows;" and certainly, had he not thus acted in his own defence, the consequences to him might have been serious. It is probable that he would not understand the phrase "muscular Christianity," or he might defend it; but although he has very rarely resorted to his physical prowess, he has an idea that,being an Englishman, he has the right sometimes to defend himself against wanton aggressors.

This picture would, however, be incomplete, without a corresponding one of a different character. Passing along Bankside one day, and feeling deep pity for those who once were his companions in sin, he began to address a few who were grouped together, and soon a goodly company assembled, among whom were half a dozen men known to him as sceptics. These men were persistent in their interruptions and reproaches; but Ned refused to argue with them, and continued declaring to them the counsel of God. There was one man among them whose conduct grieved the speaker more deeply than that of the others. He was a fisherman, whom Ned had not long before, almost at the cost of his life, saved from drowning, and whom common decency, if not gratitude, should have taught the wisdom of silence.

> "The persecution I suffered from this man," says Ned, "so overcame me that I was obliged to leave off speaking; and so, with a full heart, I buried my face in my hands, and wept tears of sorrow; my old companions laughing at me for being such a fool as to cry about it, little dreaming of the feelings of my heart about their precious souls."

Perhaps the tears thus shed by the impressible Ned may not have been altogether shed in vain!

The work of a Bible agent and sick visitor is not always the brightest. To attend the death-beds of those who have despised God, and who have departed out of the world He has created with imprecations upon their Maker, is not an employment likely to foster feelings of joy. Late at night he was aroused from his slumbers by a person who begged him to visit a dying man in a neighbouring street. Although weary with his day's work, he hastily obeyed the summons; and as he was about to enter the house, the woman begged him to go up very quietly, or the dying man would begin to swear. "But," was the reply, "I thought he wanted me to speak to him about his soul." "Oh, no, sir," said she; "it isn't he that wants you to speak, but I want you to do so." Ned tripped upstairs very lightly, and was asked, "Who's there?" Approaching the bed, the visitor replied kindly, "Why, it's Ned Wright; I've come to tell you something about some one who loves you, whose name is Jesus." The words had hardly escaped his lips, when the man replied, with a volley of abuse, "I don't want any of your b— preaching. I was not to get better." He persisted in refusing to listen to his visitor, who was compelled to retire from the room. The man died as he hid lived, an unbeliever.

> **SCRIPTURE TESTIMONY**
>
> *Jesus will never send away those who come to Him*
>
> JOHN 6:37

An infidel, dying of consumption, spent the last few days of his life in cursing and swearing, which so afflicted his wife that she begged Ned to come and see him. This he did, and going up to the bedside of the dying man, he told him that he wished to talk with him a little about Jesus Christ For a moment the man fixed his eyes savagely upon Ned, and in a tone of great anger exclaimed, "I don't want Jesus; I won't hear you, d'ye hear? I don't want Him. Damnation take yourself off, and your Jesus with you." All expostulations and entreaties were in vain. He would not listen to the gospel, and preferred to die defying his Maker.

If such cases as these made Ned sorrowful, they also inspired him with greater zeal. Failure did not undermine his confidence in the power of the gospel. He saw around him too many instances of its conquering force over the stoutest and most rebellious hearts to doubt its energy in the rescue of men from sin and woe. Looking within, he had the best evidence of what it could accomplish, and thus he was unshaken in his faith. This made him feel that no devil-beguiled creature was out of the reach of Divine mercy, and gave unusual strength to his appeals to the most degraded. It was while expressing his faith in the ability and willingness of Christ to save the lowest of men, that a tinker was aroused to a sense of his need of pardon. He had been a most cowardly and brutal wife-beater, and in his fits of frenzy had more than once left the impressions of his hob-nailed boots upon his wife's body. In bitter agony of soul he exclaimed, "Oh, Ned, can you save me?" "No," said Ned, "I cannot save you; but there is One who will save you, if you come to Him just as you are." "But, you see, Ned," said he, "I've nearly had the rope round my neck; and indeed if they had hanged me, it would only have been what I deserved." And the man wept again bitterly; while Ned offered up a silent prayer to God on his behalf. Then he spoke words of consolation and encouragement to the poor fellow; told him how, notwithstanding he himself had been a wife-beater, God had had mercy upon him. In the course of time, light streamed in upon the poor tinker's soul, and he was enabled at last to rejoice in the God of his salvation.

Ned perambulated not only the metropolis, but also the suburbs and country towns and villages, with his Bible-carriage, and of his experiences at this time many interesting chapters might be written. It will suffice, however, to indicate a few of them. In some cases, unexpected friends, mostly of the labouring poor, feeling interested in his work, provided him with food and a lodging. One day, in driving his Bible-carriage down a steep hill, he allowed it to run into a bank, and unfortunately overturning it, the body of the carriage was seriously damaged, and two large squares of glass were smashed, the broken pieces cutting several of his most expensive Bibles. Not being within sight of any habitation, he hardly knew what to do. He envied for a moment the happiness of the buzzing bee and the warbling birds, and wished be could sing as joyously as they. But there was his broken carriage; how could he be otherwise than miserable as he gazed upon its shattered frame? However, he fell on his knees, and besought God to help him in his time of trouble. When he had concluded, a labouring man stood by his side, and addressing him, said, "Cheer up, old fellow, your Father has heard your prayer, and has sent me to help you." The Bibles and Testaments were then picked up, and with the assistance of a family of hop-pickers who were returning home with their wages in their pockets, the carriage was raised from the ground. These persons each bought a Bible, selecting those that were the most damaged; then they helped him down the hill with his carriage; afterwards, they knelt together in prayer, and in that strange place God was pleased to teach some of the hop-pickers that they were sinners, and needed His grace. In about a quarter of an hour he came upon the gates of Squire B—'s park; the squire himself was outside the railings, and observing the unfortunate condition of the Bible carriage, he inquired how the accident had happened. Ned told him in a few words, and was indeed gladdened at heart to hear the old gentleman tell him to take the carriage to his coach-builder, who would repair it, and for this he was only expected to be thankful to God. While the Biblecarriage was under repair, Ned lodged, at the squire's request, at the house of one of his servants; and had many opportunities of preaching the gospel to the hoppickers of the neighbourhood.

"Passing along the road to Maidstone," says Ned, "I was told that a man was dying of consumption at the toll-gate lodge. Knocking at the door, I asked as kindly as I could whether I might see the dying man, when the old lady (evidently his wife) who answered the door, said, 'No, we don't want any of your cant here.' While trying to reason with her, a man, wearing a black hat-band, accompanied by two little children, dressed alike in black, drew near, and when the man found what my desire was, he very kindly said to the old lady, 'Ah, missus, I was like, you the other day; I wouldn't let the minister come to see my poor wife when he wanted to; but when she was dying, and wanted him, I could not get him.' However, it was no use; the old lady's heart was too hard, and in after days he died I fear as he had lived—without God.

"As I and the widower journeyed along the road, we conversed together about the work of Jesus, when suddenly my attention was arrested by a group of gips'es, to whom I gave a few tracts, and afterwards I preached the gospel to them, and while speaking of the love of God, the widower became so affected that he cried for mercy. God heard the cry, and I have every reason to believe that he was converted on the spot.

"Being very anxious one day to deliver some tracts to a number of hop-pickers, who are a most ungodly class of people, the greater part of them being illiterate Romanists, I began to present my tracts, when an Irishman shouted, 'Come here, ye lazy schamer, and be after picking hops for your living.' This they all seemed heartily to join in; so asking my heavenly Father for wisdom, I said, 'Now, if you like, I'll come and pick for you for two hours, if you will let me spend the third hour in delivering tracts among you.' This they unanimously agreed to, some of them shouting, That's a jolly fellow,' 'Now, that's something like religion.' After picking hops for two hours, I was sorry to see my friends rushing out of the rain to some place, I could not tell where. However, I prayed to God for help, and followed them, and was not a little surprised and thankful to find that they were seeking shelter to cover them in an old barn. Of course, according to our agreement, I began to give my tracts away, when the cry was raised, 'A speech, a speech!' 'All right' said I, 'but you must let me give my tracts away, then I will give you a speech; I can do it all in an hour.' To this they readily assented, and after delivering the tracts, I took my stand upon a tub turned bottom upwards, when some cried out, 'Chair, chair.' 'Stop' said I; 'my friends, you must not rob me of my half-hour, you know, by talking about forms and ceremonies; we must remember that God is in the chair, or in other words, on the throne, and we are on the earth; so that the little time we are together we must try and remember that God is here.' Feeling that there was no time for me to talk about Romanism and Protestantism, I proceeded to tell them of the dying love of Jesus. This seemed to rivet the whole of the company to the spot; and when I had finished that meeting, scores of those hard-hearted Romanists were subdued, and shook hands most heartily with me, heaping upon my head the choicest blessings heaven could give."

Having arrived at Maidstone, Ned passed by the gaol one evening, in company with a friend, to whom he remarked, "Ah, I've spent many bitter hours in that place." Whilst looking at the prison, a lad ran up, and said, "That's the place where they hang them, sir." Whilst entering into conversation with him, a number of persons were attracted to the spot, all of whom listened to what Ned had to say; and he had not been speaking for more than a few minutes, when the crowd increased so much that he began a set address. In the course of his address, he referred to his previous bad life, and how he had spent some few weeks in the prison opposite, for misconduct, as well as in several other prisons for like offences.

Several policemen and warders belonging to the prison were among the listeners, and Ned was heartily thanked at the close for his useful and powerful address.

In the course of his evangelistic work among the hoppickers, Ned was both insulted and assaulted by a Romanist who persisted in declaring that Ned had turned over from Romanism to Protestantism for what he could get. Fortunately, an old man and his wife, who happened to be in the room, declared that they knew Wright too well for that. No one would believe the Romanist, who was threatened with a "good hiding" if he did not cease his abuse. In return for his kindness, Ned spoke privately to the old man and his wife about the gospel, and on his return to London had the pleasure of visiting the man while suffering from fever, and being the means of his conversion.

CHAPTER ELEVENTH

CHAPTER ELEVENTH

URING THE three years of Ned's employment as a Bible agent, he had many opportunities of addressing large numbers of the poorest classes of South London. The mission which supported him was carried on in a suitable hall, devoted to preaching services, and here he frequently related the story of his conversion to some of the lowest characters that infest the metropolis. He also spoke at the services in the Victoria Theatre and elsewhere to thousands, who listened as if spell-bound to his wonderful story. One evening, when he had finished, a man came to him, and in a most excited manner told him that he had just been relating his own history; for his life had been very much like Ned's. The man was taken into the green-room, where Ned read and conversed with him, and prayed for his soul's salvation. It was some time before the soul-stricken man could realize the forgiveness of sins; but immediately he trusted in the Saviour, his face was lit up as with the radiance of a summer's morning. Upon inquiry, it was found that he was connected with a wealthy family; but having been decoyed from home by some companions who turned out to be expert thieves, he entered upon evil courses, and became in the end an expert thief himself. He had had a good education, and was superior in intelligence to the ordinary class of thieves. His career of crime soon led to his arrest and imprisonment for four years' penal servitude. Leaving Portland prison, he was persuaded by a Christian man to hear Ned Wright, and this resulted, as we have seen, in his conversion.

143

A gentleman generously offered to support him for three months, and this offer was accepted. At the end of that time, no other situation being found, he exchanged his suit of broadcloth for corduroy trousers and a white smock, and went gladly and thankfully to work in the East-end, to roll barrels about, at eighteen shillings per week. He was, however, soon found to be worthy of a superior berth, and was made a clerk in the countinghouse of his employer, where he rose gradually to an important post. Now he is one of the trusted travellers for a large house of business in the City, and an earnest, consistent Christian.

One of the reports of the mission with which Wright was connected, gives a striking instance of his usefulness in the conversion of another thief. We give the case substantially as it appears in the report:—

> SCRIPTURE TESTIMONY
>
> *Salvation transforms*
>
> 2 CORINTHIANS 5:16-17 · GALATIANS 6:15

"H— was a wild, reckless fellow. At the age of fifteen, he left home, and got into bad company. He started to drive what he calls a 'go cart,' a vehicle built with a very light body on wheels which could be driven without the least noise, and was used by him to convey thieves and gamblers to races, fetes, fairs, and markets. H— delighted in this wickedness. He soon became a clever pickpocket, and as great an adept in thieving as his employers. At markets he has often seen the cattle sold, and no sooner was the purchase-money in the pocket of the vender, than his hat has been pushed over his eyes, and the money extracted and made off with. What seems most surprising is the fact that H— never got detected in, or imprisoned for, any of these dishonest acts, although he has often seen his master taken off to the station and get six months. For years he continued to follow this wild course, when, having been obliged to flee to London for fear of being recognized as one of those who had robbed a lady at Ascot races, he settled down a little, and took a place as potman and general attendant at a small beerhouse, where it was his duty to wait upon those who went to play bagatelle, dominoes, cards, skittles, etc., often joining in the game, and winning by cheating. He became a skittle-sharper and confirmed drunkard. He was not particular how he obtained property. Upon one occasion, having bought a pair of stolen boots for a few pence, he was taken before the magistrates, and fined one pound. Another time he was sentenced to twenty-one days' imprisonment for having meat in his house which had been stolen by a woman. H— married shortly after he gave up his travelling life; but having no home, his wife was obliged to live with her parents, while he still lived as potman at a house in the Blackfriars Road. He was a general favourite at the beerhouses, and with a cabman, being rather a witty fellow. The publicans gave him as much drink as he required to stand in front of the bar and pass jokes. He scorned religion—church or chapel he never entered since he was a boy, except when he was married; and once, when ill, he promised, if he got well, to go and hear the minister; but his first act after getting out of his room was to go to the public-house opposite, and swallow two quarts of beer. For four years a man named K—, a converted sweep, had endeavoured, by every possible means, to get him to our meetings, but without success. H— believed there was a Deity, and he had learned, when young, that a person named Jesus had lived on the earth, and ultimately died upon a cross; but he thought it was merely to benefit, in some way, the people who were then living—he never entertained the idea that such an act had anything whatever to do with him; indeed, the heathen in the most distant parts of the earth could not be more ignorant of the ways of God than was he. Cock-fighting and prize-fighting were his chief amusements; and he was not ashamed to show his colours in this respect, having the walls of his room covered with representations of such scenes. In February, 1867, a prizefight was arranged between two men with whom H— was intimately acquainted, and in which he took much interest. It is customary, I under-stand, for the contesting parties, before the fight comes off, to have what is termed a benefit, which means the proceeds of a raffle or some musical entertainment H—, with another, had engaged to be present at the benefit, and took tickets for himself and the friend. A day or so afterwards, when he offered the ticket to the man for whom he had purchased it, he found, to his surprise, that he refused to take it, but asked him to take a ticket for a free tea. This he stoutly refused; but after some conversation, and at the suggestion of the companion to go for a good lark, and break all the cups and saucers, he consented, and went with about fourteen other reckless fellows. The moment he entered the building (to use his own words) he was 'solemnized.' Ned Wright being at the meeting, and seeing such a troop of rough fellows, called the waiters, and said in a hearty manner, 'Here, lads, these dear fellows look cold and hungry; give them plenty to eat and drink; God has sent it for them.' H— was very hungry, and thought, 'Well, he is a rough-looking chap outside, but I'm blowed if he ain't a good sort of fellow in.' Ned said to them after tea, 'Now, old fellows, I hope you have had enough, and that you will now sit quietly while I tell you something you have never heard before.' H— was surprised, as he thought of seeing and hearing a gentleman with a fine suit of clothes on. Ned preached the gospel very simply, and narrated the wonderful way God had transformed him, from a prizefighter, burglar, wife-beater, and drunkard, into a Christian man. Our friend listened attentively. It seemed as though the speaker was recounting minutely the hearer's life over to him; and he remembered the wretched state of poverty he had brought his poor wife and family to through his dissipated habits. Ned stated that once he was a bargeman, and could earn several pounds a week, which he spent in drink, while his family were starving at home, and were obliged to lie on cane shavings; which was just the case with himself. The tale of God's love in the gift of Jesus was fresh and good news to him. H— left the meeting, feeling he was a wretched sinner, and yet hoping that God would save him as He had the preacher. His conscience would not allow him to continue in his drunken habits, although he endeavoured to stifle conviction. The following Sunday he went to the evening meeting, where he again heard Ned preach the gospel. His feelings were so wrought upon, that he said to himself, 'I won't stand this any longer,' and attempted to take up his hat to depart; but in doing so he lost the use of his limbs, and was for some time unconscious. When he came to himself, he found his old friend the sweep stooping over him, seeking to encourage him to trust at once in Jesus. He got up a new man in Christ Jesus; he received the Saviour as his, and rushing home, told his wife that Jesus had died for him, and saved his soul. For days, so great was his joy, he could speak of nothing else but of the Lord's goodness to him. At night he prayed to God. His wife wondered at the extraordinary change in him, but attributed it to a weak intellect. One night, H—, thinking his wife was asleep, began to tell Jesus his difficulties, and, being out of work, asked for guidance in not a very low tone. His wife started up, saying, 'Now, I've been listening to you some time. I won't have you in the house any longer. I'll fetch the neighbours; and, please God, you shall go to the workhouse tomorrow. I won't have a madman in the house.' She really thought her husband had gone out of his mind. The threat, however, was not carried into execution. Among H—'s pothouse companions was one termed 'Dicky,' who had formerly been a keeper in a mad asylum, and prided himself on being able to detect by the expressions of the eyes, etc., where insanity existed. Not having seen H— for some days, and wondering wherever he had got, one morning he entered his cottage, and bursting out into an hysterical laugh, said, 'What do you think I've heard? Why—well, I don't know how to tell it you. They say you've turned religious and again he chuckled at the idea. H—, looking straight into his eyes, said, 'Look here, Dicky, don't you believe it, I haven't turned religious at all; but Jesus has saved my soul from going to hell, and I can't help loving Him for it.' 'Go on with you: stuff and nonsense! What! A chap like you love Jesus?' said Dicky. In the course of conversation the late keeper assured his companion that his eyes looked very bad, and there was a certain expression about his face which was a sure indication that he was going mad, and strongly advised him to go to the chemist, and prescribed for him a black draught. H— has not gone mad yet, and he reminds Dicky of this whenever he meets him. The life of God in his soul is unmistakable, and he is not ashamed to own it in the neighbourhood in which he for so many years lived the drunkard's life. The omnibus conductors, before his conversion, used to give him parcels to take to gentlemen's houses, and thus enabled him to earn a shilling when he was slack; but now they spit in his face, and taunt him fearfully, which he bears patiently for Christ's sake. A coffee-shop keeper, near where H— lives, persecuted him much; but being on his death-bed, sent for the object of his scorn, and begged his forgiveness, which was freely vouchsafed to the poor penitent, who soon afterwards passed away, owning Jesus as his Lord. In place of the pugilists and fighting-cocks, H— has representations of various portions of the life of Christ, such as the

Ascension, Blessing Little Children, etc., which he is very proud to show and explain to his neighbours."

SCRIPTURE TESTIMONY
For God so loved the world *that He gave His only Son* JOHN 3:16

The following letter from one of the men rescued from evil courses through Ned's outdoor preaching, illustrates a type of cases, of which several might be given:—

"July 1, 1866.

"MY DEAR BROTHER,

"As you wish me to give you an account of my career, I was first left to the mercy of the world when nine years of age; and when sixteen, I went in the country to Somersetshire. I used to go and hear the word of God preached at different churches and chapels, but never took any notice of what I heard. I remained there two years, and then I returned to London, and went into all the vices of every description; and yet I knew I was doing wrong. I remember a party of us was going to the Britannia at Hoxton, and I saw written up over to the door, 'To the pit.' I stood and looked at it, then I thought what an awful thing it would be for me to die in such a place—hell would be my portion. So I did not go that night, but went home to my work. Some time after, I lost my situation through drink. And then I returned to my old companions, swearing, drinking, etc., till all my money was gone and all my clothes pledged; and, at last, when they found I had not any more money left, they deserted me, and then I had no place to lay my head, and no one to give me a piece of bread, and for thirteen weeks was like that. Many, many nights I have slept on London Bridge and on doorsteps, and picked up bread in the streets. No one employed me. At last I resolved to leave London, and go on tramp. I started in September, and went to Barnet, St. Albans, Luton, Bedford, etc.; Birmingham, Coventry, Dewsbury, Chester, Birkenhead, Liverpool, Warrington, Manchester, Stockport, Sheffield, Warwick, etc.; Honden, Leeds, Hull, Driffield,

Burlington, Scarborough, Whitby, Middlesborough, etc., and so went on till I arrived in Scotland. But many were the hardships I had to go through: without food two or three days together, and sometimes not so much as a drink of water, and icicles hanging to my coat, and laid on the side of the road, with a stone for my pillow. I thought then God was punishing me for my wickedness, and I settled down for three years there, and attended church. But I never saw the Lord Jesus' love to poor sinners, of whom I was the chief, as I experienced ever since you were preaching at the corner of Short Street, when I and my wife were saved, from those words, 'For God so loved the world, that He gave His only begotten Son, that whosoever believeth on Him should have everlasting life,' and now, I am happy to say, we are both happy in the Lord Jesus, resting assured that our sins are all washed away, never to be remembered any more. The devil tries to turn us; but we keep close to the Lord in secret prayer.

"And now, dear Brother, I and my partner in life have a strong desire to go abroad, and work for the Lord's cause; we put it to the Lord, and rest it with Him, and to give us more of His strength, and guide us through life; and when we depart from this wilderness, receive us to glory, to live and reign for ever with all His dear children. And, now, my dear Brother, may God bless you and yours, and prosper your labours for Jesus, blessed Jesus. The love I have for Him is beyond description. Amen.

"I am, your brother in Jesus,—"

This man still bears evidence, not alone of the moral change which has come over his nature, but of his religious sincerity.

CHAPTER TWELFTH

CHAPTER TWELFTH

WHILE PLEASED with the nature of his work as a Bible agent, and gratified with its results, Ned felt increasingly anxious to concentrate his efforts in a neighbourhood to which his gifts were peculiarly suited. A roving evangelism had, of course, its advantages; but, not unwisely, he thought that if he were to labour in some locality where he could secure the attention of the "roughs," he might be serving God with greater usefulness. He had been hitherto greatly blest among a class supposed to be beyond the reach of ordinary religious efforts. From the first, he preferred above all places the New Cut, and having laboured for above two years with the Bible carriage, he named his desire to his employer, in the hope that a small hall might be secured for the 'peculiar services he could organize. Although not meeting with the hearty response he had anticipated, he would not give up his project; but went after the "penny gaff" he now occupies, and ascertained the amount of rent and all necessary particulars. He received, however, a denial from his employer, and thinking that possibly it was not the Divine will he should occupy the premises, he resolved to wait patiently for a more favourable opportunity.

At length he concluded three years of his labours in this field, and having acquired much experience, he was better fitted for future work. He had preached not a few times, and

> **SCRIPTURE TESTIMONY**
>
> *God using circumstances and timing to communicate*
>
> ACTS 11:11

153

addressed many thousand persons while selling the word of God. And the encouragements he had received led him to believe that God had given him a special work to do—viz., to preach to the thieves and other social outcasts of the metropolis. He therefore resigned his situation, and resolved to live dependent upon whatever the goodness of the Lord might supply him. If his way was not made plain to preach the gospel, he would go back to his work as lighterman on the Thames, and give his spare time to evangelistic effort. The very next morning a letter came by post, containing twelve shillings in postage stamps, inviting him to preach in Ipswich. This he regarded as an intimation from God to live a life of faith, and from that time to the present we believe he has never made the public acquainted with his personal needs, nor asked, directly or indirectly, for the means of his support. Occasionally he has been severely tried, but he has never been heard to complain. One of his leading helpers supplies us with some interesting facts on this subject.

At one time he went to preach at C—, and after doing so with great success, he found on leaving for his lodgings that he had only got fivepence left; and "although he had been kindly received, and urged to come again, still no one thought of asking him a word about expenses, nor did it appear as if any one cared how Ned lived or fared;" and so at half-past eight o'clock he started off to the railway station to catch the London train. Although he had only fivepence, he believed that somehow God would take him safely to London. He had not proceeded far when he was accosted by a stranger who had heard him preach on the preceding evening and received from him a sovereign, with very hearty words of congratulation. On another occasion he preached at B—, but though he was announced to speak in London on the following evening, he had not the required sum to pay for his travelling expenses. However, in dependence upon God, he went to the railway station, and on his way found he was half an hour too soon for the train. While walking about, a little child stepping up to him, said, "If you please, sir, will you take this book back to the lady whose address is inside the cover?" Ned opened the book, and retraced at once his steps to that part of the town where the lady resided. On arriving there, she expressed her great pleasure in hearing him on the previous evening, and begged his acceptance of a small donation, handing him a £5 note.

One day, while walking through the New Cut, Ned met with six of his old companions, who had just come out of the New Model Prison.

> **SCRIPTURE TESTIMONY**
>
> *God's work will not lack God's supply*
>
> PHILIPPIANS 4:19

They were deplorable in appearance, one having no shoes, another being without a coat, and another was without any covering to his head. Having afforded them some relief, and conversed with them respecting the salvation of their souls, he left them, more than ever resolved to devote his life to preaching to poor thieves. A suitable house was to be had, and as the rent was only £60 per annum, he took it, believing that the Lord would send him the money, and made at once the necessary alterations to fit it for preaching purposes.

The first person to whom he spoke on the subject gave him one sovereign, and the second £10. In less than three weeks the place was arranged to seat from 200 to 300 persons, and on the night of the opening his heart was rejoiced to find that sinners were converted. As time went on, a band of praying men and women gathered around him, and aided him in his labours. He also rented a small theatre for Sunday evenings under one of the railway arches near the "Elephant and Castle;" then a large concert hall in Bermondsey, and subsequently the penny gaff, in which he still carries on his mission. To obtain the requisite funds for carrying on this work, he appealed by means of circulars to the Christian public, his own personal support being left to those friends whom God might move at various times to help him; so that all the money contributed by the public has been wholly devoted to the mission work. If at any time he has been in need of money for the expenses connected with the hall, he and his helpers have resorted to prayer.

The communicant gives one or two illustrations of this practice. "One quarter-day the rent of the hall had to be paid, and Ned had very

> **SCRIPTURE TESTIMONY**
>
> *God provides exactly what is needed*
>
> 2 CORINTHIANS 8:15 · PHILIPPIANS 4:19

little money in hand for that purpose. He found, after he had got together all that he could muster, he was £10 short. So he came downstairs—for at that time he was living on the premises— and said to the brethren, 'I want you all to get before the Lord in prayer, for the means of paying the rent; for I'm; £10 short, and I have promised to meet the landlord and pay him tomorrow, at eleven o'clock.' The gospel meeting then taking place, it was turned into one for prayer, and each one poured his or her soul out to God for help. That night, when the meeting closed, every one present felt sure that the Lord would send the money. The morning came, but the postman passed the door, and there was no letter for Ned. Half-past ten o'clock arrived; Ned was ready to fulfil his appointment, and again he cried unto the Lord; then coming downstairs, he was going towards the hall door for the purpose of proceeding to the landlord's house, when a man entered, bearing a letter in his hand, which he handed to Ned, who, on opening it, found enclosed in a blank sheet of paper, a £10 note; so he said to the man, 'May I ask who sent this?' when the man answered, 'The Lord sent it.' Thus prayer was heard, and the rent of the hall paid; and on the ensuing evening the hearts of the members were rejoicing exceedingly.

Another time the Lord had withheld supplies, and a gas bill had been overdue for more than six weeks, which amounted to four guineas, and as Ned had no money to pay it, he came down on the night of a fellowship meeting, and asked the members to make it a special subject of prayer to God, that He would provide the money for the gas bill. One of the brethren, Robert Young, spoke up and said, 'Why, there is £6. 18s. in the poor-box, and as all the poor have been cared for, why not use it until money comes in to pay this debt? How can we ask the Lord to send us money while we have money in the house?' And so it was unanimously agreed to by over forty present to pay the money out of the 'Poor-box Fund;' and immediately after the Lord graciously sent in sufficient funds to carry on the work, and restore the four guineas back again to the purpose it was intended for."

SCRIPTURE TESTIMONY
Ask Me anything in My name
MATTHEW 18:19 · JOHN 14:13-14 · JOHN 16:23-24

One day, after preaching at Windsor, Ned managed to tear his long top-coat, of which he was peculiarly fond, because of its clerical, and as he called it Puseyite, appearance; and all the arts of his contriving wife, with her well-plied needle, could not conceal the defect. Mrs. Wright is as simple-hearted as her husband in her faith in God; and failing to hide the rent, she knelt down with Ned in prayer that their heavenly Father would provide him with a new overcoat. The next morning, the postman delivered a letter bearing the Windsor postmark, in which was a letter addressed to a well-known firm of outfitters in the West End. The unsealed letter addressed to Ned, was as follows:—

"DEAR NED,—If you will take the enclosed note to Messrs. N—, they will show you an assortment of overcoats. Please fit yourself with one, and return thanks to God for it.

"Yours, etc., etc."

The letter was anonymous, and the name of the writer is not known to this day. Ned's first feeling was that the letter was a hoax, and that some one wanted to make him a fool. His wife, however, believed that the hand of God was in the matter; and urged Ned to call upon the firm. This he did, resolving on the way, that if this were a trick of Satan's, "h would make him pay for it" by preaching Christ to the people in the shop. However, on reaching the shop, and handing the letter to the shopman, he was shown upstairs, where there was a large collection of top-coats; and the first one fitting him he hastily bade the salesman "Good morning," hurried downstairs into the street, and ran home with childish glee as quickly as possible, to report his good fortune to his wife.

Ned was now getting to be known in the country as a preacher and an effective evangelist; and so in the summer of 1867, he was invited to attend an evangelical conference announced to be held at Dublin. Before the conference was held, he preached, by invitation, in the town of Lurgan, near Belfast. On his way back to Dublin, accompanied by several evangelists of his own class, he found in the same compartment a number of Irishmen, among whom was a Roman Catholic priest. It was with no intention of annoying his "reverence" that he and his friends struck up some new tunes which they had recently learnt; but their hearts were overjoyed as they thought of the happy scene they had witnessed on the previous evening, while preaching in Lurgan. In his innocence, too, Ned concluded that not even a Roman Catholic priest would object to the singing of devout hymns; and so he sang very lustily one hymn after another, to the delight of all in the carriage, excepting the priest in the corner. At last he sang a hymn, of which he was very fond—

"O Jesus, O Jesus, how vast Thy love to me!"

which so exasperated the priest, that he jumped up from his seat, and lifting his umbrella over Ned's head, threatened to chastise him severely if he did not cease singing those words. "He made use," says Ned, "of the most blasphemous language I ever heard; had I been at Bankside, among the London Irish coal-whippers, I don't believe I should have heard worse language." Looking at the priest with great astonishment, Ned calmly said, "Oh, my friend, don't think you will frighten us with your threats and blasphemies. I tell you, sir, that you will one day give an account of this blasphemous language to my Master; depend upon it, 'Whatsoever a man soweth, that shall he also reap.' You, sir, are sowing this morning to the flesh, and of the flesh you will see corruption."

A dead calm followed, and after a little time the brethren, who, perhaps, would have acted more discreetly by not again provoking the irascible Hibernian, struck up another tune. The priest appealed to the passengers to assist him in putting down the obnoxious "ranting"; but as they rather enjoyed it, they declined. This made him yet more exasperated, and he charged them with encouraging heretics. Fortunately, they were not distressed thereat, but expostulated with him, observing that the singers were doing no harm, and that he was to blame for making such a fuss over a trifle. It was amusing to hear him threaten them, as the priest of their own church, to subject them to penance.

"How will yer Riverence prove us to be wrong?" was the quick reply. "Shure, and ain't we all of us agreed that we have done nothing, nor said anything? But, yer Riverence, ye've had all the say to yerself."

Just at this moment the train stopped, having arrived at the second station, and the priest got on to the platform, crying, as if for his life, "Guard, guard, come here! shure thim two men have insulted me, and continue to do so."

It appears that the guard was an Orangeman, and not likely to be the tool of the priest; so, having looked at the offenders, he turned round to the complainant, and observed, "These gentlemen appear to be very respectable; you can't mean that they have insulted you; I am sure they would not do so wilfully."

"Yes, guard," said Ned, with unconscious egotism, "we are very respectable gentlemen; for we are sons of the Lord God Almighty."

"Well," said the angry priest, "I will report them and you too, when I get to Dublin and with this he resumed his seat, and the train again moved on. Turning to Ned and his companions, he exclaimed, "Arrah, see if I don't make yer repint of this, when yer get to Dublin, my fine gentlemen!"

When they got to Dublin, however, the priest found he had lost his ticket during his state of excitement, and was compelled to pay over again for the whole distance—a misfortune, we fear, that aroused but little sympathy in the heart of Ned; and instead of making further complaints which might have been a little troublesome to the evangelists, the priest had to see the superintendent about his lost ticket Ned was not a little glad to escape from so ungenial a companion.

While in Dublin, Ned met with Mr. H—, an earnest fellow-labourer in the gospel, with whom it was arranged that he should return home, *viâ* Holyhead, to Liverpool.

> SCRIPTURE TESTIMONY
>
> *Preach the word, in season and out of season*
>
> 2 TIMOTHY 4:2

On the day of departure from Ireland, they found the boat crowded to excess with Irish labourers, who were leaving Erin to assist in gathering in the English harvest. As is usual at this time of the year, large crowds of these men were conveyed across the channel for the nominal sum of one shilling, and generally they huddle together on the deck, as if they were a number of sheep. Ned and his companion stood on the poop of the steamer, watched the poor fellows with keen interest, and longed to tell them the story of the cross. But they were Roman Catholics, bigoted and ignorant; and for any but a priest to venture to preach to them would be considered by them as an insult to every saint in their calendar, and to the Virgin Mary in particular. Ned dreaded to arouse their ire, as who would not that was at all acquainted with the prejudices and impulsiveness of their class? Instead, therefore, of offering them tracts, or venturing to address them, Ned and his companion silently and earnestly entreated God to deal graciously with the ungodly crew on board; and if it pleased Him, to open up a suitable way by which they could preach the gospel to them. "Open unto us, we beseech Thee, a door of utterance, that Thy name may be glorified, the gospel of Thy dear Son proclaimed, Thy will be done, and so great an opportunity neither neglected nor lost."

Confusion and noise, the clattering of tongues, crowding, fighting, pushing, swearing, blaspheming—the atmosphere was redolent with curses. What awful society for Christians! The tortures of hell could not be worse. At last the vessel was loosed from its moorings, and quickly leaving the beautiful city of Dublin behind, the steamer passed Kingstown, and steered away for Holyhead. The two Christian men looked upon their fellow creatures with deep pain, and as they observed their conduct, and heard their oaths and imprecations, it seemed as if there was not one among the dark mass of humanity before them who had not "bowed the knee to Baal." It was no small comfort to their hearts when they found that the cook of the ship was a pious man, and that there was at least one with whom they might converse. To a man of Ned's impulsive temperament, who had so much to say that was worth the saying, and so kindly a disposition to make the message pleasant even to ordinary objectors, it was no small difficulty to remain silent. The word of God was like fire in his bones. It was a hard struggle to restrain himself, and he was disposed to run all risks to gain a hearing for the gospel. Perhaps, however, if it were impossible while they were on board ship for him to preach to them, it might be his privilege to do so when they had arrived at Holyhead.

A finer day had not been seen for a long while, nor a clearer sky. As the vessel ploughed her way so gaily and gracefully across the waters, it was not anticipated that anything would interrupt their course, or mar the little pleasure they had from the beauty of the scene. When, however, they were within an hour's voyage from Holyhead, they were enveloped in one of those thick yellowblack fogs with which Londoners are painfully familiar, and it reminded Ned and his friend of the thick darkness that fell upon Egypt in the time of God's severe visitation. Ned could not discern a single person on board, nor even his companion that had stood by his side. To move a step forwards or backwards was not easy, since he could not see his own feet, much less a foot ahead. Feeling his way to the front of the poop, he mounted as best he could the skylight, and seizing the opportunity, which he believed God had afforded him in answer to prayer, he shouted out with his stentorian voice, as few men can do, the familiar words of which he is never wearied of repeating, "God so loved the world, that He gave His only begotten Son, that whosoever believeth in Him should not perish, but have everlasting life." These, to him, much-loved words were followed by other and similar passages. The Spirit of God seemed not only to bring suitable words from the inspired volume to his recollection, but to aid him in their delivery. Text followed text in rapid succession, pronounced with a peculiarly solemn emphasis; and as there was not a breath of wind stirring, nor another voice, he was heard from bow to stern, although, like Mrs. Beecher's Stowe's "Dred" in the trees, no one knew from whence the voice proceeded. Every one seemed startled. A grave silence reigned; every breath was hushed, and every ear attentive. Never man had a more willing or apparently a more impressible auditory. Naturally a superstitious people, the Irish labourers appeared to regard the voice as superhuman, and as Ned was elevated considerably above them, it required only a vigorous imagination and a cowering fear to conceive, as some confessed afterwards they had conceived, that the heavens were speaking, calling them, as if with the tongue of a trumpet, to repentance and to God.

Meanwhile the captain of the boat was considering as he stood on the bridge the best expedient to adopt to prevent a catastrophe, and to secure the cargo from damage. It was dangerous to proceed just then, as they might dash against another vessel. The speed was therefore eased, and every effort made to secure the boat from harm. But there was Ned crying aloud, "The day of the Lord draweth nigh. Prepare to meet thy God! "

Very few men would deem it prudent or wise to adopt such means for impressing the ungodly crew, as to work upon the fears of the ignorant is not the best way of bringing them to a knowledge of Christ. But Ned must not be judged by any other standard than himself. Extraordinary men, placed under extraordinary circumstances, may be privileged to use extraordinary means. The cuckoo cry of "sensationalism" is not always the wisest, and prudence may surely give place occasionally to a righteous expediency, since prudence has almost an unlimited sway. Anyhow, we are chronicling facts; and if they were unusual in character, the results were surely such as justified the means.

For twenty minutes the darkness continued, and the voice of the speaker cried with undiminished vigour. Just as the captain was about to stop the engines, and allow the vessel to drift, they suddenly emerged into a clear atmosphere and a bright sky, with the sun shining as gloriously as before. The scene of gloom had changed for one of joy and brightness. And there was the adventurous speaker, standing boldly upon the poop of the vessel, with arms uplifted to heaven, calling down God's blessing upon the human mass beneath. The poor fellows had now found from whence the strange, unearthly sounds had proceeded, and were glad to find after all that the speaker was a man like themselves.

Ned had gained their attention—what should hinder his continuing? He knew well how to interest them. The story of his own life was sufficient to do that. It was not every day that they could hear how God had met with a notorious burglar and ill-liver. They were some distance from Holyhead. The captain did not complain. The men were still attentive. "I'll go on," thought Ned, "in dependence upon the good Spirit that has helped me thus far."

And he did go on, preaching, and exhorting, and entreating, until they arrived on shore. On landing, what a different scene was witnessed from that which had been apprehended! The crowd gathered round the speaker and his companion, not to threaten or abuse the evangelists, but to shake their hands, to thank them, and to hear a little more about the message of love and of mercy which had arrested their minds.

It was evident that the people which sat in darkness had seen a great light. Some poured out their thanks profusely; others expressed their conviction that God had sent the darkness to relieve them from a still greater darkness—the darkness of sin and death; while others thanked God and His servant for the blessed tidings which that day had greeted their ears. One burly fellow wept like a child, and seizing Ned's hands, said to him, "Oh, sir, while you were quoting those beautiful texts in the thick fog, light dawned upon the soul. My eyes are opened now. My soul was darker than the black fog; but now I believe what you told us, that Jesus has paid the debt, and that He died for me; and my heart rejoices in the good news, that the blood of Jesus Christ saves me from all sin."

Ned now returned with greater zeal than ever to his work in the New Cut, and resolved upon certain plans by which he might do more specific work among the thieves of the metropolis.

CHAPTER THIRTEENTH

CHAPTER THIRTEENTH

NED DESPAIRED of securing a meeting of *bonâ fide* thieves at a religious service, by the methods ordinarily adopted to gather more reputable congregations. He had been accustomed to assist in various tea meetings for special classes of persons, and these had been successful. But even a tea-meeting might fail to allure thieves, although tea and cake would present irresistible attractions to the females. It was wisely resolved, therefore, to commence a series of soup suppers, at which the privileged guests should consist of those who were convicted thieves. None but these were welcomed; for, as a writer in the *Times* said, "The best intentions and sincerest professions of larceny will avail the visitor nothing without this formal certificate of character and proficiency from a Justice of the Peace; and if, tempted for once into untruthfulness by the too savoury fumes of the pea-soup, the respectable visitor feels inclined to pretend that he is a convicted thief, I may as well warn him beforehand, that his host will be more than a match for him. Ned Wright... has that intimate knowledge of gaol discipline and diet which only comes from a varied personal experience, and he talks the thieves' tongue like a native. In two minutes, the pretended thief would be convicted of respectability, and sent away shamefaced and soupless."

To secure his grand field nights with these deplorable characters, a number of helpers visited their haunts with cards of invitation, on which it was stated that no policeman would be allowed under any pretence to be present. Five hundred applications for tickets were received for the first night; but accommodation could only be provided for two hundred. "In the result," says one newspaper report, "the guests of the evening were roughly analysed thus: There were 188 men and boys who had altogether served in prison 142 years, four months, and two weeks; and there were seven men who had between them served sixty-seven years and four months; or a total of 195 guests, who had undergone nearly 210 years of imprisonment. One of them had been convicted no less than sixteen times, and had served seven years; against another, thirteen convictions and ten years' imprisonment were on record; and the degree of criminality gradually dwindled down from these extreme cases, until at the other end of the scale stood a boy of tender years who had been sent to prison for fourteen days, for stealing four turnips when he was hungry. It was painful to see a juvenile already in the ranks of professional criminals."

It was hardly to be expected that pea-soup, however good, and suitable addresses, however telling, would attract many of the more skilful and better-to-do class of thieves. Many of the men who are recognized in low life as cracksmen (or burglars), and clyfakers (or genteel pickpockets), are, when possessed of money as respectably attired and apparently as well conducted as a city clerk. "Snide-pitchers" (or bad money passers), "bluey-hunters," or "pigeon-flyers," (men who steal lead from the roofs of old buildings), and common "prigs," were the class of professional sinners who accepted the invitation to sup with Ned Wright. A few swell mobsmen and "opera jumpers" (men who dress in the highest style of fashion, and rob at theatres and opera-houses) were expected. For some of these men are occasionally "down in luck," and would not object to a basin of soup, although they are not accustomed, as their poorer brethren, to "a palmer's pint and three," which means a pint of indifferent coffee and three slices of bread. At the sixth supper, many notorious thieves of this class were present, and the close-cropped, repulsive-looking order of vagabonds who are as hoarse as a costermonger, were in fewer numbers. At all of the gatherings, the behaviour of the audience was good. The female thieves were at their own special meeting, placed apart from the males; but this did not cause any disturbance. One or two of the more forward indulged in chaffing observations, which were enjoyed by a few, but were regarded with but little favour by others. Ned himself was received with a round of hearty cheers, which were only interrupted by a few who strove frantically to be witty at his expense. Their good-humoured sallies were stopped when he got on the platform, and recommended his friends to take in a cargo of pea-soup." Judging from their hungry looks, they seemed equal to such an engagement, and it was necessary that they should be warned in their avidity not to deal unfairly with each other. "You're going to have a clinking clump of tommy each," said Ned, talking the thieves' tongue, "and if you make your jaws ache now, they'll be no use when you get the soup. Now, there's one piece of bread for each of you; and if any one sees his neighbour trying to take two, you must round on him,"—that is, being interpreted, turn informer—"and I will see that he enjoys his supper outside." This order was responded to by appreciative cheers; and what would have been the effect of any disobedience, it would be hard to say. And yet not very hard, if one may judge from the size of their unregenerate fists, and from the fact that Ned himself had to use a little physical persuasion forcibly to exclude some "smashers," whose company had not been invited, and for whom no provision had been made.

The clamour during this part of the proceedings was, as might be expected, great, and the chaffing and shouting uproarious. The bread was eagerly seized, and quickly devoured, as though it were a luxury to their empty stomachs. With all their eagerness and keen appetites, they were remarkably obedient, and not a little patient, as they sat on the rough forms awaiting their turn to be served. At last came the soup. Loud were the shouts of approval and of welcome as the first basin of soup, all steaming hot, was brought in by one of the waiters. A rush might have been expected, but it was not made. Some lingering sense of propriety, or a feeling of respect due to the host, or perhaps a fear of being put down by ridicule or physical force, kept the visitors in their seats. One wild-looking, bullet-headed fellow, who was inclined to be obstreperous, was fenced effectually when Ned, pointing to him, said, "If our friend in the white jacket were to do that in Wandsworth, they'd know what to do with him, eh?"

"Three days' bread and water, sir," was the immediate response. And the company cheered, the gentlemen on the platform smiled, a few winked, and the offender appeared ashamed.

It is not always easy on such occasions to secure the attention of the guests after the meal. Some may wish to leave, and many excuses of an outrageously absurd description will be offered to avoid remaining to the short religious service. Others will persist in cracking jokes and indulging in horseplay. A strong hand may sometimes be needed to put an end to interruptions. But few displays of ill-temper have been witnessed at these peculiar gatherings. Having been one of their own class, they feel an interest in Ned; and are curious to know how he will speak, and what he will say. The proceedings were commenced by the speaker asking them to take off their caps, which was promptly done, a small bare-headed boy in the gallery shouting out, "But suppose we ain't got none." This was evidently deemed an exceptional instance of poverty, for no reply was thought needed. Ned then commenced,

"Now, men and boys, although I know you are a don't-care set of fellows, I want you to show you can do what I ask you tonight. Now, I suppose you're most of you out of work, and without any characters to lose; if not, you've no business here, for this meeting's intended only for those who've got into trouble. Now, I dare say there are many of you who'd like to have a coster's barrow, with a stock of goods on it. Well, I've got some thing to say about that before I've done; but first, I want you to sing a hymn with me."

A demand was here made for hymn-books—for the "Gospel Hall" has its own special penny hymn-book— but this was politely denied to the audience, on the significant ground that so many had "forgotten" to leave the book behind on a previous occasion. A hymn was then sung, more expressive of Ned's own experience than of the feelings of those who joined heartily, though not melodiously. Few hymns, indeed, could be suited to such a unique gathering. A short prayer followed, and then came the address.

Ned is an effective speaker, full of good points, and always vigorous. The few chapters he has learnt to read well, he gives with considerable dramatic force. Few who have heard him read the fifty-third chapter of

Isaiah, or the story of the Prodigal Son, or the narrative of the Trial and Crucifixion of our Saviour, will readily forget the impressive and forcible style of the speaker. As to his discourse, the *Daily News* observes that at one of his soup suppers, it was "half-speech, half-sermon, and in some respects neither one nor the other. Wright, though essentially a street-preacher, and having many of the faults, and most of the characteristics of that class of orator, is still something more than a street-preacher. Though sometimes inappropriately vehement in his manner, he can be really earnest and truly impassioned. His better manner is the colloquial, and he is at his best when he is delineating some scene, or repeating some incident in which he has himself taken part, or in contrasting his own sufferings, or those of his hearers, with the tortures and indignities endured for their sakes by the Saviour of mankind. His matter is not well arranged, his transitions from one branch to another being somewhat too abrupt, and probably rather puzzling to people unused to religious discourses of this class; but he keeps his main subject well in view throughout, and his points are, as a rule, clear and telling. Of one thing there can be no doubt—he commanded the ear of a body of thieves, affected them visibly, made them, at a word, bend their heads meekly while he offered prayer; called forth the tear at one moment, and the smile at the next, and played upon their feelings as a master who commands every string. The secret of this success, for which so many educated and wise in vain sigh, was very apparent—simplicity and earnestness. The speaker did not preach to his hearers so much as talk to them, and the touch of nature, after a little management, made them all kin."

To this it may be added, that Ned's great *forte* is not so much preaching, or even expounding the Scriptures, as delivering fiery, impassioned appeals to the unconverted. He is, *par excellence*, an evangelist, and one of the most sensible and able of that class of orators. A judicious critic, who has heard him preach more than once in Brighton, thus writes of the man and his work:

"His muscular power is great; he has a very powerful voice, and he speaks with a great deal of vehemence and dramatic force. He is young, and has a physical organization which many of us might envy. As an outlaw, as a

Philistine, as one of those who are described with their hands against every one, and with every one's hand against them, he must have been an ugly customer. He gives you an idea of immense uncultivated capacity. If the system of Fourrier be adopted in the Christian Church—to every one according to his capacity, and to every capacity according to its work—his place can be no common one. He can pray, and preach, and sing, as if he were possessed. Out of the dark depths of his own experience he can point his moral, and adorn his tale; and sometimes he does this with wonderful effect, as when illustrating the sufficiency of the Saviour, when bearing the punishment of our sins, he describes his own feelings, his agony, his remorse, his despair, when sent to gaol for three months for an offence of which he had not been guilty. Very few and simple are his ideas, but he seems to hold and utter them with Titanic force. He clings firmly to the physical theory of another life; abstract truths, I fancy, have little charms for him. In theology he is the exact opposite of the sentimental mystic or the contemplative Hindoo. His theology is fearfully concrete, his heaven is to be taken by storm; outside there is the lion that seeketh whom he may devour; outside there is the burning flame and the bottomless pit: outside there is the worm that never dies, and the torment that knows no end. In a moment—in the twinkling of an eye—sudden as the lightning's flash, Christ comes to you, and you have passed from death unto life. You are now inside; for you there is the golden crown, and the shining robe, and the victor's palm; the joys of heaven and the melodious song of Moses and the Lamb. Christ follows you every step; there is no friend like Him. Well, this doctrine is Scriptural, but it may be stated extravagantly, and misunderstood by ignorance. As Wright sometimes states it, Huntingdon might have stated it. Once, as a lighterman, Wright told us he was in peril when going through a London bridge. Instead of trying to avert it, he fell on his knees and besought the Lord Jesus, and Jesus came and guided the barge safely through. The writer has no wish to criticise any one harshly. The harvest to be gathered is plenteous, and the reapers are few. The best of us can but poorly apprehend spiritual truth, and it is poor work stopping to quarrel about terms. And if Christ is thus to step in and save from danger, what are we to think when a good man loses his life by a railway accident, or when such a fearful catastrophe as that of the loss of the *London* occurs? Is it well to tell the least educated and the least reflective classes of the community that all things, temporal as well as spiritual, are wrought by faith in Christ and fervent prayer?... His mission appears to be to the roughest and rudest of our race—to men whom most would pass by as irreclaimable. Can these dry bones live? Yes, replies the testimony of Scripture, and the experience of the Christian Church. Of such was I one, says Wright, 'I was all that was infamous and bad. I committed crime after crime against man and God; and now I have found Christ, and will preach Him whenever and wherever I can—if not in the consecrated church, or to the men of intellect and culture, then by the roadside or in the humble schoolroom, to the companions of my sin and shame; to those whose poverty and crime would forbid their joining in a more regular worship.' To the thief, to the harlot, to the public sinner, he seeks to preach Christ His language is that to which they are accustomed; it is the Saxon of the rough and rude; his style and manner are the same. But all will see he is sincere—Christian in his life; and there are many in all parts of the country who will for ever have reason to rejoice that they went to hear Ned Wright."[1]

There does not seem to be any difficulty in securing the attendance of the class of persons invited to Wright's soup suppers. The only fear entertained by the thieves was lest any policeman should gain admit-

> **SCRIPTURE TESTIMONY**
>
> *The heart of the believer, like Jesus, is full of compassion*
>
> MATTHEW 9:36-38 · GALATIANS 6:2 ·
> EPHESIANS 4:32 · COLOSSIANS 3:12

tance to the hall. After the first supper, the receivers of stolen goods, terrified lest "the hope of their gains" should be gone, circulated a report that the police had apprehended two or three men who had been long looked for, and that Ned's only object in gathering them together was to afford facilities to the police to "spot" them. To "spot" a thief is to make him known to a brother detective. The helpers, however, assured the thieves upon whom they called that the reports were wholly false, and that no fear of the police need be entertained. Some believed, while many assailed the

---

1   Christian World, April 5th, 1867.

visitors as traitors, and threatened them with ill-treatment if they came again. However, in spite of this opposition, two hundred men and lads accepted the invitation, and attended the second supper. At the close of each service, Ned requested all who desired to lead a new and honest life to call upon him on the following morning, when he would see what could be done for them. He soon found a larger number of cases than he could help. The most deserving men were therefore selected, and their immediate wants relieved. Employment was found for others, and help promised to those who could not then be assisted. Meanwhile, ten thousand small bills were printed and circulated in the metropolis. The bill was as follows:

"HONEST EMPLOYMENT FOR THIEVES.

"SIR,—Permit me to solicit your helping hand to temporarily rescue poor thieves from their miserable position, hundreds of whom are at this moment ready to work at carrying advertising boards in the streets, also delivering circulars, etc., at a small return; information of which may be obtained upon application to Edward Wright, New Cut Gospel Hall, 24, Lower Marsh, Lambeth, twenty-five doors from Westminster Road (see lamp over the door). Boards and men always in readiness.

"Every care will be taken to see that the work is done well.

"Letters of a private nature to be addressed to 20, Carlton Square, Pomeroy Street, Old Kent Road; letters of business, to Gospel Hall, 24, Lower Marsh, Lambeth.

"N.B.—Some portion of the moneys earned will be thrown into a fund, out of which the deserving will be helped into a position when they can honestly help themselves."

Orders soon came in for work, and the men gladly accepted the employment offered them. Some were engaged as bricklayer's labourers, others were put to general work requiring no special skill or technical knowledge, one man became a carman, and a lad was sent to sea; but the majority were, as might have been expected, put only to casual work. The men showed a strong disposition to help one another, and thus presented an example, as Ned well says, to many an honest man who had not lost his character.

Two men, who were happily in employment, lived themselves upon twelve shillings a week each, and contributed seven shillings a week each towards the support of those who had been less fortunate than themselves! This was noble generosity, which spoke well of the genuineness of their moral reformation. One great preliminary object which Ned had in view was to prevent any who were desirous of retrieving their characters, returning to their old haunts. Some, too, were homeless; and before anything could be done for them, it was necessary to provide them with a temporary lodging. The only available place was the green-room of the "Gospel Hall," né penny gaff. This room was in a very dilapidated state; but some of the thieves, who understood a little of carpentering and bricklaying, at once set to work, and in a short time the apartment was made fairly comfortable, and five men were at once lodged there out of the twenty who made application. As these men found employment they hired lodgings elsewhere, and thus made way for others who were destitute. This method of rescuing men from their dishonest career has thus far been eminently successful; although it is Mr. Wright's prayer and hope that a new building may be erected, in which thieves may be lodged until they attain a respectable position in life. Trucks of an improved construction, with trays, etc., for light goods, are now being built, and a portable Bible carriage has been put into service in the metropolis, that portions of the word of God may be circulated, at the lowest possible price, among the poorest classes. A similar Bible barrow, with a pony, is also employed in circulating religious literature in the villages.

The meeting for female thieves deserves special mention, and the following description from the *Daily News* will afford the best idea of the character of that unique gathering: "Although the countenances of one or two of the male thieves in the gallery seemed to indicate recollections of the crank, and to suggest possibilities of the lash, they behaved upon the whole very quietly and orderly. Once or twice while Wright was speaking he felt it necessary to call them to order, and at last he asked some of 'our navvy brethren' to go and sit among them. We are ignorant of the exact authority enjoyed or exercised by a 'navvy brother but their presence in the gallery was sufficient to procure complete silence among its occupants, and Ned had no further occasion to rebuke them. The women, who, as we have said, numbered about seventy, were of all ages, from sixteen to sixty, or probably more. Babies—and one there was so wizen and so wan, so small of size, and so pinched of feature, that it seemed not like the offspring of a human mother, although all trace of humanity was not yet beaten out of the features of the thin pale girl who held it in her arms, but rather like a juvenile ape or monkey which by some freak of Nature had approached more than ordinarily close to a resemblance to mankind—we do not include in this calculation. All the women and girls were, to judge from their appearance, thieves of the meanest and most miserable kind. There was no show of success or pride, or even bravado, about them. They did not include among their number a single specimen of the gentle-mannered, elegantly-clad 'lady' who filches a purse in an omnibus, or whips a roll of costly lace from a counter, or of the stalwart, flaunting, audacious 'blower' who holds a foolish 'fast' man with her arms while her pal knocks him on the head and rifles his pockets of his watch and valuables. All had the appearance of petty paltry pilferers, and pilferers with whom pilfering had gone very hard, and to whom it had brought few gains, many punishments, and much suffering. With the exception of two or three girls on one of the front benches, who wore bright wraps round their necks, and showy feathers in their jaunty hats, the clothes of all were mean, and poor, and scanty; their faces were pinched and drawn by want and hunger, and their manner was watchful, timid, and cowed. Of the few girls who looked better fed and better clothed, who still retained some of the freshness of girlhood, and some of the daring mirth of youth and innocence, two or three were afflicted with racking coughs that shook them at times from head to foot, which told a sad tale of constant exposure to wind, and rain, and storm, and threatened in unmistakable tones a speedy termination of their miserable careers. The supper which was provided consisted of large bowls of strong pea-soup, replenishable at the will of the consumer, and huge lumps of good wholesome bread. The girls in the front places did not appear greatly to relish their entertainment. They laughed loudly, almost contemptuously, among themselves when the huge bowls of steaming soup were presented to them; and although they ultimately stowed away the 'toke' in pockets or, shawls, they hardly touched the steaming liquid. Not so their older and more experienced fellow-criminals. With them the pangs of hunger were sharper, the doubts as to tomorrow's meal evidently more serious. Soup and bread disappeared with equal rapidity, and more than one poor woman asked for and received another and yet another allowance. The eagerness of their appetites seemed to increase with their advance in years, and the old nursery maxim that "the eldest should have the most was strictly, though unintentionally, carried into practice."

A thieves' supper was given in Manchester, in May, 1870. In that city private efforts have for some time past been made to find employment for convicted thieves. The Rev. Wm. Birch, a worthy Baptist minister, has, up to the present time, been surety for their good behaviour when work has been obtained. One, a ticket-of-leave man, wrote from prison, begging for work the moment he came out, in order that he might be saved from his old companions. "Nobody," says Mr. Birch, "would employ him, and I had him on my hands some time, but eventually got him a place at a large workshop, and became bail for his good behaviour for two years. Altogether, he cost me about four pounds. He worked steadily, paid me instalments of the loan until it was cleared off, and is now an honest working man." Such instances prove the possibility of reclaiming these persons, and of evoking from them feelings of undying gratitude. At this Manchester thieves' supper Ned gave the story of his conversion, and preached Jesus Christ, and many were touched to the heart. A letter of Mr. Birch's in a local paper mentions eleven cases of persons who were present that night, to whom good was done. One was a lad, a convicted thief, influenced by circumstances to evil, but not hardened in crime; he is now at work, and likely to prove a faithful servant. "Another, a strong and well-built man, who has been convicted eight times, and has twice suffered penal servitude, told me he had tried hard for work, but no one would have him, on account of his previous history. I obtained for him a promise of work, and it was understood that on presenting a letter from me he would be employed. He was out of bed at 4.30 a.m., and told me afterwards that it was the happiest moment of his life. He had now the prospect of being a respectable man, and he knelt to thank God for this blessing. Long before the time he was at the gates; but some of the work-people knew him, and the poor fellow returned with the following note from the manager: 'Your note came to hand per bearer this morning—he was here before six o'clock; but I am sorry to say he is known, and it would not do, therefore, for him to work here. In order that a man may have a fair chance of living honestly and uprightly after 'servitude,' he should be among strangers. I am exceedingly sorry for this man. God help him.'" There is no help for it, it would seem. The only course open to such a man is emigration, although Mr. Wright thinks that such men may do better in the old country, because they require to be kept in hand, and under the influence of some visible authority.

Another man, who was willing to work at any honest employment, was a strong young fellow, who had followed the trade of a burglar. His mother was a good woman, as not a few thieves' mothers are, but he was led into crime through evil associates. He has been frequently in gaol, and has found the way of transgressors to be hard. "A few weeks ago," writes Mr. Birch, "out of the proceeds of a burglary, he bought a pair of trousers for 8s. 6d.; but he said, 'I got the money crooked,[1] and it did me no good. It's always the same. The money we get does us no good at all. I was starving the next week, and sold them for 4s., and bought these things I have on for one shilling. To get food and lodging I must now sell my boots, unless I can get work. I will not go out again."

Other men have long sought for opportunities of beginning again the battle of life, but have not found any. "There is no one knows," said one poor wretched fellow, "how hard it is to fight the uphill fight, to repair the character when once it is gone." Two others were men of superior education. One had been in gaol three, and the other, four times, the latter having associated with thieves and vagabonds in all parts of the country. He says: "I have tried to pray to God, but my heart cannot. Oh, how wretched I am! I have gone to such an extent that my friends will not look at me, and I am an outcast in the world. I can go to no one for advice, except old companions, and you know what theirs will be. I have walked about the streets two nights rather than go back amongst them,

---

1   Dishonestly

and have had nothing to eat for two days except the bits of bread I have been glad to pick up out of the streets. Alas! What must I do? No money, no friends, no work, no character! Who would even allow me on their premises? O God, suffer me not to fall back into my life of crime. My first situation was with —, where I had always a pound or two in hand for payment of foreign letters, and even then I began to pilfer, but was not found out. Oh, how tired I feel of my past life! And what a terror comes over me when I think of it, and death! I cannot give you my address, as I have not got one at present, but I will endeavour to get a lodging this afternoon, although, no doubt, it will be difficult, as I have no work, and no money, and no prospect of honestly obtaining any. God forbid that I should again do so dishonestly."

It is clear from these instances, which are typical of thousands of others, that the life of a thief is so miserable that, when in his sober moments, away from his evil associates, and in the company of honest men who would do him a service, he would gladly quit his sinful courses. "When they have good plunder," says Mr. Birch, and our narrative of Ned Wright's dishonest career abundantly confirms the testimony, "it has to be spent very quickly, for fear of being put in gaol before they are half through their ill-gotten spoil; and after spending it they are careless whether apprehended or not. Half of their time they are in hunger and fear, and any night may have the policeman's bull's-eye on their bed, be bidden to dress, and taken to the station-house on suspicion. Of course, there are some whom the police neither know, nor can they find them when wanted. They are generally men of good education, but they will eventually descend, and their sin and the detective will find them out."

CHAPTER FOURTEENTH

CONVERTED AND REFORMED THIEVES.—THE HADDOCK-
SMOKER.— A REFORMED THIEF.—AN UNCONVICTED THIEF.—A
LITERARY BURGLAR.—A REFORMED IMPOSTOR.— LETTER FROM A
RESCUED MAN.

CHAPTER FOURTEENTH

ALTHOUGH VERY much of the good done by Ned as an evangelist among the lowest classes of society must, of course, ever remain unknown, except to the God who enables him to scatter the seed of Divine truth, yet, happily for his encouragement, he has many mementoes of the saving power of the gospel as preached by him. Many degraded thieves have been restored to their friends, made decent members of society, and converted to a new and higher life. Statistics of spiritual results are delusive, if not obnoxious, to a Christian reader. Remarkable cases of usefulness may, however, be given with propriety.

A haddock-smoker has been a changed man for a few years. He was a convicted thief at nine years of age, and he states that from that time to his conversion he was in and out of prison all his life. "I am now twenty-five years old; I have been a drunkard, gambler, wife-beater, and great swearer and scoffer at God and the gospel I used to attend fairs and races for illegal purposes. I did not believe there was a hell, but now I know that Jesus Christ died to save me, a great sinner, from going there. It was on the 2nd of March that I went to a house with Mr. K—, where he got some bills. I said, 'Shall I give some away?' He said, 'No, it will do you no good, because if anybody was to ask you whether you loved Jesus—' 'Then,' said I, quickly, 'I should say No.' "Then I went to Flint-street schoolroom with him and my mate. My mate was converted the same night. What struck terror to my heart was my mate crying loudly. When Ned Wright had done preaching, he came to me. He saw my eyes full of tears. He said, 'Now, old fellow, how is it now?' "'I said, 'No how.' He said, 'Can't you believe?' I said, 'I am too bad.' "He said, 'He (*i.e.* Christ) died for the like of you and me, who have been so bad.' Then I said, 'I will believe.' My heart was broke, and I was crying. Mr. K— said, 'Now, you have professed to believe; I hope you wilt.' I cried all the way home, but I got up next morning rejoicing in Jesus as my Saviour. Then I prayed for my wife, and the Lord answered my prayer; for on the 19th of the same month she was converted."

One poor fellow who attended a soup supper for male thieves, in a letter to Mr. Wright, says: "I write to you to express my thanks for the supper I received on Wednesday night I have come to the determination to alter my mode of living, if possible. I have been living an honest life these last six years; but, falling out of work about a month ago, I have been compelled to return to my old habits. I would gladly avail myself of your kind offer of work, to save myself from further trouble. You spoke in your discourse about Arthur—, and you said there were some among us who knew him. You were right I knew him well. He was a pal of mine, and I felt the force of your remarks, so much so that I would gladly avail myself of this opportunity of saving myself from his fate. The first of my career was twenty-one days at Brixton for orchard-robbing; the next was six months at the Old Bailey for uttering [base coin]; then fourteen days at Wandsworth for an attempt; then two months for an assault; then six months at Coldbath Fields, of which [charge] I was innocent; next twenty-one days for an attempt, at the same place; then twelve months at the Old Bailey for an attempt at uttering; besides no end of remands. I should have applied to you on Thursday, as you said, but I was so destitute that I was compelled to go to St George's Workhouse to get three hours' work to supply my immediate wants... I had to walk about all last Wednesday night, and I refrained from wrong-doing, so that I might have a chance of communicating with you. I shall be very thankful if you will assist me in obtaining work before it is too late." This man is now in employment, and is a reformed character.

An unconvicted thief was at the same mournful meeting. "I am," he wrote, "a poor backslider from the truth. I have yielded to temptation twice, and stole, but I have had to suffer deeply for my sin. Today I have been tempted to take my own life, for I am homeless and friendless." This man begged for Mr. Wright's prayers, and sought a helping hand to save him from destruction. He is now a happy Christian.

Ned's fame has evidently reached America; for we find that a burglar of literary pretensions has favoured him with the following amusing epistle:—

"N. I. S. P. *Trenton, New Jersey*, U.S.A.,
"February 17th, 1870.

"FRIEND NED,

"Press bravely on; philanthropic millions mortal and immortal, are your anxious, admiring observers.

"Your labour is solemnly vast—let your soul catch the inspiration of its greatness, undismayed by its gigantic proportions, though the Prince of Darkness environ you with obstacles mountains high.

"Be not deceived; our greatest foe ever lurks within. The moral sentiments, glowing with a momentary activity, or with the fraternal impulse of the hour, I ke the tides, have their ebb and flow. Former instincts want a constant guard, else will they rise upon their masters to fetter and destroy. With unrelaxed vigilance, time will confirm you in your chosen path, wherein the passions, long scorned, will but feebly and vainly essay to retard your advancing steps.

"Faithful to your holy purpose, and not intimidated by reverses, nor vainly elated by success, your old age will arrive, with footsteps unperceived, crowned by the never-fading glory of noble and fruitful deeds.

"For a number of years I have been a pariah, a burglar, being at present an inmate of the State prison, entangled in a chain of circumstances which has swept me along through a cycle of painful years. I have cherished a growing repugnance to my detestable vocation, besides being a careful and thoughtful observer of all the phenomena springing from, or affecting, all within the range of my observation. These observations, and the legitimate deductions accumulating from them, I am about to lay before the public, in a

12mo. volume of 300 pages. Think not, then, that you are wholly abandoned to labour alone for the elevation of a miserable class but too little understood, and too long subjected to remedies inefficiently and indifferently applied.

"In brotherly sympathy I extend you my hand, though Atlantic's restless power long stretch her abyss between.

"Please acknowledge the receipt of this communication, and enclose your correct address; for I would like to send you a volume of the work referred to as soon as it is issued from the press. Stand faithful, and history will award you a glorious meed.

"With brotherly love,

"I am yours,

"C— F—

"Mr. Edward Wright.

> "'The man who has it in his power
> To practise virtue, and protracts the hour,
> Waits till the river pass away. But lo!
> Ceaseless it flows, and will for ever flow.'"

HORACE.

M— was respectably brought up, and received a fair education. He lost his father when a lad, but his mother enjoyed a small annuity, and was "clever at the needle." He was put into an auctioneer's office in London, and eventually became a clerk at a banker's house. His good fortune, however, proved his ruin; for, aping the manners and aiming at the position of other clerks who were better paid, he found an income of £90 per annum insufficient; and to meet certain exigencies he kept back £5 10s., intending to replace it when his salary became due. This has often been with city clerks the forerunner of delinquencies for which they have had to suffer, and in too many cases the money retained has never been replaced. The deficit between the bank books and the receipts was at once and unexpectedly discovered, and M— was immediately dismissed, but not prosecuted, as it was found that £10 were due to him on account of salary. Perhaps if he had been prosecuted, it would have taught him a useful lesson; but, as he confesses, "to let me escape punishment, seemed like offering me a premium to go and do the same thing again, as indeed I did, in the hope that I might get off as easily the second time as I did at first" His degradation involved that of his mother, who was housekeeper in the chambers of the bank; not, however, that she had been acquainted with her son's extravagances and visits to the music halls of the metropolis. They were compelled, therefore, to take lodgings, and for some time M— lived upon the earnings of his mother. Instead of being desirous of making amends to her for the misery he had brought upon her, he actually stole the poor woman's rent money, and with it determined to go to America; but finding the sum insufficient, he spent it in visiting theatres and concert rooms. He was, however, soon brought to beggary, and compelled to lodge with a number of low characters, among whom was a thief who had been in a good position which he had lost through embezzling sums of money belonging to his master. "This man was living by his wits," said M—. "These said wits suggested an idea to him; but not being educated enough to carry it out with any probability of success, he proposed the plan to me, and said if it succeeded, I should have half the money we received. The plan was to form a Despatch Agency Company, taking the name of a firm which, in former years, when he was in service, was in existence. Very few persons seemed to have known of the discontinuance of the firm, and thus we felt that we should be free from detection on that account. Our plan was to go round certain streets in the West-end of London, and put down the numbers of the houses and the streets in which the shutters were closed, that being a sure sign of the master or mistress being away from home. The next thing to be done was to look in the 'Directory,' to ascertain who lived at the houses; and if they were persons of consequence, we put their name upon a printed envelope, and putting a sheet of foolscap paper inside, we sealed it with a seal, purporting to come from 'Dawson's Despatch Agency, 392, Strand, W.C.' This, together with a printed receipt, containing the amount charged (either 6s. 9d. Or 7 s. 6d.), and also the place from whence it was supposed to have been issued, I would take to the houses on my list. Thus, in one instance, I asked if Lord E— was in; of course the man-servant said he was out of town. Whereupon I said, 'You must send this on to him directly; it has come this morning from Florence in Italy, and is very important.' I then handed him the letter, knowing very well that he dared not open it, as it was addressed to his lordship, and then I said, 'There is 6s. 9d. to pay; I have got a printed receipt for the money.' The man directly paid the money, I suppose out of some left in his hands for any parcels that might come, and I came away, and went to the Marquis of —'s."

This system of imposture was kept up nearly one month, when a letter appeared in the *Times*, warning the public against the dodge. The consequence was that M— was arrested by a butler, who was also a special constable, when attempting to carry out the same trick, and was taken before Mr. Arnold at the Westminster policecourt, and committed for trial upon three separate charges.

The late Assistant-Judge Payne tried the case, and sentenced M— to twelve months' imprisonment, with hard labour; a light sentence for so grave an offence. In consideration of his exemplary conduct in prison, he was entitled on leaving to the sum of seven shillings and sixpence. This good conduct, however, did not last long after quitting prison; for, meeting with his old companion, he was treated by him to places of amusement until gay society and excitement became irresistible. In vain his mother faithfully warned him; he persisted in his evil courses, and ultimately went to live with his associate, who was soon after arrested on an old charge. M— was now thrown upon his own resources, and he resolved to commit another theft. "Having the latch-key of my mother's house in my pocket, I watched my opportunity; and when I knew she was out, I went up to her rooms, and took away a box of clothes belonging to a gentleman who lodged with her. Then I went to Greenwich, and sold the articles for half their value. When the money was all gone, I did not know what to do with myself, and so I went to Marlborough-street police-station, giving myself into custody for the theft I had committed, and was sentenced to six months' hard labour, though in my own name this time, and not in a fictitious one as in the former cases.

"My mother came to see me when I was in prison, and said she could not think of deserting me in my trouble, although I had returned her such base ingratitude for her many kindnesses; and if it pleased God to give her the means, she would have me home again when I was released.

At my discharge I went home, and the Scripture reader at the prison took me before the magistrates, who gave me ten shillings as assistance towards getting a fresh start in life. This sum, and a few shillings that mother gave me, enabled me to purchase a small stock of magazines, periodicals, etc., with which I managed to earn just enough to keep me alive for nearly four weeks. But having had two or three days' bad sale of papers, I was obliged to encroach upon my stock-money until it nearly all went, and mother not being able to supply me with any more ready money, I was compelled to give up that chance of getting on."

He was brought this time to great destitution, and at the end of one day, after walking the streets fruitlessly, he was asked to hold a horse for a gentleman, near Charing Cross. For this, having been kept one hour, he received one shilling, which provided him with a lodging for two nights. The next day being the Sabbath, after attending the Young Men's Christian Association in Great Marlborough Street, he suddenly determined to go over the water, and find out "Ned Wright," of whom he had read. Accordingly he went, and heard Ned preach, more out of curiosity than desire to profit. He felt that the speaker was the man to whom he could state his case, and ask for a little assistance; and Ned kindly treated him, and was the means of saving him from his dishonest career. "I sincerely hope," says the penitent, in a letter before us, "that it may not be too late for me to repent of my sins, and that the ever-merciful Redeemer may pardon me my many transgressions, and that through faith in our Lord and Saviour I may eventually be brought to a knowledge of the truth as it is in Jesus. O Lord, may Thy word indeed be a lantern unto my feet, and a light unto my path—that strait and narrow path which leadeth to eternal life; for then indeed shall I be able to exclaim in perfect sincerity, 'The Lord is my strength and my song, and has become my salvation.'"

One evening, in 1867, Ned gave a free tea to about six hundred men and women in Flint-street school-room, Walworth. The noise and confusion which prevailed during

> **SCRIPTURE TESTIMONY**
>
> *God answers prayer*
>
> LUKE 18:7 · JOHN 15:7 · ACTS 12:5 · JAMES 5:15

the fore part of the proceedings augured so unfavourably for the success of the service, that Ned went on to the platform while the laughing and jeering were going on, and fell upon his knees, and cried to God for special power from on high, that these men and women might not be allowed to resist the appeals that were to be made to their consciences. The novelty of such a procedure, and the intense earnestness of the speaker, silenced them at once; and the addresses which followed were interrupted only by the sobs and cries of those who were suffering from sincere conviction of sin. Ned believes that not fewer than thirty souls were brought to a saving acquaintance with the gospel that night. The writer of the following letter was one of three men who had separated from their wives, all of whom professed to have been saved through that evening's service. We give the letter *verbatim et literatim:*—

"September, 1867.

"BELOVED BROTHER IN CHRIST

"Soon after my conversion I promised you, with the help of the Lord, I would give you a brief scetch of my past carreer. I now, with the Lord's help, take up my pen to do so, not, at the same time, wishing to boast of my bad and wicked deeds, but hoping that it may be the means of showing to some other poor sin-stricken soul that there is none too bad for our blessed Lord and Saviour, but that He is willing and will save any poor sinners, however bad they may be, that fly to His open arms. I shall not go back to my very early days, but give you a little skitch of the last fourteen years or so, and from this you will see what a very wicked sinner I was; but I can now truly say that my black and long catalogue of sins have all been washed away by the precious blood of Jesus Christ! At the time I am going to speak from, I was in the Chatham Division of Marines, where me and my late master, 'Old Satan!' were shipmates together. Ah! My dear brother, the depredations that I carried on were truly frightful; for I neither feared nor cared for no one, or nothing; my whole delight was in making myself as agreeable as I could to my chums, and so winning their good wishes, and robbing of them up hill and down dale. Me and my old master used to lay our heads together so nicely, that detection would seem impossible almost, except to God alone. Ah! My beloved brother, I have seen other men punished for crimes that I have committed, but that did not touch my hard heart. Oh, no; as long as Jack got off scot free, no matter who suffered. After having served some years, and being paid off from my ship, I bought my discharge. I then came back to London, where, being rather a noted character before I entered the service, I found many old pot companions. I then went to work as a carman; but it pleased the Lord to lay His almighty hand upon me in the shape of a very severe accident. I was made foreman over all the carmen in the firm (after I recovered from my accident) where I was employed. Here I began to put my thieving abilities into practice with the aid of another one, whose duty it was to check my expenditure; but instead of that we used to row in the same boat. I will just tell you how we used to work together. It was my place to put the carmen on (if any were sick) in their place. Sometimes I would have as many as seven or eight away at the time, and then I would let their horses stand still and do no work, but take good-care to draw the money for the extra men, who were never employed, and so pocket this sum every week. I likewise organized a society, and after getting about sixty pounds in hand, I stuck to it. I then left this employ, and turned horse-coper. Oh! My dear brother, I could make your hair stand on end. I made it my whole study whom I could cheat. Ah! Many an aching heart have I caused at this game; for I used to be one of the cleverest hands there was in what we call ramming people, and macing. We used to do it in this fashion: I would have a horse in the market or fair, and as soon as I saw any one that I took to be a flat looking at it, I would ask him a very long price. Perhaps he would say that he could not afford to give so much. I would then tell him, if he could find anyone in the fair that would vouch that he was a respectable man, I would not mind giving him a little accommodation. Of course the man would think it very kind of me, and would find some one who knew him. I would, in the meantime, get out of him how much money he had about him, and he, thinking I was going to trust him, would tell me. I would then sell him the horse, taking care to draw what money he had about him. I would then treat him, and during the time that he was drinking, my pal would come in the booth, or wherever it was, and pretend to ask me if I had sold my horse to the man I was drinking with. I would say, 'Yes.' Then he would say, I hope you have got the money for him, as the man was a bankrupt a little while ago? Of course the man would be taken all aback, and declare he was innocent; but we took fine care that we kept the money we got, and the horse too, perhaps the last penny the poor man had. But this is nothing to some of my crimes; in fact, I bested a sergeant of police once when he came to take me; for you must understand that I got imprisoned several times for being too clever.

"But my poor wife was the greatest sufferer for my misdeeds, until it pleased the Lord to take her from me for a while, and place her in an hospital. I then sold off my home, and when she got well she had no home to go to; but the Lord, in His great mercy, provided for her, and I hope, by His help, we may soon be united again.

"Of course my conversion at Flint Street is well known to you. Of course, my dearly beloved brother, I have been many times tempted to go back to my old master; he has offered me some good chances; but our Blessed Master has kept me from him. I would to God and His beloved Son that every sin-stricken soul may be brought to the feet of our Blessed Saviour! For I can truly say, as Paul did, that I was the chief of sinners; but I now thank our Blessed Saviour that I was not too bad for Him. Oh, the blood of Jesus! It cleanses from all sin. I must say, dear brother, that our dear Brother M— has been the means, with the help of the Lord, in keeping me constantly looking at Jesus. May the Lord bless you and him too, and all his dear children; and may the Lord, in His great mercy and love to me and my poor much-abused wife, let us be united again, so that we may love and serve Him truthfully, in our journey through this wilderness.

"Yours for ever in Christ,

"J— S—."

CHAPTER FIFTEENTH

The boys of London.—William H—'s bad training.—The boy criminal.—A company of blacklegs.

CHAPTER FIFTEENTH

ALL THE education which many a boy living in the metropolis gets, is that obtained from the streets. Thousands of little fellows practically live in the streets year after year, and are sent out to hawk "cigar lights," to sweep crossings, or to sell newspapers. They rarely get a substantial meal, and before they can eat any of the scraps they buy so cheaply at common cook shops, they must earn the coppers with which to purchase them. Not a few dwell with their parents, cooped up in a pigeonhole sort of garret, with perhaps half a dozen brothers and sisters, and are ill-treated if at the end of the day they return home without having disposed of all their little stock-in-trade. Their natural love of play induces them to dispose as quickly as possible of their goods, or to realize— honestly or not, is soon with them a matter of indifference—an average sum of money, that some of the hours of the day, or all the hours of the evening, may be spent is boyish amusements. Their love of gambling, and the dexterity with which they cheat each other, combined with a passion which in some is uncontrollable to gain money, and in others to spend it, gives them a taste for dishonest tricks which eventually brings them to prison and to disgrace.

William H— was one of this numerous class of boys who are sent from home to earn their livelihood when they ought to be in an elementary school. When a young man, he was employed to carry deals in the docks; but the evil lessons he had learnt as a child in the streets had prepared him for a life of crime. He combined with others to plunder systematically his employers. This was done by loading the waggons with more wood than the order required, or the invoice specified. The extra quantities were disposed of, and the money spent in drink. At last they grew so bold in their robberies as to be suspected; no direct proof, however, could be brought against any one of them, or they would have been prosecuted. But they were discharged, and William H— had to bear his share of the punishment he deserved in being out of employment for nearly twelve months. During this time he wandered the streets, failing to find work, and was brought into the direst poverty. Starvation at last staring him in the face, he resorted to petty acts of pilfering, but avoided detection. A good opportunity was afforded him to retrieve his lost character when he obtained work on the Midland Railway works, which were then in course of construction. He was removed from his old associates: and if his wages were low, they might have sufficed to maintain himself and wife comfortably. Unfortunately, in spite of better intentions, he became involved in difficulties, and resolved in an evil hour to abstract a cashbox from one of the wooden sheds on the line. He gained admittance into the shed by means of a crowbar one evening, at nine o'clock, and stole seventeen shillings in postage stamps and thirty shillings in silver. The robbery did not occupy more than two or three minutes, and he left, as he had entered, unobserved. Soon after gaining the main road he encountered, near a public-house, the watchman of the works, who saluted him with "Good night, William; why, ain't you home yet?" "No," was the reply; "I'm just off." In order to prevent suspicion he deemed it prudent to call at the public-house, so that he might be able to say that the watchman could not have seen him, since he was at the time drinking at the bar. He therefore went inside, called for liquor, and just as he was leaving, he met a policeman at the door. "Hallo, William," said he, "what brings you here at this time of night?" For a moment the guilty man was confused; but at length replied, "Oh, I've not been home yet, since I left work." "Nonsense," said the officer; "why, I saw you go home with the other men." "Oh, no," was the audacious reply, "you must be mistaken; why I've been drinking here all the evening.

Will you have a pint? I'll go and fetch it; but you see I've had plenty myself." Upon saying this he hurried to the bar, called for a pint, and threw down a shilling for payment. "Oh," said the landlord, "you're well up tonight, William, ain't you? It's well to be you. Why, this is the third shilling that you've changed tonight, and you've only had three pints of beer. Suppose you give me coppers; for I'm rather short of change." The policeman overheard the landlord; and when William went to him, and proffered the beer, he said to him, as he placed his hand upon his shoulder, "Oh, never mind the liquor now; I shall apprehend you, for I am satisfied there's something wrong, since I know all about your previous character, and did so long before you came here." At this moment the landlord came to the door, and addressing the policeman, begged him not to run away with one of his customers, as he had only been at the bar a quarter of an hour. This still further increased the constable's suspicions, and William was taken to the station-house, where the stamps and some of the money that had been stolen were found upon him, and at his trial he was sentenced to six months' imprisonment with hard labour.

All his prospects in life were now blighted, and, as he felt, his character was irretrievably lost. His industrious wife, who had laboured hard

> **SCRIPTURE TESTIMONY**
>
> *Salvation transforms*
>
> 2 CORINTHIANS 5:16-17 · GALATIANS 6:15

to maintain him and the family while he was out of work, felt degraded. She regarded it as a great calamity to be the wife of a convicted thief, and could hardly bring herself to believe her husband guilty. When he left prison, and again came to London, she besought him to promise not again to transgress, and he resolved to lead in the future a more honest life. He was, however, soon after ensnared by a receiver of stolen goods, and resorted to his old haunts, spending his days in drunkenness and thieving. Like many others of this class, all was not sunshine with him, and the money he gained dishonestly he spent so readily that at times he was reduced almost to starvation. The heartlessness of some of his small acts of robbery was cruel. He even stole some of the garments of the poor persons who lived in the same house in which he lodged; and sold them for one-tenth of their value.

Fortunately he was induced to attend the second of Ned's soup suppers.

"During the evening," says Ned, "I noticed that he seemed greatly impressed by what he was hearing; and when the meeting and supper were over, one of the friends called me to him, when I found him deeply concerned about his soul. I put the gospel before him simply, and he left the place completely overwhelmed. I had invited those who were desirous of changing their course of life to come and see me the next day, and he was one of those who came. I gave him a little present help, and having taken down his address, I visited him in his own home. I found his wife hard at work, making small baskets, and three or four children were round her, all huddled together in one miserably furnished room. They seemed to be in the most abject state of poverty. I spoke to the wife concerning her husband, when she said he was a great trial to her, that they would all starve were it not for her own industry, and that she had to work very hard to get bread enough for the children; but she would not mind that, if he would only be kind to her; for his temper was almost too much for anyone to bear. I asked her what she thought as to his soul, when she replied, that since the previous night he had been in a most wretched state of mind, but had not been so cross with her; he only seemed wild with himself, as if he hated himself. I learned that he was labouring under conviction of sin. I was enabled to help her with a little money for their immediate wants, for which she expressed her gratitude, and after commending the family to the Lord in prayer I left, promising to use my best endeavours to obtain some employment for her poor husband."

At the next soup supper he was also present, and it was on that occasion he found relief to his soul. With a heart full of joy he ran home, and embracing his wife, told her that the Lord had that night saved his soul, and that, although he had been a bad man and a cruel husband, he meant, in dependence upon God's Spirit, to act differently. The next morning his eldest daughter, who was about nine years of age, asked her mother,

"What is the matter with father this morning? He speaks so kind to me, and he never did so before."

"Oh, nothing, my child," was the mother's reply.

"Ah, but I know there is," persisted the little girl; "he was never like this before. Oh, mother, is father going to die; for he has been crying and reading the Bible, and he's never done that before."

" No," answered the mother; "your father is not going to die, he is going always to be kind now; for he means to love Jesus, and go to chapel."

"Oh! " cried the little one, joyfully, "won't that be nice? For then, I know, he'll take me to chapel; and I want to love Jesus, too."

The next Sabbath he attended the house of God, with his eldest child, and joined the Bible-class in the afternoon. Employment was ultimately found for him, although at small wages. His wife is now a consistent Christian, and the family is as distinguished for its happiness as once it was for its misery.

F— A—, as in the preceding case, received nearly all his education in the streets when a child. He was brought up in a western city. His father was a good tradesman, but of grossly intemperate habits, and his mother strove hard to provide sufficient food for her children. At eight years of age, F— had to go out to work, and he soon associated himself with a gang of rough lads who trained him for a criminal life. As an errandboy at a grocer's shop, belonging to one of his father's boon companions, he was noted for his sharpness, and soon he was put behind the counter. Here he began to steal, sometimes robbing his employer to the amount of thirty shillings a week, his unsuspecting mistress blaming her husband for taking the money from the till with which to procure more drink. F—, however, was not content with these thefts, nor with the quiet life he then led. To be compelled to serve behind a counter, though an employment for which he was well fitted by natural gifts, was irksome to a lad who loved to roam about the streets. After a few months he was determined to be released from his confinement; and leaving the shop, he joined a gang of young thieves in the city, and went into training for house-breaking. They would go out at night, and practise upon several houses, learning how to open doors and windows without making a noise, sometimes stealing from the halls and passages a few articles, but rarely entering the houses at all. Their doings ultimately attracted the notice of the police, who suspected them of stealing as well as merely opening the doors of the houses. They managed, however, to avoid detection, until one morning, after a night's "good hard drilling," the police met them as they were returning home, and took the gang into the station, on suspicion of being concerned in a robbery. They were remanded for a week; but nothing could be proved against them, for they had thrown into a canal their burglar's tools, when in sight of the police.

The magistrates, however, committed them for three months' imprisonment with hard labour, as rogues and vagabonds. On their liberation they intended to start for London, where they might complete their training; but F— was persuaded by his father to remain in the city. Shortly afterwards he was employed as a bargeman, and he remained in this situation until he finally removed to London. At Christmas he was induced to visit a brother of one of his late companions in crime, and on quitting the house he left a new pocket-handkerchief behind. In the following Whitsuntide he was called into his master's office at Bristol, and there he found, much to his amazement, two detective officers. One of them said to him, "Do you know — of Bath?"

"Oh, yes," was the reply.

"When did you see him last?"

"Christmas time."

"Where?"

"At his mother's house."

"Did you leave anything behind you, then?"

"Yes, a new pocket-handkerchief."

"Would you know it again if you saw it?"

"Yes," was the ready answer.

"Is this anything like it?" Asked the officer, as he held up an old washed-out and tom handkerchief.

"No," said F—, "mine was a new one."

"Well, is it anything like yours?"

"No; at least I really cannot say yes or no."

"Well," rejoined one of the officers, "— is in custody for a robbery, and this handkerchief was left; and his sister and mother declare that it belongs to you, and that you left it there at Christmas; and unless you are prepared to swear that this was the one you left there, we intend to take you for being concerned in the robbery of the 1st of April."

"You may take me," said F—, "but I was not at the robbery, and I can prove it. I was at Devizes on the 1st of April. I remember it well, for we were loading a barge with wheat on that day; but I will not swear to that handkerchief."

He was thereupon taken to the police-station, and committed for trial, with three others, for robbery, he alone being admitted to bail. Eleven weeks afterwards he stood at the dock with the other prisoners. Conscious of his own innocence, he was startled by hearing a witness swear positively that he saw him carrying on his back the sack in which the stolen property was found, and that he saw F— standing outside his own door on the morning of the same day. In spite, however, of these assertions, he was fortunately enabled to prove an *alibi,* and was therefore honourably acquitted.

The trial had taught him a lesson it was needful for him to learn—viz., to avoid keeping bad companions. He was sickened of their influences and society, and resolved at once to remove to the metropolis, and labour honestly for the future. This he did, gaining respectable employment and excellent wages. For a season he prospered, but was suspended for one month for insubordination. During this time he was tempted once again to steal, and longing for some more money to add to the little store he had managed to save through his industrious care, he resolved that evening to pick someone's pockets.

Evening, however, did not come before he fell ill of the small-pox, from which he suffered so severely as to be blind for several days, and unable to resume work for eight weeks. Although he was but poorly acquainted with scriptural truth, he knew that God's omniscient eye had been upon him, watching his career, and that He discerned all his evil thoughts. He remembered some of his mother's wise admonitions, and the recollection made him feel very uncomfortable. On his return to work a city missionary began, and carried on at stated times, a religious service among those men who could not, or would not, or from various causes did not, attend the house of God on the Sabbath. F— went to this simple service, and his attention was arrested by the reading of the parable of the five wise and five foolish virgins. He felt self-condemned. His conduct had been through life foolish, and his end, he feared, would be as sad as that of the virgins whose lamps had gone out. The words of Jesus Christ sank into his heart, "Watch therefore, for ye know neither the day nor the hour when the Son of man cometh." The parable forced upon him the duty of self-examination, and as the result he was greatly troubled. He now determined to think more of the needs of his undying spirit; and as he had never been to either church or chapel, he felt a disinclination to begin to attend a place of worship; so he resolved to listen to some of the many street preachers who take their stand in various parts of South London, and accordingly he listened night after night to some of the men connected with the Gospel Hall; and hearing from one of these speakers that "Ned Wright" was to preach on the following Sunday evening, he made up his mind to hear what Ned had to say. He did so, and his feelings, while listening to the preacher's story of his life, and exhortations to his hearers, were such as led him to believe that his past career was known to him. In his simplicity he concluded that God had communicated to the people around him all the particulars of his life. The preacher's testimony was the means of F—'s conversion; and for four years he has had cause to bless God for the mercy extended him that evening. Like most of the labouring men who have been saved through the word preached by Ned Wright, he began soon to attempt some work for God. He frequently spoke about the love of God to sinful humanity, and it is still his delight to tell the story of the Cross to his fellow-workmen. Nor have his humble efforts been fruitless. The second foreman on the works was brought to the meetings by his persuasions, and F—'s heart was delighted to find that he, too, had become a partaker of Divine grace. And among the men on the works F— is still known as an earnest, simple-hearted, God-fearing man, whose daily life illustrates the lessons which often flow from his lips.

E— P— was the son of respectable parents, his mother having had £15,000 left her on her parent's death. Her first husband was a dissolute character, and spent her money. At his decease she was compelled to seek a situation in a large metropolitan hospital, and while here she was married to one of the surgeons, the father of the subject of out present sketch. E—, however, lost his father when seven years of age, and was sent to the pauper's school at Lewisham, where he remained until he was eleven years old. With a few other lads of about his own age he got into an orchard, and stole some fruit. For this he was to have been corrected; but he escaped from the school, and walked to London, calling upon his mother, who was cook in a family in Newington. He was taken back to school; but the master refusing to admit him, his mother found him a situation as doctor's boy. His early life was a series of mishaps. He accidentally broke one or two of the panes while cleaning the doctor's windows, and was discharged. He dropped a pie-dish when taking it to the bakehouse, and his employer, a blind-maker, angry at losing his batter-pudding, dismissed him his service. He was accused falsely of stealing half a crown at another place, and was once again thrown upon the world. He was then apprenticed to a shoemaker for seven years. After two years' service had expired, his employer, deeming him to be trustworthy, sent him to purchase leather. This was indiscreet, and the young shoemaker, who only had an allowance of threepence per week as pocket-money, soon found the opportunity to cheat too favourable to resist. He began to buy an inferior article, at threepence per pound cheaper than he was told to pay, and at last his misdeeds were discovered by his master, who would have prosecuted him had he not otherwise been a good servant.

Some time after this he was put in prison for using a knife with intent to do grievous bodily harm. It appears that a quarrel arose between himself and a fellow apprentice who had the misfortune to be near-sighted. The latter, in the heat of passion, raised his hand to strike E— a blow on the head, but did not see a knife that was in E—'s hand. When E— saw the hand about to fall, he up raised his own to guard himself, when the knife entered his assailant's arm above the elbow, making a severe gash, and opening one of the arteries. E— remained at Newgate nearly six weeks awaiting his trial; but the grand jury ignored the bill.

When he attained the age of manhood, E— earned good wages; but, alas! He spent all he earned at the concertroom and theatre, and in gay amusements. Being a good singer, his company was much sought after by the frequenters of music-halls and public-houses. He spent his Sunday evenings at the Eagle, surrounded by his pot companions who admired him, and his money not less. Often would he spend thirty shillings on one of these evenings in drink and in treating his flatterers.

It was thought that his marriage would be the means of his reformation; but as his wife was fond of amusements too, he still continued in his wild career. His friends set him up in business, which proved to be lucrative; but, as before, all his gains were misspent. Business became neglected, the trade fell off, and he was greatly reduced in circumstances. After a time he returned to shoemaking, and chose for his evening companions the men who are known as "blacklegs," many of whom were thieves. His wife set up a receiving house, and purchased of her husband's companions the goods which she well knew, because they confessed it, were stolen. The police suspected some of these men, and E— was persuaded to become a spy. He was therefore engaged to purchase goods of the thieves, and hand them over to the detectives, in order that they might compare them with other goods, and thus get a clue to the real offenders. One night there was a great jewel robbery to the amount of £13,000. Rightly or wrongly it was believed that E— knew who were the guilty parties, and that he was afraid to divulge the secret for fear of being murdered. On one occasion he bought a waggon-load of leather, and was introduced into a "thieves' garret for, good reader, the most successful thieves are the least happy, and live mostly in the deepest obscurity. Here he saw at the top of a house, in a room, an entrance to which had to be gained by means of a ladder and a trap-door, the home of a gang of notorious burglars, who could find no securer place than this to hoard their ill-gotten gains. E— purchased the whole of the leather they had stolen, and worked it away by degrees, selling it in small quantities very cheaply, but succeeding in making a large profit out of the bargain.

Cards, gambling, drinking, and other vices were followed greedily at this time, and E— began to be known in the neighbourhood in which he lived as a confirmed drunkard and notorious blackguard. He was also a great scoffer at all holy things, and the deeper he descended into sin, the stronger were the words which he employed everywhere to express his detestation of religion. At last, however, he lost a child of which he was very fond, and this loss was followed by other family bereavements. His wife's sister, who was a member of a Christian Church, died, and E— had to attend the funeral service. The minister's discourse deeply affected him, and, determined to change his life, he became a total abstainer from alcoholic drinks. It was a good resolution; but while the heart remained unchanged, there was little hope for a radical reformation of the conduct. He commenced again to rail at religion, and, like many other cowardly enemies of the saints of God, he persecuted those whose purity and godliness were a protest against his own sinful life. That which he could not understand he blasphemed; and those who sought to bring him into his right mind were scouted as fools and intermeddlers with his peace.

One day, while in a state of deep poverty, he was seized with typhus fever. Friends, however, were kind; and when he became convalescent, they removed him to one of the bye streets in the Blackfriars Road. In the removal, however, a relapse occurred, and his life was despaired of. While in this condition he was visited by two Bible-women, who endeavoured to arouse him to a sense of his condition as a sinner. His feeling, however, was that he had not done harm to any one but himself, and that all through life he had only been his own enemy. When he recovered his sickness, he was invited to a tea meeting for the poor of the district, and he and his wife accepted the invitation. Both husband and wife were convinced that night of their need of the Divine forgiveness, and they realized its power. This occurred nearly five years ago; and now E— is one of the most active and useful men who, in connection with Ned Wright's work, labour to bring souls to the Saviour.

E— may be heard preaching nearly every Sabbath evening in the New Cut, both indoors and in the open thoroughfare.

CHAPTER SIXTEENTH

THE THIEF CONJUROR.—HIS POETRY.—THE REFORMED LAD.— TOM THE
SHOEBLACK.

CHAPTER SIXTEENTH

E— c— was born in a village in the West of England, in the year 1836. Naturally of a roving disposition, he left home at an early age, in spite of the remonstrances of a praying mother and gentle friends. When fifteen, he associated himself with a gang of thieves and burglars, and was concerned in several robberies in and about Plymouth. If he succeeded in his nefarious designs while in the company of more expert hands than himself, he soon failed when he dissevered himself from them; for, having entered the dwelling-house of a respectable draper, and stolen some jewellery and a quantity of wearing apparel, he offered a black silk-velvet mantle to a second-hand clothes dealer, who purchased it and exposed it for sale. The police made inquiries; the shopkeeper remembered from whom he had obtained the stolen article, and the thief was captured and committed to prison, and at the end of five weeks was sentenced at the assizes to four months' imprisonment with hard labour, fourteen days of which were to be spent in solitary confinement, and he was ordered to be flogged twice. This being his first experience of the severities of gaol discipline, he soon bitterly deplored his fate, and repented of his misdeeds. The flogging made him feel acutely his degraded position, and as the cat-o'-nine-tails had to be administered both on entering and leaving the prison, he was ashamed to look his fellow-prisoners in the face, for fear they should be saying to themselves, "That is the chap who was flogged, and has to be flogged again."

211

Solitary confinement for fourteen days in a cell in which he could see only the bare walls and ceiling, is likely, if anything, to bring a youth not wholly inured to evil to serious reflection. At first the punishment seemed trivial; but as time grew on, and he began to estimate the value of speech, he deemed it far more golden than compulsory silence. The heavy tread and unconcerned expressionless look of the turnkey as he passed by the cell, or handed to the prisoner his food; the arrival of Christmas Day, and thoughts of the home and friends he had lost, increased his wretchedness, and filled his mind with despair. He sought release from melancholy by reading the few books that had been placed in his cell. Fortunately, Bunyan's "Pilgrim's Progress" was among these, and this he read with avidity. Christmas Day was spent in tracking the history of Christian's progress from the city of destruction unto the gates of the celestial city; and when the evening shades drew nigh, he threw himself upon his straw pallet, and began to reflect upon what he had read. He wept and repented of his sins, and vowed he would reform when he left the prison. Day after day he read and read again the precious volume, and found it to be increasingly interesting. The second flogging was less endurable than the first, although the lashes were fewer; for his back was still tender, and he had to witness beforehand the infliction of a similar punishment upon another prisoner.

When he left prison, he resolved to go home to his friends without delay. but thinking of his degradation and of his recent severe punishment, he deemed it better to wait a while. There could be no harm, he thought, in visiting some of his old companions, if he did not enter into their evil practices; and he was quite resolved not to suffer himself to be dragged into their sinful courses again. A false step, however, will not lead to right ends; and no sooner had he taken this unwise course, than he forgot all the lessons of the past, with its penitence and vows, and became a drunkard and a thief. Then he went to Bristol disguised as a beggar, sometimes wearing a pair of pants and a sailor's shirt, and representing himself to be a shipwrecked mariner. Notwithstanding his various disguises, he was soon suspected by the police, who watched his conduct narrowly, and ultimately, failing to arrest him on any other charge, he was taken before the magistrates, and sentenced to fourteen days' imprisonment as a rogue and a vagabond. Afterwards he found employment as a stable boy at a circus, and becoming notorious among the company for tricks displaying considerable ingenuity, he was taken into the employ of a conjuror and ventriloquist, who taught him his business, in which he became so great a proficient as to entertain audiences for two hours together with his "tricks and patter." Having quarrelled with his master on pecuniary matters, he resolved to set up in opposition to him as the "Chinese Wizard." He did not succeed very well in the same town, and so he went on his "provincial tour," taking care in each case to forestall his old employer. For some considerable time he performed in all the principal towns and in some of the more important villages in the South of England, engaging halls and rooms, and, wherever he could, evading payment for their hire. When he arrived in London, he found his services not likely to be so well appreciated, and he therefore accepted engagements as a comic singer at various music-halls. Evil company and love of drink again reduced him in circumstances, and eventually he was compelled to wander about the streets singing and selling the last new popular song, and lodging at threepence per night in one of the many low lodging-houses which abound in the metropolis. One day, however, he happened to meet his sister, who took compassion upon him, gave him half a sovereign, and extracted from him a promise that he would call upon her next day, when she would present him with a suit of new clothes, that he might try and secure a new start in life. Unfortunately, he spent the half-sovereign in drink, and ashamed again to meet his sister, he started off for Brighton, where he raised money by means of a begging letter, representing himself as desirous of travelling to his uncle's home to obtain relief for his widowed mother and family, whose house had just been burnt down.

At length he reached Bristol, and journeyed towards his home in Devon. On a previous visit, when acting as a conjuror, he astonished the natives by his tricks of legerdemain, and made himself an object of gossip by securing the affections of a young woman, to whom he now felt considerably attached. This acquaintance induced him to attempt once more to become honest and respectable; and so he settled down in Bristol as a rag and bone merchant, in which business he might have done well. But prosperity did not shine on him long; his old drunken habits returned with even greater force, and he spent every farthing he had saved in getting drunk night after night for a whole fortnight. Quitting his business and the neighbourhood, he obtained employment in a paper mill in one of the midland counties, where he soon became a foreman over one of the departments. While here, he married the young woman to whom he had been engaged, and for more than two years he attended a Wesleyan chapel, and taught children in the Sabbath-school. There was a change in conduct, but not in heart; and his self-righteous pride was so intolerable, that it was feared it would lead him into open sin. These fears were soon realized; for he began secretly to indulge in drink and to ill-treat his wife; then he fell openly into sin, and in one of his fits of intoxication he stabbed his young wife with a pair of scissors. Had it been a knife, and had the jury known how the deed had been perpetrated, he would have been put on his trial for attempted manslaughter. He was only sentenced to six months imprisonment with hard labour, and bound over to keep the peace at the end of that time, himself in £200, and two sureties in £100 each. The required sureties were obtained, and shortly after his liberation from prison he came to London, and eventually obtained a situation in the Royal Arsenal at Woolwich, where he remained for eight years. During this time he still indulged in drink, and was frequently threatened with his discharge.

Having resigned his post there, he removed to London, where he became much reduced in circumstances; his wife was taken ill, and ultimately died in an hospital. For sixteen years he led the life of a confirmed drunkard, obtaining money at one time by painting, and at another by selling cough lozenges in the public streets. Then he became conductor of an omnibus, and got married; but drink again reduced him to beggary, and his wife was compelled to go to service. It pleased God, however, at last to bring him to his senses; and when he felt how greatly he had sinned against the Lord, his mind was filled with remorse. Some one had most injudiciously told him that he was "too late for salvation," and this preyed so greatly upon his mind as to drive him to despair. In his broken-hearted condition he attended the services in the Gospel Hall, where he obtained the relief he had so earnestly sought. His story, as given at one of the meetings, is very interesting.

"Surely, I may well say, how wonderful are the ways of the Lord! How mysterious, and yet how good, in drawing on guilty, sin-stained

SCRIPTURE TESTIMONY
Holy Spirit convicts people of their sin
JOHN 16:8

man until he stands face to face with his Saviour! Truly may we say, 'God is love.' It was on the eve of the new year that I made the resolve to lead a steady life. I fancied that, if spared until the forthcoming year, I would show the world the results of a temperate life. I had built splendid castles in the air, and in my own mind and strength I was about to enter the new year a sadder but a wiser man. I had strolled in here, where earnest prayer was being offered—the sort of prayer that makes one tremble and weep. I mean, in my simple way, that it makes you feel somehow that you cannot get away. You feel uneasy; it brings to your recollection a mother's heartfelt prayers. That faithful monitor, conscience, told me that I had been a most wicked and unprofitable servant. The battle then waged fearfully in my breast; I was determined to quiet conscience, if possible, and conquer this seeming weakness that possessed me. I had not been here long, however, before the cry was raised of 'Fire,' and I hastened with the giddy multitude outside to the scene: it was in Upper Ground Street. The thought of fire in my wretched condition of mind was very painful. I have been in prison, awaiting my trial; and when in my solitary cell, it has been sad for me to think that perhaps I might soon be banished from my friends, my home, and my country: but still this feeling was nothing to that which filled my soul when God appeared to say to me, the wicked shall be turned into hell, and all the nations that forget God. These were some of my thoughts on that memorable evening. But finding my troubled spirit could not find rest, I retraced my steps to this place. I came hither, not of my own free-will—of that I am positive; but somehow I was under an influence which I could not resist. I went sorrowfully home that night, and wept and prayed. It is true that I weep now; but they are tears of joy; for I am now on my way rejoicing in a loving Saviour, who has graciously plucked me as a brand from the burning. It is free grace and never-dying love that has made me happy; for I am saved through the atoning blood of Jesus Christ.

Oh, to think and to know that God condescends to save a poor wretch like me!—A poor fellow who has been branded twice with the burning 'cat-o'-ninetails,' imprisoned for various crimes; a Sabbath-breaker, a drunkard, almost everything but a murderer! Yea, I have even been very close to that; for I once suffered a term of imprisonment for maliciously wounding! And yet the blood of Jesus Christ, God's Son, has cleansed me from all sin. What a blessed thought is that to me!"

Since his conversion, this man has meekly received the word of God, has grown in grace, and it is hoped he will be usefully engaged in the Christian Church. A friend at once communicated the good tidings to his brother in the country, and the news caused great rejoicing among not a few Christians who had for ten years prayed for the conversion of the drunkard. Ned, after preaching in the town, related to his brother the story of this remarkable conversion, when the latter exclaimed, "Yes, prayers have been piled up, pile upon pile, for him, and God has answered them all at once." When his mother heard of it, she burst into tears, and cried with joy, "At last, at last, the prodigal has returned."

Poetry, or rhyme-making, seems to be a tender passion with not a few converted thieves. Ned Wright himself has been guilty of this innocent amusement; and E— C— has followed in his wake. We give a sample, not on account of its intrinsic worth or rhythmical beauty, but as illustrative of the deep religious feelings of the writer:

GO AND TELL JESUS!

Go and tell Jesus when sorrows o'erwhelm thee—
    You will find Him a friend, both loving and true;
He will patiently listen to all that concerns thee,
    And will teach thee in life the things thou shouldst do!

Go and tell Jesus, anxious one, I implore you!
    He is watching you now with His dear, loving eye;
He is waiting to love and gently caress you;
    Then fly to His arms, for He's ever nigh.

Go and tell Jesus, weary one, I entreat you!
　　Oh! Tell him your weakness—rest your head on His breast;
He will come to your help, and sweetly will kiss you,
　　And then make you happy by giving you rest.

Go and tell Jesus, suffering one; for He ever
　　Will pour out the balm on your sorrowing soul!
He will bind up thy wounds, and forget thee—oh, never
　　For He longs to speak, "Peace," and to make thee all whole.

Go and tell Jesus, tempted one; for thou knowest
　　Thy Master endured it when He suffered below;
And if thy proved sword that Friend thou once showest,
　　And speak of His blood, thou canst vanquish the foe

Go and tell Jesus, happy one; for His favour
　　In loving thee first, then teaching thee love:
Adore Him, dear one; for He's a sweet Saviour,
　　Who ere long will take thee for ever above"

Among the many young lads who attended the thieves suppers was one who manifested intense anxiety to change his mode of life. He confessed he had been "a very bad and wicked boy;" had been convicted of stealing in the city of Bath, and was imprisoned there for some time. After his release he tramped to London in search of employment. In this he failed, and therefore applied to Mr. Wright for help. A benevolent friend in Folkestone had applied to Ned for a convicted thief desirous of reforming his life, to work in the coal trade, and this lad was sent, and his services accepted. He is now likely to become an honest and industrious young man; and his life has hitherto well tested his sincerity. Two days after his departure the following letter was received from him:

　　"DEAR SIR,
　　　　"I now take my pen in hand to write these few lines to you, hoping you are quite well, as it leaves me at present, and I had

a very pleasent journey and Mister G— met me at the stasion safely, and he is a very nice gentleman and he took me to Miss A— she is a very nice lady to and, I think folkstone is a very nice place and the vessell wich I am goen a board is at bolougne, and I am goen thear this evening Monday 18th and I shall very often come to folkestone and I am very thankful that I have such great friends to com and see when I com a-shore and I don't no how to thank you a nuff for your grate kindness to me and I will promise to keep a way from public houses, en I and i'll trust in the Lord to help me through all my little difekeltys and dear Mr. Wright

"You must forgive me for riten so bad, for I have had no schooling and give my love to all the young men at the hall, and I am very happy now and i hop i shall get on nice and comf bull and i will keep a way from bad company, so i havno more to say at present and I will send a nother letter when i get on bord, as soon as possible, so good-bye for the present.

"from your

"Affectonet friend,

"A— G—"

In a subsequent letter, addressed to a lady at Folkestone, who received him previous to his going on board ship, he writes:—"I have a very good captain, and he is very kind, and he is one I can get on with very well indeed; and I thank you very much for your kindness to me. I don't know how to thank you enough for your kindness, but I will try to do my best while I am here, and I think I shall get on very well indeed."

SCRIPTURE TESTIMONY
Do good to those who hate you
MATTHEW 5:44 · LUKE 6:27

Tom—, a shoeblack of the New Cut, was one of the most desperate of the young lads who infest the neighbourhood. From his earliest years he seemed to delight in mischief, and was determined to live a dishonest, vagabond life. He was well known to the police in the district as an expert young gambler, and as a consequence he received no favour from them. His favourite game was "pitch-and-toss," in which he indulged in the street when the police were out of sight, with his blackingbox by his side, which served as a "stall," or disguise. His language, as a swearer and blasphemer, was only equalled by those who had acquired greater proficiency in blackguardism. This habit became so great upon him that he could not utter a sentence without either an oath or the use of some filthy expression. In the evening he was always to be found patronizing a low theatre, and on the Sabbath he did little else but gamble, seeking for all the "flats" within a given radius. He manifested a malicious pleasure in annoying the open-air preachers, and taxed his ingenuity to the utmost in scoffing at religion. If a prize had been offered to the worst lad in Lambeth, Tom would probably have been the successful competitor. His mother, however, was determined to rescue him from the streets, and to put him to some trade. This was the first step towards reformation. He found honourable employment to ward off many a temptation, and to him it was a new experience to have his mind set a-thinking by hard work. Working at the bench by his side was a young lad of quite a different character—quiet, shy, unassuming, and meditative. He was never known to join in the blasphemies of other lads; he always refused to drink with the workmen, and was noted for his love of industry. He was a Christian! That was enough of itself to secure the dislike of the ungodly workmen in the shop; but their hatred of him was increased all the more when they found the foreman honourably approve of his conduct and attention to work. It was thought that nothing would annoy the consistent lad more than impure language, and Tom was urged to vex his righteous soul as much as possible in this way. Tom was very proud thus to show off his diabolic skill, and sought incessantly to arouse the temper of the young man. Greatly to his surprise and disappointment, however, every art and provoking allusion failed, and Tom was compelled eventually to give up assailing him. One day it happened that Tom was in difficulty about his work, and although the workmen knew well enough how to help him out of it, they declined to render him any assistance or offer him any suggestion. Not so the persecuted lad, who volunteered his help; and when Tom had conquered the difficulty, he was quietly invited to come at any time for "a lift". Tom was staggered, and became speechless, and so unable to thank, as he would have done, his unexpected friend. While looking at his friend with a wondering stare, a hand was laid on Tom's shoulder, and the young man said, "I have hope in you yet; for I have prayed very much for you."

"Prayed for *me!* Prayed *very much* for me!" thought the astonished Tom, "why, what does he mean?" Though he went about his work heartily, and set about his amusements in the evening, yet the words would ring in his ears, "Prayed very much for me." The plane in his hand seemed burdened with the same words, as he used it, and the saw seemed to echo the same mysterious language. Whenever he attempted to swear, or to use foul speech, he was gagged as he thought of the words, "I have hope in you yet; for I have prayed very much for you."

The young Christian observed with joy that Tom did not swear at, or otherwise annoy him, and he hoped that the words he had said to him had touched a secret chord in his heart. In vain did his cowardly companions now urge him to assault his new friend.

"Give him a peal, Tom," said an old man, as he passed Tom's bench.

"What for?" asked Tom; "he never annoys me."

"Oh," said the other, "he's a religious bloke, he is. Why, he ought to be burnt, and all such sanctimonious —. I'd burn them all, if I only had my way with the crawlers."

"I'll tell you what," was Tom's sharp, bluff reply, "he's the quietest young chap that we've got, and the civilest too: so you may say what you like; but I won't abuse him any more, and I think you had better let the man alone."

"Bravo! Tom," exclaimed a voice by his side. Turning round, Tom encountered the foreman, with an approving smile on his countenance. "Bravo, Tom! I am right down glad to hear you say so. I wish you were all like him. Why, I shouldn't have half the trouble I have, if you all were; well, well, I've hope of you yet, Tom. To tell you the truth, I had thoughts a day or two ago of getting rid of you, as an incorrigible fellow, but now I have some hopes of you." And with this the foreman moved on.

"Thanks," said Tom; "but you've not done for me what he has done,— 'prayed very much for me.'"

The foreman had passed out of hearing; but the object of his remarks observed in a quiet tone, "Praise the Lord, I do, Tom."

"Well," said he, "I don't know why you should; for I've been a regular torment to you ever since I came here; but I'm very sorry for it, and promise that I'll never do it again, and so I hope you'll forgive me, though I have been so bad to you."

"I forgive you," was the quick response, though you must ask God's forgiveness, and you cannot do that unless you know Him; but if you come to Jesus, God will forgive you for His sake."

This struck Tom as strangely mysterious. "Don't know Jesus," he replied. "Come to Jesus! how can I come to Jesus? He won't have anything to do with me. It's only good folks, that go to church or chapel."

"But," said the other, "God loves you."

"No, He doesn't," said Tom, respectfully. "He only loves good folks."

"Ah, no, Tom," said the Christian workman; "it was not the righteous, good folks, but sinners, that Jesus came to save."

Tom's curiosity was aroused. He began to think soberly about all that had passed. He longed for the dinner-hour to arrive, when he could talk a little more with his friend.

True friends indeed did they become. Tom learnt now the way of salvation, and was interested for the first time in religious truth. On the Sunday he was taken to the once despised "Gospel Hall," to hear Ned Wright. That night became the most remarkable night in his history. Bitterly did he weep, as he felt deep penitence for sin; joyously did he sing when he found all his sins forgiven. He went home praising God.

But he went home to ungodly relatives. Neither mother nor father loved or feared God, and his younger brothers were neglectful, while the eldest of them all was a lover of every vice. But he did not hesitate to tell them of his conversion, and on retiring to rest he prayed, as well as he could, for the salvation of the whole household. Somehow, though he did not place any merit in his prayers, or believe in the efficacy of any of his words to his parents, he felt convinced that his brethren would be saved. On the Monday morning he went to the workshop, with the intention of maintaining silence about the great change, lest he should not be able to brook the persecution which would be inevitable if he openly avowed that he was a Christian. But, to use a Bunyan phrase, "as God would have it," one of the workmen, who happened to be present at the service on the previous evening, cried out, " Oh, here comes one of —'s pupils."

"No," said Tom, "not —'s pupils, but one of Jesus Christ's pupils, I trust;" and before all the workmen he boldly confessed that Jesus was his Lord.

His after conduct abundantly proved the sincerity of Tom's professions, and his earnestness won respect. At this time he could not read. Hundreds of Christians amongst the lowest classes are not able to read a chapter in the New Testament when first converted to God; but one of their earliest efforts after conversion is to secure instruction in the spelling-book. It was so with poor Tom. With perseverance he soon succeeded in his task, and was able to read his much-loved Testament. Having received some further instruction, he was requested one evening to tell the story of his conversion to a number of poor people in the hall. He did so, and Mr. Wright has since met with not a few who were "savingly convinced of the truth as it is in Jesus" that evening. On another occasion his father and mother were in the hall, and seeing them present, he made a personal and affectionate appeal to them, which God was pleased to bless to their conversion. Tom has now the joy of knowing that his prayers have been answered; for all the household are now serving the Lord.

CHAPTER SEVENTEENTH

THE CONFESSIONS OF A THIEF.

CHAPTER SEVENTEENTH

I WAS BORN, says one of the reformed thieves who has for some time been under Mr. Wright's teaching, within the precincts of the city of London. Though my parents were in humble circumstances, they sent me at a very early age to school; and when I was eight years old, I was transferred to a parochial school, where I received a very good education. My parents were kind, afforded me every encouragement to learn, and set me a worthy example. I received the clothes as a charity boy, and at twelve years of age I was made the head boy in the school, wearing the highest number, 'One,' on the breast of my coat. When I was fourteen years old, I was sent out into the world, a gentleman where I had been cleaning knives and boots in my spare hours having got me a situation at the West-end. Here I was away from my parents' influence, and in the matter of remuneration for my services I was illiberally treated. After serving him nearly two years, I was sent on the traveller's rounds; but my travelling expenses—one shilling a day—not being sufficient, I took, in an evil hour, a shilling of my employer's money. That was my first step to ruin; and as I was not detected, I soon committed myself again, and eventually became utterly regardless of what I spent I had become an expert at bagatelle, and to satisfy my thirst for this amusement I robbed my employer of his money and his time. At last I was discovered, and should have been prosecuted but for my youth. I was, however, discharged his service, and thrown upon the world without a character. Still in a few weeks I got temporary employment in a house of business, where several of the men were constantly getting drunk. I was now fairly launched into crime, and the example set me every day increased my thirst for drink. To enable me to live in vice, I was obliged to resort to other than honest means of obtaining money. I was advised by one of my drunken companions to get orders from some of the customers I had known in my former situation, and draw some money on account, though the goods were never sent. This I did for some time without detection. At last a gentleman gave me employment to solicit orders; but this did not satisfy me. I was so initiated into evil ways, that I was unhappy when away from the public house, or apart from my evil associates. To enable me to do this I would take things out of the shop and pawn them, and this continued until one day I was taken hopelessly drunk to my employer's shop. Not knowing where I was, or to whom I spoke, I discharged a volley of abuse upon my employer, who threatened to turn me out of the shop. But the Almighty ordered it that my guilt should be discovered; for in putting my hand into my pocket to get something out, I dropped a pawn ticket relating to some of the property I had stolen. I was not aware of having lost the ticket, which fell into the hands of my employer, who did not say a word to me until Saturday night, when he said, calling me by my name, 'There is your salary; I have no further need of your services.' I stammered out, 'Why? but he refused to give me any reasons, and so I left, and walked home to my lodgings with a heavy heart, feeling myself a ruined man.

"I took to drink to drown my reflections, and removed as far as I could from the shop, being ashamed of my misdeeds. I became acquainted with a regular old 'sot,' whom no one would employ on account of his dissipated and irregular habits. I went about with him for a fortnight, getting a shilling or sixpence anywhere we could; my clothes being pawned, and my landlady pressing me for the rent, and threatening to turn me out, and take the few things I had. However, there was not much for her to take, and I only valued one thing, viz., a box that belonged to my poor mother, which had been in the family for years. I was determined, at least, to retain that, and so I stayed out that night, and went to my lodging the next morning, telling my landlady to keep the place as quiet as she could, as I required rest, having got a situation at an employment which kept me out all night. This she readily believed, and having promised her payment as soon as I got my first week's money, I was allowed to go to my apartments. I then put my few things into my box, and when all was quiet I descended the stairs, and opened the street door; but missing my step, I fell down headlong, box in hand. Fortunately, I regained the use of my feet, and as the landlady was at the back part of the house, I managed to escape.

"The next day, while wondering what I should do, I met my last employer in the street, who was good enough to pass the compliment of the day to me. I resolved to go at once to him, and beg his forgiveness, and entreat him to give me another chance. This he was kind enough to do; for he was a Christian man, as good as I was bad. He sent me out soliciting orders, and the same day being Saturday, gave me more money than I was enti-tled to receive. I was resolved to do my best to show my benefactor some gratitude; but, alas! It was poorly carried out; for I began to drink again. I kept myself honest for a time, and I was assisted to get better clothes, my employer thinking it would give me a better opportunity of doing more business. After all this kindness and good feeling, one would think it impossible to be so basely ungrateful as I was; but love of drink was so strong that on one occasion I got so tipsy as to pawn a parcel of goods. I was told not to come to the shop again until I was sober. The next week the other traveller discovered that the goods I had pawned had not been delivered, and he told me he could not do otherwise than acquaint my employer with the fact. I then took my flight, and got employment as a canvasser where no character was required. I went to work with a good will for a short time; but soon I began again to go to my old associates, became as bad as ever, and having been trusted with some property, I again made away with it. Detection followed; but even this gentleman did not like to part with me, as I was considered clever at my business. So he made a debt of my defalcations, to be paid so much weekly; but he would not trust me to deliver any more goods; and as he was determined to have the money, I tried another way of obtaining it This was my plan: after the goods had been left at a customer's, I would go to the house and get them back, on the pretence that it was the wrong parcel, or that I had a particular order for that class of material, and if they would let me have them, they should have some of the same kind on the following day. In many instances they gave me the goods back, and when my employer went the next week, he found I had taken back the goods. One Monday evening, while engaged in skittle-playing, and just as I was making a bet on a floorer as they call it—which means knocking down the whole of the pins—a policeman seized me by the arm, and told me I was wanted for stealing articles, the property of my employer, who was standing by his side. I was then for the first time in my life taken to the police station. On the way there I begged for mercy; but it was too late—my employer was inexorable, and the day of retribution had come at last.

"After the charge was booked I was searched, and every article taken from me. The next morning I was taken from prison to the police-court, and after hearing my case I was remanded for a week. At five o'clock the van arrived to take us to the House of Detention. Each prisoner has a box to himself, and after squeezing yourself in, the door is locked, and you are fixed, not able to move either way till the door is opened. Glad enough was I when let out, though my eyes beheld at once one of the corridors of the prison. I was afterwards placed in a reception cell by myself, which cell was about four feet wide by ten feet long. During the evening I was weighed and measured, and any particular marks about, my body were taken notice of: these precautions are taken in the event of a prisoner making his escape. Then I was taken to the baths, and on looking in I observed the water to be rather dirty, and told the officer so, but was politely assured that if I did not go in at once he would put me in. After bathing, the prisoners were all put in a row, and a square tin, in which was a pint of gruel, and a little brown loaf of bread, weighing six ounces, were handed to us. We were then told off to our different cells, and upon arriving at mine I found my bed to consist of a hammock and two blankets. I had no sleep that first night, but gave way to reflection. Oh, what would I not have given to have my liberty again! I wished I had never left the paths of honesty. I had cast off Christ; I had rejected His salvation.

"At a quarter to seven the next morning a bell was rung, and a few minutes after came a tremendous kick at my door, and a husky voice shouted, 'Now, out of that, or you will come out of it quicker than you went in.' But I was out of the hammock before he could finish his sentence. According to the rules, I was to do up my bed, and clean my cell; if this be not done, prisoners are deprived of seeing their friends, and a punishment is awarded them of so many days' bread-and-water diet, which is hard upon a prisoner whose guilt has not been proved. At ten o'clock you go to chapel, at twelve you are allowed to see one friend for ten minutes—this friend may bring you any plain food and one pint of porter. If you are not fortunate enough to possess such friends, you must be content with the prison diet. My poor old father came to visit me; it was the first time he had ever set foot in prison, and I felt now that I was bringing his grey hairs with sorrow to the grave. After a further remand of a week, I was found guilty of illegally pawning a pair of trousers, and sentenced to two months' hard labour. I was then taken to Coldbath Fields' prison, where my hair was cut short, and I was put into a room with about a hundred other prisoners. At dinner-time those that were near me eagerly watched for my provisions; for, knowing I was a new-comer, and thinking I was not likely to want such coarse food as was presented me, they sought to obtain my bread. Of course they were afraid to ask me for it, since silence is enjoined; but when I turned round to look at my fellow-prisoners, my loaf vanished, and I found an empty tin in front of me. A companion in trouble gave me to understand, as well as he could, that he would pick all my oakum for me if I would 'sling him my toke.' Anything a poor fellow would do to get something more to eat. The next day I was put on 'the wheel' for fifteen minutes on and fifteen minutes off—-a dreadful punishment. I have seen the prisoners become so exhausted that they have fallen on to the ground.

"At the termination of my imprisonment I was received home again, and was treated with the greatest kindness. I was ill for several days, owing to my having partaken of too much food on a weak stomach; for I grew weak on the prison diet of twenty ounces of bread and two and a half pints of gruel per day, which I had half the time I was there. I now received a letter from one of my shop-mates, stating that he had been fortunate enough to get into partnership with a friend, and that he would give me a trial. A week after my discharge I commenced travelling for this person. I did very well, but soon forgot all my good resolutions; and one day, being sent out with a parcel, I pledged it for a small sum, spending the money in drink. The parcel was redeemed, but I made away with a larger one. My employer discovering this, did not tell his partner, but arranged that I should pay him back in instalments what I had stolen. I did not like what some people call working on a dead horse, and I soon committed myself again, and had to flee to escape punishment I then shared the proceeds of some extensive robberies which were committed by a young man upon his employer, who was also a relative. For about eight months we lived in this way, getting drunk, and associating with the vilest characters. One day I met my last employer, but took no notice of him, and had hoped that he did not recognize me; but after walking a little distance I started running as hard as I could, when some boys playing in the road cried out, 'Look at them men having a race.' It was a race indeed for me, and one in which I was bound to lose; for, on turning the corner of the next street, I met two policemen coming towards me. I turned quickly round, but only to fall into the arms of my employer, who had raised the cry of 'Stop thief!' Thinking I might have a chance still of getting away, I knocked him down, but was speedily grasped by the police, and once more taken to the police-station. I was sentenced to twelve months' imprisonment this time, and I did not get through my punishment as easily as before. One morning the chief warder wanted men for the mat-room. I was selected for one, and was set to work. The officer over us was very hard with me. As I had never worked at mats before, my progress was very slow, and I was being continually reported, and, as a consequence, was put on bread and water. I became quite tired of this, and being told to take a mat to pieces, I deliberately cut it to bits. For this I was sentenced by the governor to three days' bread and water, and to work in solitude for twenty-eight days. For three of these days I had no labour to perform; but the next day the warder brought me my oakum to pick; but having offended him, he reported me, and I had again to live on bread and water, though it was in the depth of winter. Afterwards I was sent, with twenty others, to Bedford Gaol, where I found to my sorrow it was all solitary confinement, excepting during the time of exercise and in chapel hours. I got very ill through catching a severe cold, and began to think once again of God, and prayed to Him in my wretched position, confessing my sins, and asking for pardon. Night and day I cried to Him for help to endure my punishment, and to keep me from the cravings of hunger. My prayer was heard; for I was sent into the kitchen, where a fellow-prisoner gave me four large pieces of meat and two half-pounds of bread, telling me I must now look after myself, and 'nail' anything I could. There being no restrictions in the kitchen as to speaking, I soon gave way to lying and bad language.

"I now got my entire liberty again, and though I found employment, I began again my evil practices, stealing parcels belonging to various persons. Then I got into trouble, this time being innocent. On Whitsuntide holiday I had been drinking, and having spent all my money, I pledged my coat, and being without one, I went to a young woman I knew, to borrow her father's. I was in the public-house close by, with the coat on my back; but as I got so very drunk, I did not take it back until the next day. When the father came home at night, the daughter was afraid to tell her father that she had lent me the coat; so she told him that I went into the house, and stole it. I sent the coat in, and went into a public-house close by, and was drinking with some companions when a constable came up and took me into custody. I was only sentenced to two months' imprisonment, the magistrate thinking it was a drunken spree. My case, however, was reported in the newspapers, and I fully expected to be retaken upon my discharge for acts of robbery. The morning came, and I was now contriving how I could disguise myself. While we were all together exchanging the prison dress for our own, I saw a man who had on a long smockfrock and an old wide-awake. I thought if I could get him to exchange with me for my coat and hat, I should be able to accomplish my purpose. This he did, on my explaining to him the fear I had of being taken. I then put his clothes on, and sallied forth, hardly knowing where I was going, my old companions not even recognizing me, and I got clear away. I was told afterwards that I had a narrow escape, as I was being looked after.

"I again gained employment on commission, and again rogued those who employed me, spending the proceeds in the same evil way. Being reduced to poverty, I tried to get orders and a deposit on account I had several narrow escapes, one in particular. I called once upon some people down a mews, when a man asked me if I was taking orders for coals. I told him 'Yes.' He very kindly asked me into the stable, and calling to some companions, told them to fasten the doors. 'Now,' said he, 'I have got you at last; you had three shillings of a friend of mine yesterday, and I mean taking you to his place, and the first policeman I meet I shall give you in charge. I was then taken by the collar, and walked into the Bayswater Road by two men, when we met a constable. They told him I had been receiving money by false pretences, and begged him to take me into custody. I consented to go, and they thereupon released their hold upon me, and I, pretending to be most willing, started off in another direction, and managed to outrun the whole of them. Still, it was a sharp race, as one of them was a tall, active man, and nearly succeeded in catching me.

"Some time previous to this occurrence I was asked whether I would get members for a burial society. I was allowed all the entrance fees as commission, and a salary, provided I secured twenty members in a week. It was, however, very difficult to persuade people that the society was genuine; and as the day had now come when I should receive my salary, I found I had only two members towards the twenty. I therefore put down the names of all the relatives I could think of, and went into the office with about twenty-five names, all false but two, and received the salary agreed upon. I took care not to call there again, but went elsewhere, and called upon a house for orders. A boy answered the door. I inquired if his mother was in-doors. He replied, no, there was no one in the house, and no one would be at home until the evening. I then told the lad that I had come to measure his father for a suit of clothes, and that, as he was out, if he would let me see his best clothes I would measure them. He asked me in, and produced the clothes, which I pretended to measure, but made the excuse that I thought I had better take them to the shop, then no mistake would be likely to arise. The lad allowed me to take away the clothes, and of course did not see any more of me. One day I had succeeded in getting a coat from two lads, and had walked half-way down the street, when a woman asked me what I intended doing with the coat. I told her the same story as I had told the lads; but she said it was all lies. So I thought it best to give her the coat back, and get away as quickly as possible, deeming myself fortunate in being able to escape so easily. At another time a girl asked me if I had come for the rent I said 'Yes,' and she asked me in the room, and gave me eight shillings, with the rent book, which I receipted, and went away. One day I knocked at a door, and asked the boy if his mother was at home. She came downstairs, and immediately recognized me as having taken an order from her before, and received a shilling from her. Finding she was determined to give me in charge, I turned to run off, when she seized me by the collar, and in my struggle to release myself my coat was torn open behind from top to bottom. In this state I ran away, amidst the cries of 'Stop thief' and pursued by two policemen, who succeeded in capturing me. I was taken to the station, but was let off on the ground that as the charge was a misdemeanour, it was necessary that a summons should be taken out against me.

"In this way I went on for some time; one day I was in a neighbourhood where all the houses are let out in apartments, and I asked and obtained leave to go over one house to solicit orders. I accordingly proceeded to the first floor, knocked, and asked a man in bed whether he wanted anything in my way, and was told to call when his wife was at home. On coming back I saw in the front room a large glass decanter, which I put under my coat, and then left the house. I had, however, been watched by a woman who had lost some things in the same way before; and I had not proceeded far when a constable laid hold of me, and asked what I had got under my coat. I struggled hard to get away; but it was of no use; and I was taken to the police station, and charged with the theft. The next morning I was taken before the magistrate. While in the waiting-room, who should I see but a detective to whom I was well known? Seven years' penal servitude now stared me in the face. I was afraid every minute he would turn his head round to the corner where I was sitting, trembling and shaking like an aspen leaf. To my great relief, however, he walked out of the room, wishing some of the other constables 'Good morning.' I was now taken into court, pleaded guilty, and as nothing was there known against my previous character, I was sentenced to three months' imprisonment with hard labour.

"When I came out of prison, it was with the determined resolve, if I could get employment, to keep honest; but I soon found that no one would assist me, and, instead of praying to God to keep me from temptation, and trusting to Him for my temporal wants, I soon went astray, and commenced again my old pilfering habits. Again I had a very narrow escape; for on passing down a street a person called me back, and accused me of having swindled her some time back of 3s. 6d. I denied all knowledge of it. Some of her friends coming up at this moment, they told my accuser not to let me go, but to send for a policeman. I now found it rather dangerous to stop, so I started off; but in doing so, two or three women caught hold of me by my coat, one at each tail, and in struggling against them I pulled them along with me a little distance—indeed, until they were compelled to let go, when I made my escape. Another time a woman who answered the door said, 'Oh, yes, you came to me with the same tale before, when I was living in — street, and perhaps you have come to pay me the two shillings back you then had of me.' Of course I denied that I was the man; but she said she could swear to me by my front teeth; so, telling me I had better be off, I took her advice, and decamped.

"After continuing at this kind of game for a considerable time with varied success, I thought, as I had been to every place I could think of within seven or eight miles of the city of London, I would now try my fortune in the country. So, early one morning I left home, and worked my way to a large town some thirty miles from home, where I commenced taking orders for coals, making use of a gentleman's name in the town. I obtained three or four shillings in this way in about an hour, and I then went into a public-house to get some dinner, when a sergeant of police opened the room-door, and looked round, and went out again. In a few minutes he returned with a man from whom I had taken an order, though he did not give me money, as he thought I was a swindler. 'That's the man', said he; and the sergeant then sat down opposite me, and taking a pencil and book out of his pocket, he asked me if I was authorized by Mr. So-and-so to take orders, and receive money. I told him 'Yes.' He then asked me my name. I gave him a false one, and a false address as well. He wanted to know if I had received any money from any person. I told him 'Yes as I knew that I had received something at the next house to where the man who watched me lived. He then left me in charge of another constable, and knowing I was again in the hands of justice, I drank up a glass of rum, called for another, and had also a pint of ale, believing it would be a long time before I could get any more. The sergeant came back with a warrant for my apprehension, and I was taken to the magistrate. Upon a detective saying that there were other charges against me, I was remanded, and then committed to the quarter sessions. These were held the next week, when I pleaded guilty; and as the prosecutor did not wish to press the case against me, I was sentenced to only one month's imprisonment.

"When I left the gaol, I was met outside by a detective, who showed me a warrant upon another charge, and told me I must go with him to London. The handcuffs were again placed upon me, and I was taken to the townhall, where I had to wait until a train arrived to convey us to London. I was this time sentenced to twelve months' imprisonment; and just before the expiration of this term, I wrote to one of the gentlemen from whom I had stolen, begging for employment when I came out of gaol. He sent me a very kind letter, saying that he had no vacancy then, or he might have given me another chance, and hoping that I would do better in the future. Dreading to go back to my old ways, I wrote to another person, but did not receive an answer. I was now left to do the best I could; without employment, I struggled on for a month, till absolute starvation drove me again to steal. I could not see my wife and children starving any longer; but though I did commence to steal again, it went against my grain, and I was determined only to take enough to purchase food, and not to commit such crimes as I had done before. However, on several occasions, when opportunity came across my path, I was tempted to take advantage of it, until, tired of so dishonest and miserable a life, I resolved firmly not to steal any more.

"Taking up a newspaper one morning, I saw an account of Ned Wright's soup supper; it made a very deep impression upon me, and as I was now resolved to lead a new life, I applied to Ned Wright, who readily assisted me as far as lay in his power. I now feel that I would rather suffer my hands to be cut off than take anything that does not belong to me. I earnestly hope that all I have wronged will forgive me, even as I hope we all may be forgiven of our heavenly Father. I trust now that my sins are washed away with the blood of Jesus Christ, whose blood cleanseth from all sin.

> "'The dying thief rejoiced to see
>   That fountain in his day;
> And there may I, though vile as he,
>   Wash all my sins away.'"

CHAPTER EIGHTEENTH

CHAPTER EIGHTEENTH

"I T'S NO matter, Mr.—; it's no matter. George has been christened in the true religion of our holy Church, and they may convert him to what they like, the power of the holy water will bring him back to the Catholic faith."

This was said by a priest in the Romish Church to the father of a boy who had become a Christian and a member of a Protestant Church.

"Then you think, Rev. Father, the boy is not totally lost to the Catholic Church; it's all his mother—I blame her for this; she always was a Methodist. I have dared her at her peril to go to the Protestant places of worship; I have threatened her time after time what I would do if ever I found her out: but now, since this Fenian movement, she has left me, and got the youngest child with her. She thinks she will do as she likes. I tell you, Rev. Father, I'll have the boy from her altogether, that I will; and that is why I have come for your advice, if you'll only say the word."

"Never mind," said the Romish priest; "let him stop: depend upon it, he'll come back. I never knew any go away from our holy Church after they had been christened, but what the power of the holy water brought them back again. But let us have the girl christened; get her under the power of the water."[1]

---

[1] That Roman Catholics do credit their so-called " holy" water with marvellous powers, will be seen from the following extraordinary document which is said to be affixed over the vessels of "holy water" in the church of S. Carlo Borromeo in the Corso, at Rome:—

The man to whom these words were addressed was an Irish Roman Catholic, who during his courting days had represented himself to be a Protestant, and had not openly avowed himself to be what he had all along been secretly, a Papist, until he had a goodly number of children around him; when he commenced a cruel persecution against his wife, forbidding her to attend any Protestant service, and commanding her to abandon all Protestant society. When the youngest child was born, it was christened according to the rites of the Romish Church, and when the lad, whose name was George, grew up, he was sent to a Roman Catholic school, where he formed the acquaintance of a number of boys whose parents were Irish. Some of these lads were of the most depraved tastes, and George soon learnt to be as cunning as they; indeed, he had not been in the school more than two years when he became a ringleader in their misdeeds. They formed a thieving band, George trying his pren-tice hand by robbing his mother of small articles, and combining with others to steal a bundle of riding whips. Other petty thefts were also committed to raise funds to go to the playhouse or penny gaff. At one time an unfortunate baker, who left his barrow in the street while he waited upon his customers at their houses, was watched by the juvenile

---

"Holy water possesses much usefulness when Christians sprinkle themselves with it with due reverence and devotion. The holy Church proposes it as a remedy and assistant in many circumstances both spiritual and corporeal, but especially in these following:—

"ITS SPIRITUAL USEFULNESS:

"1. It drives away devils from places and from persons.

"2. It affords great assistance against fears and diabolical illusions.

"3. It cancels venal sins.

"4. It imparts strength to resist temptations and occasions to sin.

"5. It drives away wicked thoughts.   .

"6. It preserves safely from the passing snares of the devil, both internally and externally.

"7. It obtains the favour and presence of the Holy Ghost, by which the soul is consoled, rejoiced, and excited to devotion, and disposed to prayer.

"8. It prepares the human mind for a better attendance on the Divine mysteries, and receiving piously and worthily the most holy sacrament.

"ITS CORPOREAL USEFULNESS.

"1. It is a remedy against barrenness in women and in beasts.

"2. It is a preservation from sickness.

"3. It heals the infirmities both of the mind and of the body.

"4. It purifies infected air, and drives away plague and contagion."

gang, whilst one of their number stole his bread. This act being successful, it was tried on succeeding occasions, the bread in each case being sold, and the money spent in the penny gaff. As they were eventually caught at this trick, they changed their tactics, and began robbing orchards and fruit gardens, filling several bags with fruit, and selling them, and with the proceeds attending the theatrical representations in the New Cut. At the Victoria Theatre and in penny gaffs they acquired a still further taste for lawless adventure by witnessing such favourite pieces as Dick Turpin and Jack Sheppard; and no play was considered to be worth their attention unless it was highly seasoned with deeds of blood and broad allusions to criminal intrigues. At school hours these stories were minutely discussed, the merits of the different actors criticised, and their exploits applauded. In course of time these lads became notorious in the neighbourhood as incorrigible rascals, and their conduct was frequently complained of to their parents, whose incredulity was marvellous when it is considered that proofs of their misdeeds were so abundant. Their not crediting the tales told of their boys' misconduct only encouraged them, until they grew almost hopelessly hardened in sin.

George's father was, however, very severe in his treatment of his boy, and would frequently inflict upon him a punishment which might have tamed a less spirited lad into submission. But the severest discipline seemed lost upon his high spirits, and he grew more stubborn and determined than ever. His mother was not acquainted with all his doings; but she knew enough to trouble her mind as to what his end would be. The attractions of the theatre were so strong upon him that he dared the violence of his father, and defied the entreaties of his loving mother, and resolutely determined to continue his evil practices. The wretch who received the goods stolen by the lads trained them to thieve on a still larger and more daring scale, giving for articles worth several shillings only the few halfpence which would enable the young thieves to attend the playhouse. The consequence of their early career was, that when they were put to employment on leaving school, they continued their acquaintance with each other, and stole, not only their masters', but also the workmen's tools. On one occasion they concerted a plan to break into the shop where one of the boys was engaged. They obtained a false key, and in the evening the lad within unbolted the door, and just as the boys without were about to gain admittance, they were interrupted by the master, and thus the burglary was prevented.

At length George's father listened to his mother's persuasions, and decided upon removing him away from his evil companions. He accordingly took him to work at his side in Sevenoaks, and fed him only on dry bread for a week. This punishment, so far from proving salutary, made the lad feel determined at any cost to escape from his father, and having obtained a shilling, he watched his opportunity, purchased a ticket at the railway station, and returned to London. He was followed by his father, and found at his mother's home, and was very severely chastised, and taken back to work. In the evening of the next day he ran to the station, and, without a ticket, jumped into a train. Arrived at the Elephant and Castle Station, he showed the ticket collector a hole (which he had only just cut) in his pocket, observing, "Look here, I've lost my ticket through this hole here." He was asked what station he had got in at, and replied that it was Camberwell. He was asked for the fare, which was only twopence, which was all the money he had in his possession.

About this time George's mother separated from her husband, and was thus relieved of the visits of the priest, whose talk of the efficacy of holy water did not commend itself to her judgment. If, however, she had sufficient enlightenment to disbelieve in the juggleries of priestcraft, she was not so well informed upon the way of acceptance with God. If she attended a place of worship with regularity, and took her children with her; and if she honestly resolved to sin no more, but to go on to moral perfection, she might attain unto, and fully merit, life eternal. This was her hope, and she set about working for her own salvation. In this state of mind she once went to hear Ned Wright preach in a hall at Camberwell, out of a feeling of curiosity, much prejudiced against the man whom her friend had designated as a "converted burglar." Ned was declaring, with his accustomed simplicity and energy, how that "Jesus Christ came into the world to save sinners," and how it was by relying upon His atonement that men could be saved. "Dear friends," said he, "it is the blood of Jesus Christ that cleanseth from all sin. Christ shed His blood on Calvary for our salvation. He Himself declared that His work was a finished work, and what you have to do is to believe on this finished work of Christ.

> "'Cast your deadly doings down,
>   Down at Jesus' feet;
> Stand in Him, in Him alone,
>   Gloriously complete.'"

This was a new kind of gospel to the stranger. She had been in many places of worship, but somehow had never heard the matter so plainly and so forcibly stated before; the message seemed so very simple that it suited her, and as she had endeavoured to gain the peace of mind which passeth all understanding by the deeds of the law, and had found no justification therefrom, but only perplexity, she would venture, if she might, to look to her Saviour for pardon and peace. She went home a happy, joyful woman, and began at once to pray for her children, especially her rebellious boy. George was pressingly invited to attend one of the services. For some time he declined, telling his mother that he wanted "tin," not Ned Wright; but at last yielded to her solicitations. He felt during the evening that the preacher was doing nothing else but talk about him; that he could mean no one else, and so he determined not to attend again. At the succeeding meeting, however, he was present, and felt again that the preacher knew all about his past life. "Surely," he reasoned, "mother has been telling him about me; and yet mother does not know scarcely anything that I have done, but Ned Wright knows it all." On the third occasion he was miserable in mind, and as the preacher discoursed of the terribleness of God's anger against the unrepentant, George's heart began to melt. The preacher, pointing, it seemed, to him, said, "My lad, do you love Jesus?" "I burst," says George, "into tears; for I was quite overcome. I felt I was such a sinner whilst Mr. Wright was preaching. He was telling us how that Jesus died on the cross for us sinners, and I wondered whether Jesus died for me; and when he spoke, and pointed to me, I could not help crying." A gentleman by his side addressed the young lad—at this time he was not more than fourteen years of age—and seeing he was affected, spoke words of encouragement and consolation to him.

"Are you a sinner?" said his friend.

"Oh, I'm a great sinner," was the heartfelt reply, "an awful sinner."

"Well, Jesus Christ died for sinners, and His blood cleanseth from all sin."

"But, sir, I'm such a big sinner," said George, as he sobbed aloud.

"There's power in the blood of Christ," said the gentleman, "to cleanse all your sin, be it ever so vile. Only believe in Jesus Christ, that He died on the cross for our redemption—for *yours*. Can you not believe that?"

It seemed as if the light of heaven had dawned upon George's mind. He felt that he could say without presumption that Christ died on the cross for him; and he went home praising God for his salvation. The next morning he called upon his old companions, the Irish boys who had led him into so much mischief, and told them that since he saw them last he had become a reformed lad; that the previous night God had been pleased to convert his soul, and therefore he could not enter upon any of his old evil practices. They threatened him that they would go to his father, and tell him about his conversion, but George was not afraid. They carried out their threat, and his father went to the priest, with what result we have already stated. His conversation about the power of the "holy water" was duly reported to the young heretic, who only replied, "Blood is stronger than water; I am saved by the blood of Jesus; and the power of the blood that saved me can keep me, and will keep me, praise the Lord."

George now began using his leisure time in distributing tracts to persons in the streets, feeling that he ought not to be ashamed of his profession as a soldier of Jesus Christ. He also conversed seriously with his senior sister, whom the priest was so anxious to put under the power of the water. This young girl had been convinced of sin under her Sunday-school teacher, in a Baptist chapel, and had sought in prayer a realized sense of forgiveness. She says,—

"While I was in this sad state of mind, seeking, but not finding, I did not know what to do. I went to father, who immediately placed me under the care of a nun named Sister —, at a nunnery in —, as a day-scholar. Here I was instructed in the Roman Catholic catechism, and in other books, to prepare me for being christened in the Catholic faith, and to prepare me for confession. It was arranged between my father, the priest, and the sister, that as soon as I was christened, and finished in the lessons of the catechism, I was to be sent to France to become a nun. Easter Monday, in 1868, was the day fixed for my christening, and I went to the chapel that day for that purpose. I dreaded it; but I was told that I must go to confession as soon as I was christened, and I thought I could never tell anybody all my sins. If I could only get away, I should be so glad.

"When the priest came to hear me say my catechism, I was frightened of him; he spoke so sharp and so unkind that he frightened all I had to say out of me, and I could not get on at all. So he put me back to learn my catechism more perfectly, especially the seven sacraments, and more particularly baptism and confirmation. As soon as I got out, instead of going home to father, for I dreaded his anger because of my not saying the catechism, I ran to Mrs. —, and after a while to mother.

The anxious feeling wore off, but mother was converted under you, Mr. Wright, and then my brother got converted also, and they would sing hymns, such as 'The blast of the trumpet'

> 'The blast of the trumpet, so loud and so shrill,
> Will startling re-echo o'er ocean and hill,
> When the mighty, mighty trump sounds,
> Come away, Oh, art thou prepared for that solemn day?'

Oh! I hated that hymn. I always got out of the hearing of that hymn: it terrified me so. I used to think if the trumpet was to sound, what would become of me? Then all my sins would rise up and terrify me, and make me miserable again.

"One night I was sent on an errand to your house with some work mother had been doing for one of the children, and Mrs. Wright began talking to me about my soul, and said Ned was going to open a new gospel hall in the New Cut on the next Sunday, and she invited me to come. At first I felt I would not do any such thing; but she pressed me so strongly and so kindly that I could not refuse her; so I promised I would do so, and I went to dinner and tea at your house, along with my mother. After tea you began to sing 'The blast of the trumpet' I could not bear to hear it I said to mother, 'There's that horrid hymn again;' but I could not get out, so I was compelled to hear it. At night you preached, and you spoke so sweetly of the love of Jesus, and so many looked so happy, I wished I was like them. Mother and every one seemed happy, except me; still I thought I loved Jesus, yet I could not get rid of this load of sin. When you finished, you gave out that hymn, 'Christ for me;' and you observed, 'Young men and maidens, can you say, "Christ for me"?' I wished I could. Although I sang it with my lips, I did not feel it in my heart.

"At the close of the service you said, if there were any anxious ones there, if they would follow you upstairs, you would be glad to sit by their side, and point the word of God out to them. So I went up with the others, and you began to read the third chapter of St. John's Gospel to us, and when you came to the 16th verse, 'Whosoever believeth m Him should not perish, but have everlasting life', you showed so clearly that 'whosoever' was me, and that it was not feeling but believing, that I believed in Jesus, obtained forgiveness on the spot, realized peace through believing, and have been rejoicing in the Lord ever since."

Young George felt a happiness that night which was inexpressible. His feeble prayers for his sister's salvation had been heard. He was transported with joy, and they all wept and praised God. The mother is now very useful in connection with Wright's "Mother's Meeting," and has been the means of leading several mothers to Jesus. "As a visitor," says Mr. Wright, "she has been untiring, going into the darkest parts of Lambeth and South London, visiting Roman Catholic families, reading and talking to them about Jesus, visiting the sick whenever she has an opportunity, for she has to earn for herself the bread that perisheth. Her daughter labours hard, and George is working with one of his teachers, and promises fair to become a very useful Christian."

Ned has been brought into contact with many Roman Catholics, and in not a few instances he has been useful in their spiritual enlightenment.

Interesting communications have been received from several of them, after conversion; the subjoined we give *verbatim:*—

"August 22, 1866.

"Dear Brother,

"Now i must rite a few words to you; before my conversion i was a Roman Catholic, and for a long time i like others used to worship the priest more than the Lord, for I was ignorant of what the Lord had done for me; but I was under the conviction of sin for two years, and about 2 years ago I was afflicted with apperplexy and several times I went to the Oritary at Brompton to be cured by the holy relic that is 40 priest. My Husband never had my faith in it but i did, but it was dead faith, for how can a man that is blind show another one how to see? I have been prepared fore death by priests different times when i had been taken with fits. May the God of all show the priests their blindness that they of themselves can do nothing, for it is all God's power and none but Jesus can do helpless sinners good. In last march the Lord laid it in my heart to go and hear the gospel preach by Mr. C— but he was not there but one of his helpers was there, that was dear brother Wright that preach the gospel, for i was under the conviction of sin for 2 years and i thank God that dear brother Wright was the means in God's hand of brining pardon and piece to my guilty sole.

"I thank God me and my dear Husband were saved both in one night, and we are now happy in Jesus.

"May God bless dear brother Wright and his dear wife in there own souls for ever. Amen.

"J— W—.

"'Let carnal men blaspheme,
   And worldly wisdom mock;
The Saviour's cross shall be my theme,
   And Christ Himself my rock.'"

SCRIPTURE TESTIMONY

*According to your faith
be it done to you*

MATTHEW 9:27-31

Mr. Wright visited this woman's house, which he found to consist of a top attic, in which she, her husband, and three children lived with her mother, who was a bitter opponent to Protestantism.

"At a glance," says Ned, "I saw by this woman's face that she deemed me an intruder; so I thought it would not be prudent to speak directly to her, but endeavour to strike her two or three very severe blows by way of speaking to her daughter. So I began to inquire as though I had heard nothing as to the dealings of the priests with the woman, who was subject to fits; and she began to tell me about the inability of the priests to perform a miracle. They had attempted a miracle, twelve of them gathering together for that purpose. At this, the old woman in the corner jumped up in a rage, and censured her daughter for daring to speak of the insufficient power of the priests to take away her fits, from which she had suffered many years, sometimes having three of them in one day. I now felt that the time was come for prayer; so I said, 'It is very evident that whatever the priests can do, they have hitherto failed to take away your fits; therefore, as the Bible says, there is but one mediator between God and man, and that is Christ Jesus; and so let us proceed to ask Him to accomplish that which the priests could not do.' We then fell upon our knees, and I prayed to God that He would exert His power, and show that He alone can forgive sins or cure fits. When I had finished, the poor wife cried to God, that He would take away this troublesome complaint, for the sake of His Son Jesus Christ, and so prove to her mother that Romanism was a delusion. Since then, not only has the poor woman's outward circumstances somewhat improved, but she has never had a return of her fits."

Most of the cases of conversion which come under Mr. Wright's notice are of a more or less striking character. The case of an aged shoemaker is in point. He was an habitual drunkard and a fearful blasphemer—scoffing at anything approaching a religious sentiment. One day his wife stepped into the Gospel Hall, and God was pleased to meet with her there. She became a Christian; and this change led to a series of cruel persecutions. Nothing could exceed the brutal behaviour of her husband; the Bible she had bought he forbade her to read, and dared her to take it from the dusty shelf on which he had placed it; and the meeting-house she attended he designated by opprobrious names, charging her with inconstancy whenever she had attended it. Sometimes, when enraged by drink, he would watch outside the hall, and as she came out would swear at, and otherwise ill-treat her. Still, none of these things moved her from her purpose; she persisted in reading the Scriptures, and sought every favourable opportunity to attend the means of grace. On the Sabbath he would work all day that he might faithfully observe St. Monday, and when in his drunken fits his conduct inspired terror in the minds of all his neighbours.

On one such evening his poor wife, presuming he would not return until midnight, ventured once more to go to the Gospel Hall, and towards the close of the service was pained to hear her husband's voice outside roaring like a maddened bull. She trembled with fear, believing that her husband's visit would

> **SCRIPTURE TESTIMONY**
>
> *Believers suffer for Christ,*
> *not common crime*
>
> I PETER 4:12-19
>
> *A man's foes will be those*
> *of his own household*
>
> MATTHEW 10:34-39 · MATTHEW 12:48-50 ·
> LUKE 8:19-21 · LUKE 9:59 · LUKE 12:49-53

create an unseemly disturbance, and that, infuriated at finding her there, he would kill her. He had so frequently threatened "to knock Jesus out of her," and to murder her, if she darkened the walls of the hall again, that she believed he would carry out his threat. She therefore went up to Ned Wright, and begged him to prevent her husband from entering the building, so that she might slip out unobserved. Before Ned could reach the door, however, the drunken fellow came staggering into the room, calling out most vociferously, "I want my wife; where is the —?" Ned sought to pacify him, but he failed; and seeing the poor trembling woman, her persecutor swore at her, and threatened to cure her of attending such a place. It was felt to be extremely undesirable, in his then state of mind, either to expostulate or in any way interfere; and so prayer was offered to God on the poor woman's behalf, that the violent hand of her wretched husband might be restrained.

Finding that he would not quit the building without her, she hastened out of doors, her tormentor assailing her all the way with awful imprecations and curses. Ned cried after him as he went along the passage,

"Be sure your sins will find you out! Be sure your sins will find you out!! Be sure your sins will find you out!!!"

"Find me out, eh?" said the retreating man, as he heard the warning words the third time; "find me out, eh? Well, we shall see."

Hurrying home, the agitated woman left her drunken husband to stagger along as he could; and having reached the house, she carefully hid every dangerous thing that he might turn into a weapon of attack, and knelt down in prayer that her heavenly Father might grant her special protection. What was her astonishment when, on her husband's arrival, she found he did not offer to assail her, may be imagined; her wonder was still further increased when she saw him sit down in a chair, and heard him mutter, "Find me out! Be sure your sins will find you out! What does he mean, eh?—find you out."

Throughout the rest of the evening he was in a semi-delirious state, every now and then repeating the words which Ned had addressed to him. The next morning he was quieter; and when he sat down to his work he seemed lost in thought, and during the whole of the forenoon he did not say a word, save when he whispered, as if to himself, the words which had so seriously impressed him.

Meanwhile his wife was silently crying to the Lord, that He would have mercy upon her husband; and whenever she heard him repeat the passage, "Be sure your sins will find you out," she begged that it might even be so, that he might see their enormity, and be rescued from the consequences of continuing in them. Towards evening he became sociable, and said to her, "Are you going to the hall tonight?"

"I should like to go," she meekly replied, "if you would allow me." To her joy he at once gave his consent. She longed to ascertain from him the state of his mind, but was for some time afraid. At last she ventured to inquire why he had asked about her going to the hall that night.

"Oh, nothing," was the reply; "but will Ned Wright be there tonight again?"

"Yes, I believe so," said the wife.

"Well, I'll go and see the fellow," was the rejoinder, "and ask him what he meant by hollering after me, 'Be sure your sins will find you out!'"

"I hope, however, you won't go to make a row there."

"No; you know I would not make any row when I'm sober: it is only when I get drunk, and then I'm a fool."

His wife was glad to hear so honest a confession from his lips; and although half afraid lest all might not end so well as she hoped, she left him and her cause with God, praying that that night might witness the conversion of her rebellious husband.

Although he was an old man, he had not been with his wife to the house of God since his marriage; everything was therefore new and strange to him, and the service naturally excited his curiosity. Ned Wright was the preacher, and, as usual, the sermon was charged with simple, forcible, evangelical truths. The stranger listened with an attention that was indicative of the great interest he took in the subject; and at the close he astonished every one by bursting into a flood of tears. Ned went and sat by his side, and explained to him how even a vile sinner could find mercy of a long-suffering and gracious Father. The man was as much affected by the story of the Saviour's love and willingness to save as he had been by feeling the greatness of his own iniquities; and when he felt in his heart the joy of salvation, his exhilaration of spirits was extraordinary.

His life now became very different. For the last four years the habitual drunkard has been free from his once besetting passion; and not only has he permitted his wife to become a Bible-woman, but he himself renders good service to the mission by acting as door-keeper.

CHAPTER NINETEENTH

CHAPTER NINETEENTH

O UT OF the very large number of letters received by Mr. Wright from persons who have been brought to the Saviour by his ministry, we propose now to make a selection. In some cases we retain the original orthography. In every instance care has been taken only to publish the letters of those who are now leading a consistent life.

The writer of the following letter is a seller of watercresses in London, who is well known in one district in the south of the metropolis as "Happy Bob." Prior to his conversion, he was one of the most dirty and ragged lads in the streets; but as soon as he was a changed charac-

SCRIPTURE TESTIMONY
Salvation transforms
2 CORINTHIANS 5:16-17 · GALATIANS 6:15
Followers of Christ care for their own household
I TIMOTHY 5:8

ter, he became remarkable for a most scrupulous tidiness and cleanliness. Instead of being a lazy vagabond, he is now a hardworking, cheerful young Christian; and through his industry he has kept his mother from entering the workhouse.

> "DEAR FRIEND,
> "I was invited into the Deptford theatre by a workingman, a gambler, a swarer, a skittle-player, a seane-shifter in this very theatre, were i was converted, and if any body ofended me no sunner the word than the blow, i work for the devil in the Deptford theatre

for 12 months, and now I serve the Lord of Lords witch is Jesus.
13 months ago i heard Brother rite lifting up Jesus on the Gosple
Book, and if God had cut me down, i set i should have gone to
hell, were hope and mercy never comes, the verce of schriptoor
that God blessed to my soul through my Brother Rite's lips was
this—"God so loved the world, that He gave His only begotten
Son, that hoosoever Believeth in Him should not perish, but have
everlasting life. He that Believeth on the Son hath Everlasting life.
He that believeth not on the Son shall not see life, but the wrath
of God abideth on him." The Blood of Jesus Christ, God's Son,
has cleansed me a 10 hundred pence deter from all sin.

"May the Lord bless you wherever you gow, and helpe you to lift
up Jesus like He did the night when God bless'd this one word to
my soul. May the Lord Bless you and i ask you to pray for my poor
deluded brother who i have to put up with much perchicushun
from. I was the first one the Lord saved in this theatre. Good bye.
I wish you God speed. Your brother in Jesus,

"R— R—."

The following epistle is from a very warm-hearted believer:—

October, 1864.

"DEAR FRENDS,

"i have bean one of the wust of Drunking Blasthemer and i
neither fearing God or man, but got stoped one night, and goin
long Dockhead wen i heard Nead Rite teling what God had done
for his soul, and ther for the first time in my life i knew that i
was a sinner, and from there God led me into a room and there
i heard that gospel Preched and heard that the blood of Jesus
Christ cleanses from all sin and there i felt i was a sinner in the
site of God; from that i was lead to the place called cal very and
there i found Jesus bearing my sins on the cross. Then i prased
God for his goodness toward a Rech like me Dear Friends i can
praise God now Becase god saved poor man poor Drunking man
like me, and from that time i praid for my wife for the saving of

her soul and God hear and answer my prayers and i also praied for my mothers soul answerd my prayer and now we can prais him togear, and now we are all pilgrims on our way to God and i can say I see Jesus for He Revel him self to me and now i can say precious Jesus precious Jesus precious Jesus thou art all in all to me

"yes i have been very happy ever since.

"R— W—."

The following is a letter from a backslider who lived for some years in sin:—

"Dear brother,

"I was converted at an early age, having been brought up in the fear of the Lord. I had the advantage of pious parents, was a Sunday scholar, and afterwards a teacher in the Baptist chapel at Cardiff, and, when a young man, played the clarionet in the singing; but subsequently I went to sea, and soon went into the depths of sin and degradation. I became a drunken blasphemer, a noted fighter, and one of the worst characters in the ship (except being dishonest).

"Miserable in my soul, I stifled my conscience with the drunkard's cup—even to giving up all thoughts of God; and in one of my maddened hours I offered to sell myself to the devil, that I might get money to rid myself from the man-of-war, and enjoy the unrestrained pleasures of this world.

"For years I continued in this state, until about two years ago I was working at a shipbuilding yard at Greenwich, when one Sunday night, in Deptford Broadway, I stopped to listen to a young man preaching; and when he was done, he announced that a converted burglar would tell how he was captured, at the Deptford Theatre at seven o'clock that night, I followed the crowd, as they sung, down to the theatre, and I went in, and there heard Ned Wright.

"During the address Mr. Wright asked a little girl that was near him on the stage if she was afraid to die, and the child said, no, for Jesus died for her.

"Mr. Wright then addressed the mothers, and urged them to pray for their children, for this child had been saved by a mother's prayers; and then addressing sinners, he spoke of some there who had praying mothers. I thought of my mother's prayers for me—conviction seized hold of me, all my sins arose before me; I was miserable. I saw my position before God. I left the theatre a changed man. I resolved to give up the drink from that hour, to leave off swearing and blaspheming, and to turn over a new leaf. Although happily for me I kept these resolutions, yet I could not find peace for my soul. I was wont to say, and that very often, 'Ned Wright was a great sinner, but I am a great deal worse than he.'

"During November, 1869, I removed to Lambeth, and one night I said to my wife, 'next Sunday night I will go to some place of worship.' Accordingly, on the night in question I strolled into Surrey Chapel; but observing the minister (the Rev. Newman Hall) ascend the pulpit in a white surplice, and commence reading the prayers, I thought it was the Church of England, and so took up my hat, and walked out, and went up the New Cut.

"When I got to No. 15, I observed a lighted lamp, with the words 'Gospel Hall,' 'God is love,' 'What think ye of Christ?' upon it; so I thought I would go in here for a little; and when I got in, I was surprised to find my old friend Ned Wright. I resolved to attend this place regularly, and on the third Sunday night I observed on the wall a large paper text, with the words 'Have faith in God' upon it. This was a message from God to my soul; it was a nail driven in by the Master of assemblies. I went home that night repeating that text, 'Have faith in God'. I retired to bed; but still, in the darkness of the night, I heard those words, 'Have faith in God'. Sleep left me, and during that night I was restored to God's favour.

"H—."

The subjoined note is appended to this letter by Ned Wright:

"Shortly after this man's restoration he went to work with his whole heart, sometimes hardly giving himself time to eat his food. He had not been restored to God long before it pleased the Almighty to lead his wife to the Cross. He now became very much concerned about his son at sea, and would seldom offer a prayer in the meeting without calling upon Him to protect his son who was away from home. Some of our crochety friends more than once said they did not think it necessary to be always praying about one thing; but, undaunted, our warm-hearted friend continued to wait upon God for his son's salvation, until one evening I observed, sitting beside this man, a sailor lad, apparently about seventeen years of age. The preaching being finished, I called upon two of the brethren to pray for the anxious souls. The words had hardly escaped from my lips, when this man arose to his feet, and exclaimed, evidently with a heart full of praise, 'I thank Thee, O God, that Thou hast heard my poor prayers, and saved my poor sailor boy!' This scene melted the whole of us to tears, and before we parted we saw several souls brought to know the pardon of their sins through faith in the finished work of Jesus. This man and his family have removed to another part of London, and are, I believe, living consistent lives."

The next letter is from a person who desires Mr. Wright to excuse "his educakson:"—

"Jennuary 30th, 1869.

"MY DEAR CRISTON BROTHER,

"I rite to you in the name of our Lord and Saviour jesus Christ, stating the state of my soul since i have ben caming to your hall, scence November, last year. That was a happee day for me, prays the Lord; I felt my sins was forgiven, thank the Lord for that, for if ever I love Jesus it is now, God bless is name. But, my dear brother, my reason for riting to you his to tell you that I have felt so happee in my mine everey since last Monday eveanin and Wednsday eveanin, and I should like to hear Christon brothers like yourself and them everey eavenin prech, if it was possible, for the benefit of all poor sinners like me. May the Lord make me thankfull for all his goodness to me.

"Pardon me for riting to you.

"I am, R— H—."

The three following letters are from persons who have now been exemplary Christians for four years past:—

"August 21st, 1866.

"DEAR BROTHER WRIGHT,

SCRIPTURE TESTIMONY
For God so loved the world *that He gave His only Son*
JOHN 3:16

"At your request I will try and tell you how Jesus found me one Sunday morning, while in school. Two others and myself were sitting on a form, and I asked them if they would come for a walk when we came out, and we all agreed; and I said to the two others, 'Will you come to the Surrey to-night?' They all agreed; and as we were going to the Surrey, I said to them, 'I will go to all the theatres that are open for preaching;' and they all said, 'So will I.'

"We went into the Surrey, and stayed about ten minutes, and then we all came out to go to the Victoria; when we got there, the brothers would not let us in; so we agreed to go along the Westminster Road, and over the bridge, and go home by the Strand; and as we were going by Astley's, I heard some of the brothers preaching outside, and when they had finished, they went into Wilcock's, and so we went in too, and sat down.

"Brother Wright was speaking, and so I sat still listening, my heart very nigh broke. About eight o'clock the other two asked me to come home, and I said I would stop until it was over; but they went out, and I followed them; and when we got outside, I said, 'That man very nigh broke my heart;' they said the same. I said to them, 'I will go next Sunday night;' they said the same (I was not converted then).

"The next Sunday night came; I called for them, but they would not come, but promised me they would go the following Sunday. I never went that Sunday, and so I called for them the next Sunday; then they would not come, and so then the devil wanted me to stop back; but I went by myself, and that same night I was converted. Brother Wright was speaking about God so loving the world as to give Jesus, and that whosoever believeth on Him should be saved; and so I thought my name was there, and I believed on Him and was saved; and I have been happy ever since that Sunday night (before Good Friday); but before, I was miserable; I used to dread night coming; and, oh! When I laid my head down, I used to think if I was never to open my eyes no more on this earth, where should I spend my eternity?

"The devil used to say, 'Oh, never mind, you will be a better boy tomorrow;' but when that tomorrow of his came, I was worse than before. Dear brother, when you are speaking, tell the people about me; tell the people that I could never find any peace anywhere, until I found peace in Jesus. I have been converted about five months, and was never so happy in all my life as I am now.

"Do pray for my father and mother to the Lord to save them.

"Believe me to be, yours affectionately,

"H— S—."

"July 23, 1865.

"MR. WRIGHT.

"DEAR SIR,—I write these few lines in grateful thanks, and the love of God to you, for the kind manner in which you

SCRIPTURE TESTIMONY
Believers have peace with God through the finished work of Christ
ROMANS 5:1-2

addressed me, and told me about the Lord Jesus. Blessed be God, I have realized that He died for a poor sinner like me on the cross, and bore my sins. Oh, Mr. Wright, you know I stood

before you a poor, miserable, drunken sinner, nearly lost. Oh! If
the Lord had cut me off in my sins, where would my poor soul
be? Oh, my soul, thanks be to God for Jesus. Blessed be His
name, he bore my sins on the cross to save my poor soul, that I
might live. Oh! He is my Saviour. Oh! The sinner ought to love
Him, and have faith in Him; He loves to save poor sinners; in
Him I have found peace, joy, and happiness, which I had not
till I found Jesus. Oh, Mr. Wright, before I met with you, I can
assure you the devil had fast hold of me; but the blessed Lord
Jesus has saved my soul.

"H— W—."

"August 24th, 1866.

"Dear Friend,

"When about sixteen, I left home, which was not a very
good one, and began gambling, such as bagatelle, dominoes,
and other things of vice, which of course wanted a good deal of
money to carry out, and my earnings were not enough; so, with
companions as bad as myself, I took to thieving, and was taken
up twice, found guilty, and had three months' imprisonment.
When there, I formed some good resolutions, thought I would
not pick up with my bad companions again but it was only in
myself, so it did not last long, and I was; as bad as ever again, or
even worse, always wanting to be going to the theatre or concerts,
or some gay place of amusement; so about this time, having a
brother in London, I thought I would go; so I told my mother
my intentions, and, she, thinking it best for me, as I should be
away from all my companions, consented to let me go; but after
I came to. London,, I was as bad as before, going into all kinds
of gay company, the theatres, and concerts, and every other gay
place; but after a time I was walking along the Blackfriars Road,
when I saw a young man preaching the gospel. I stood up to
hear him, and he said, 'Sinner! God loves you.'

"It quite struck me, although I did not know what it meant; but still I kept always thinking of those words; they seemed meant for me alone, but they were not so; for there were many more present. Then he began to read the 16th verse of the 3rd chapter of St. John: 'God so loved the world, that He gave His only begotten Son, that whosoever believeth on Him should not perish, but have everlasting life.'

"But the word 'whosoever' he kept calling out, it was not some that were called, it was all that would believe; after a short time he said they would sing a verse or two of a hymn, it was that one which begins

SCRIPTURE TESTIMONY
For God so loved the world that He gave His only Son
JOHN 3:16
Bad company corrupts good morals
I CORINTHIANS 15:33

with 'I do believe, I do believe, that on the cross He shed His blood for me;' after that he said he was going to the Victoria Hall which was close by. I went home, got the Bible, found the verse, and read it, and found the words he had repeated were the same. Then I began thinking how God could love such a helldeserving sinner as I had been, so I fell down on my knees, and prayed to Him to show me in what way I was to know that He loved me, and how I was to love Him. I continued praying and praying until Sunday evening. I went to the Victoria Theatre, and heard a dear young man preach, one who had been as vile a sinner as myself; and there I thought if God could forgive him, one who had stolen, and been a prize-fighter, He would forgive me; so, going home, I prayed, and continued praying all the week, asking God to forgive me; and the next Sunday I went to the Victoria Theatre again, and heard the gospel preached, and stayed to the prayer-meeting. It was then that I knew my sins, which were many, were all forgiven. Then the young man that had preached the gospel to us took me by the hand, and began singing that beautiful hymn,—

'There is a fountain filled with blood
　　Drawn from Immanuel's veins,
And sinners plunged beneath that flood
　　Lose all their guilty stains.'

"I then went home rejoicing in the Lord, and told many what He had done for me; and ever since I have been much happier than before; thank God for it!

"I am, dear friend, yours most truly,

"A— A—.

"Mr. E. Wright"

CHAPTER TWENTIETH

CHAPTER TWENTIETH

M R. WRIGHT still continues his evangelistic labours in the country. Although the metropolis affords a wide scope for his peculiar gifts, he deems it better not to confine his efforts to the great city. To preach Sabbath after Sabbath in one hall would be a tax upon his powers which they might not sustain. He is confessedly an evangelist, an itinerant missionary or preacher. "And He gave some apostles; and some, prophets; *and some, evangelists*; and some, pastors and teachers; for the perfecting of the saints, for the work of the ministry, for the edifying of the body of Christ." The office of such evangelists was to preach the gospel where it was not known, and their diocese was the world. This is the object of Ned's ambition. He does not aim at the instruction of those who are already Christians; his one absorbing purpose is to declare the gospel to those who may be attracted by his plain, forcible language. He knows the peculiar temptations which beset the lowest classes of society; he can enter into their feelings, meet their difficulties, and gain their rapt attention. It would be a pity, therefore, to confine such a man to one particular district, or even to one city, however large its dimensions. Let those who can arouse the uncultured, the ignorant, and the criminal, be thrown loose upon the country, to storm as best they may, and as God shall help them, some of those frowning ramparts of sin which a more regular ministry cannot always so successfully assail. Such men are among the best helpers of Christian ministers, and as such should be welcomed and encouraged.

In some of the large towns he has visited, large audiences, composed of all classes, have awaited him. Men of culture have listened with profit to his earnest eloquence, and have thanked him for his honest and searching appeals to their consciences. In one town he visited, a magistrate was converted to God the through his instrumentality; and numbers whose religion was but a thin veneering of piety, just enough to be recognized by man, but insufficient to meet with the approbation of a jealous God who abhors lukewarmness and a frigid profession of faith,1 were led to a higher and truer Christian life. Men and women who could boast of little else but their morality have been awakened from their sleep of death; while many, whose lives, on the score of morality, would not bear inspection, have become earnest and exemplary believers in Christ.

Of Ned's visit to Ireland we have already given some incidents, and others might be recorded. At *Dublin*, the preacher aroused the wrath of a critic, who favoured him with the following choice epistle:

"Dublin, 4th Oct, 1866.

"RESPECTED FRIEND,

"I was in the Metropolitan Hall last night, for a few minutes, while you spoke of the abandoned life you led before (as you say) your conversion; but in my opinion I do not think it right for men like you, with only a small amount of education, to stand up in the place of a minister of the gospel, and attempt to expound the Bible. What use would there be in a college such as Oxford, or Cambridge, or Dublin University, if any one could stand up? A few months ago a fellow got up out of a coalpit, and told us he was a ruffian, and so forth, and that now he was a saint. After came a blacksmith; and you come—a prize-fighter. No wonder for the Church of Rome to sneer at us Protestants. I do not at all want to hurt your feelings, or to daunt you; but let me tell you that you should first go to college, and then preach. And when you told us that many a time when the devil was in you that you would strike your father to the ground, you might have kept that

---

1   Revelation 3:14-18.

to yourself; for it well showed the audience that you were unsuitable to stand up and preach to an enlightened audience. Besides, you said there was *plenty* of people in the hall whose hearts were black in sin. Now, sir, how do you know that they were black in sin? Anybody knows that a preacher's life is easier than a baker's.

"I remain, with all respect,

"Your friend,

"A PROTESTANT.

"P.S.—I will be in the hall to-night, and will answer if you call me.

"A P.

"Mr. E. Wright."

Accordingly Ned called for the Protestant baker to avow himself, but received no answer.

At *Paisley*, Ned encountered a Protestant baker with other results. This man, after conversion, manifested an enthusiasm for souls which God was pleased to reward with several conversions. He sought with earnest persistency the salvation of both grown-up people and little children. He took his son to one of Ned's meetings, and also a man who had been a confirmed drunkard, and both were savingly converted the same evening. This occurred while Ned, in company with another evangelist, was on a month's preaching tour in Scotland. "I had a little room engaged in Paisley," says Ned, "where we met for prayer before the Sunday. By the Saturday night we had well covered the town with handbills; but to make sure of a good meeting, I hired a large bell, and walking slowly down the streets, ringing it, I shouted as I went along, 'It's to-morrow night, at the Abercom Rooms, at half-past six o'clock, seats all free, and there's nothing to pay.' In answer to a question from an old man, I said, 'There's a man come down here from London, who has been dead for five and twenty years, but he has been brought to life in a most mysterious way, and he's going to appear at the Abercom Rooms to-morrow night.'" By these peculiar methods of advertising, Ned succeeded in getting an audience on Sunday night of six hundred persons, to whom he related the deeply interesting story of his conversion after being "dead in trespasses and sins" for five and twenty years.

At *Glasgow*, he found a little difficulty in his way. For some reason all the halls were closed against him, but the Queen's Rooms; these the landlord would not let unless Ned's soberer companion pledged himself to preach a quiet discourse. Ned, at this time, was inexcusably noisy, and his stentorian lungs and basoon-like voice were scarcely acceptable to the quiet folks of Glasgow. However, Ned must be himself; and as this was in the earlier part of his career as a preacher, he could not be restrained. A good opportunity for preaching the gospel presented itself to him as he was walking one day in the streets with two of his companions. To use his own expression, he was "boiling over" to speak. "Directly I stopped in the middle of the road, and shouted out the most solemn passages of Scripture I could think of, my two friends quietly walked on to the pavement; and not caring to part company with them, I moved on too, keeping on shouting; but at this my two friends began to trot. So, thinks I, Ned must trot too; but not caring to be seen by the landlord of the Queen's Rooms in company with such a noisy character as myself, they took to their heels, and ran for it. Seeing this, I did the same, shouting, as I did so, 'Stop 'em, stop 'em!' Of course, as I ran, the people did the same, and so I continued to cry out, 'Stop 'em, stop 'em!' My friends at last stopped short, thoroughly exhausted, at the bottom of a steep hill, and I ran at once to them; and, thinking that was the only way by which I could accomplish my purpose, I put my hand upon Howard's arm, and cried out, 'I've got them, I've got them!' The people soon gathered round, and in less than five minutes there was a large crowd. My two friends were ready to burst with laughter; but I managed to keep my countenance, and commenced addressing them." Beginning by turning his race and capture of his friends to good illustrative account, he went on to speak of how Christ came to seek and to save that which was lost. The other speakers aided Wright, and the meeting proved successful.

At *Greenock*, the preaching party went to a fair, where they purchased an egg-chest, which served as a platform, from which Ned delivered addresses to the pleasure-seeking crowds.

A series of meetings held at *Brighton* were greatly owned of God. The Oxford Music Hall was crowded to excess, hundreds being unable to gain admittance, and several most interesting instances of the power of God's grace were brought to light. Similar results flowed from preaching in *Ipswich*.

At *Wilton*, he preached in the Independent Chapel, which was thrown open for working people. "It was cheering," says an account which appeared in the newspaper, "to see these poor men and women coming up by hundreds to hear one from among themselves. On Monday the people again came by hundreds, some from a distance of eleven miles." A young woman had left the meeting convinced of sin; in the middle of the night she got up, saying to her mother, "I cannot lie any longer; I must see the preacher." Accordingly the mother went to Ned's lodgings, just as he was falling asleep, and begged him to see her daughter at once. He did so, and after prayer the girl professed to find peace.

At *Folkestone*, several services have been held at various times, and very pleasing reports have been furnished of good done there. Several young people were brought to the Saviour,

SCRIPTURE TESTIMONY
Be reconciled to your brother   *before going to the altar*
MATTHEW 5:23-24

one who was a Sabbath-school teacher. Two boys, living in the town, had quarrelled, and they retired to a convenient spot where they might indulge in a fight. At last one of them was so severely thrashed that he had to give in, though he vowed vengeance upon the adversary who had beaten him. In the evening, led by curiosity, both lads unexpectedly met at the townhall, where Ned Wright was preaching. In the course of his address, Ned alluded to an incident which occurred in his own life that was in direct contrast to these lads' behaviour to each other. The narrative deeply affected the defeated, but vindictive lad, who stretched out his hand to his companion, and bursting into tears, said in a broken voice, "I'm very sorry indeed for what I said to you to-day up yonder; but I hope you will forgive me, and let us be friends again." It is not every boy who had vowed vengeance against an antagonist, 'who would submit voluntarily to make an apology; but the other boy was as manly in his reply, when he said, " I was as much to blame as you, and I hope you will forget all that has happened, and let us be firm friends for the future."

Some of the letters received by Mr. Wright from persons who trace their conversion to hearing the gospel he preached at Folkestone are very affecting; and, as a token of their appreciation of his services, a number of persons presented him with a very handsome dressingcase, accompanied by a letter, which said,

> "We, the undersigned, wish to present you with a token of our deepest gratitude and affection for the many blessings which God has made you the means of conveying to us; above all, for that greatest of blessings, the knowledge of a Saviour's love, of which many of us have been ignorant up to this time.
>
> "We trust that we shall live in your memory and in your prayers, as you will in ours. May God bless you more and more in the sphere in which he has placed you; and that we may all meet at His right hand in glory is the prayer of all who love you."

The testimonial is signed by eighteen persons.

After preaching one evening at a country place about sixteen miles from London, Ned, needing refreshment, called at a public-house, and had a bottle of ginger-beer in the tap-room.

SCRIPTURE TESTIMONY
No one can serve two masters
MATTHEW 6:20-24 · LUKE 12:22-34

"As soon as we entered," says Ned, "we found four or five men smoking their pipes, some at the table, and one young man sitting in the chimney corner, who at once took his pipe from his mouth, and concealed it with his hands; but the smoke oozing out between his fingers, I said, 'Go on with your pipe, old chap; don't be afraid of me.' 'Amen,' cried one; 'So be it,' said another; but our young friend said, 'Well, sir, I am not like these here; I know that I have a soul, and that it is unsaved, and I am on the road to hell.' I found out that he had been listening to me on the night previous, so I pointed him to Jesus; and taking advantage of the opportunity, I dropped down upon my knees, and poured out my soul to God for his salvation. On opening my eyes, after I had done praying,

I found all the pipes were out, and the landlord and his wife were kneeling by my side. Before I left the house, both the landlord and his wife, and also the young man, professed to have found the Saviour. And the following day, just before I left the place, I learnt that the landlord had sent an advertisement to a local paper, announcing his intention to sell his public-house: his reason for doing so was that he could not serve two masters, and so he meant to quit the business altogether."

Of the character of Ned's work in the metropolis, we have given many illustrations, as also of his special efforts among thieves. The services in the Gospel Hall are conducted by his many helpers during his absence. Some of these helpers are earnest and intelligent men, who have gained the ear of the poor, and know well how to tell the story of the Cross. Special meetings, in addition to those for the dishonest, have been held at various times. Tea meetings for mothers, for costermongers, and others have been highly successful. In 1869, a few young converts clubbed together to pay the rent of the Milton Hall, near the Elephant and Castle, for a few weeks, that Ned might preach there. Two "midnight meetings" for fallen women have been held—the second being protracted till eight o'clock in the morning, when Ned accompanied twenty-one of these poor creatures to a home. It was a bitterly cold morning, a severe north wind, rain and sleet falling heavily. Some of the girls had borrowed either their bonnets, or shawls, or boots, and had to send them back before they could go to the home. It was a pitiable sight to see them trudging along the Blackfriars Road, some without bonnets and others without shawls, and most but ill-clad. The "way of transgressors" did seem hard. One poor girl, fair as a flower, was admitted to Guy's Hospital, where she died, rejoicing that "her sins which were many, were all forgiven her."

Many incidents that occur in the course of some of the services at the Gospel Hall would startle the reader as unheard-of novelties in religious worship. Interruptions, however, occur but rarely. Sometimes urgent requests for prayer are made. Thus, a young man pencils a letter to Mr. Wright, asking as a favour that he would pray for him. "I am sure," he says, "your prayers will be heard. I have been out of employment ever since my conversion; but, thanks be to God, I am not sorry for my conversion. So

I hope you will offer up a prayer or two, and God will answer them. Bless the Lord for everything. So I now leave it with you. From a young convert that is in the meeting at the present time. Amen."

Cases have occurred in which, under the influence of powerful appeals, persons have even screamed aloud for mercy. One evening, while Ned was solemnly discoursing on the terrors of the lost, a lady-like woman shrieked as if in agony, and cried for Heaven's forgiveness. Her terror of mind was fearful, and awakened sympathy in the breasts of all present. The same evening, however, she professed to have found the Saviour, and her radiant face spoke of the hidden calm which had possessed her heart. This woman had belonged to good society; but one false step in life had divorced her from her husband and all her friends. For twenty years she had bitterly repented of her sin, and had been told by a clergyman to whose ear she had confided her sorrowful history, to go on repenting; but it was not until she heard Ned preach that she learnt that there was forgiveness with God, that He might be feared. Her means were very limited, and she had contracted debts which, it is believed, have now by her industry been entirely paid.

Sometimes Ned is favoured with letters by persons who for various reasons do not desire to give their names and addresses; and these communications relate to the good impressions which they have received from his preaching. A desire to test the sincerity of the change which they hope and believe they have realized, induces some of them to suppress for a time their names. One correspondent thanks the preacher for so plainly preaching Christ, and begs that he will ask God to reveal Himself to the writer's distracted heart; another complains of spiritual deadness, and manifests the energy of his religious life by deploring the evil to which he fears he is subject; another has been perplexed by difficulties of a doctrinal type, and has been harassed by theological doubts.

> **SCRIPTURE TESTIMONY**
>
> *At the right time, Christ came and died for sinners*
>
> ROMANS 5:6

One young woman, brought up with those who had espoused an extreme Calvinism, was in much distress of mind as to whether she could be "one of the elect." Ned had met this young woman at a Night Refuge, and finding her to be a moral and upright person, though in the deepest distress, he took her home with him, and Mrs. Wright speedily procured her some food. "When this was placed before her," says Ned, "although only a piece of broiled haddock, with a cup of tea and some bread and butter, it was with difficulty we got her to eat: the cause of this, no doubt, was the natural effect of going without food for three days and two nights. However, after two or three attempts, she managed to consume the meal, when I thought it my duty to speak to her upon the more important question of her soul's salvation." In the course of conversation, Ned found that not only was she well acquainted with Scripture—she had almost learnt "the Psalms" by heart—but was able to reason very speciously. It was some few weeks before the stranger felt the power of the gospel.

"It was wonderful to see the rebellion of this precious soul against the truths of the gospel. At times she would start up and exclaim, 'Does not the Bible say, "Elect according to the foreknowledge of God," "Predestinated from before the foundation of the world"?' In answer to which I said, one night, when she had been with us about three weeks, Can you tell me whether this special class of persons for whom Jesus died had any particular name by which they might be distinguished or not?' At this question she hesitated, and noticing her hesitation, I said, 'now, I believe that the special class of persons for whom Jesus died, and rose again, are called by a particular name, the two first letters of which are I shall say no more about it tonight, but leave you to guess between this and the morning what this name really is, and whether you are included among the number.' I and my dear wife had no sooner adjourned to our bedroom, and closed the door, than we both knelt down and cried to God that He would awaken this most precious soul to see her lost and ruined state. The morning came, when, as a family, we met for prayer and reading, at the close of which I abruptly asked my young friend whether she had found out the name the people were called by for whom Jesus died. Tears started from her eyes, and rushed down her cheeks, as, with utterance half-choked she said, "The only name I can think of—and I have been thinking of it all night—to which the initials refer, is that of sinner.' 'Then,' said I, do you think you are included in that little word?' To which she exclaimed, 'Yes, I believe it; I am a sinner, and I can believe that Jesus died for me.' And we all praised God that the lost was now found, and the lame had been made to walk."

This young woman was put to honest employment, and aided to emigrate. This is not the only distressed person whom Ned has befriended, and saved from poverty and crime. Even in his poorest circumstances, the friendless have shared his meals with him, and have been sheltered by his worthy wife, until they have gained work. Indeed, labouring, as he does, among those who have sunk into the deepest poverty, it is essential that help should be afforded them. The missionary to the poor must help them when facing starvation, if he desires to succeed in his spiritual mission. Whatever may be the faults of indiscriminate charity,—and there is a danger of magnifying them,—the relief that is granted to those who are personally known to be deserving must be humane and Christian. We hope that Mr. Wright may not fail to receive, in carrying on his good work, that measure of support which a Christian public is not loth to give to a deserving and philanthropic object. For his soup suppers, relief agencies, and the rent of the buildings in which he carries on his labours, he is necessarily dependent on public aid, and feels at liberty to appeal for such a purpose, although for his own and his family's maintenance he is, as we have before said, supported by those who feel moved at various times to keep him from want.

He is now treating with a railway company for the rent of a capacious arch in a district where many dishonest persons reside, at £10 per annum. To fit up this arch for public meetings, the modest sum of £30 only is required; and this, in addition to serving as a hall, will afford shelter for Bible barrows, and answer as a stable for ponies and donkeys, a few of which he proposes sending round the villages with the barrows, the hand barrows being used entirely for London. It is also in Ned's heart to employ carpenters in this arch, who have lost their tools, in making Bible barrows and other articles, which will enable them to gain other tools, and thus aid them in a fresh start in life. Above all is he solicitous that the gospel should be preached to the poor, the social outcast, to those who doggedly profess to have no confidence in either ministers or missionaries, of whom there are, alas! Too many amongst the lowest classes in the great city. In this noble work our prayers follow him. "We have confidence in the Lord touching him," that in all his enterprises for God's glory and man's welfare he will be led, guided, and sustained by the Good Hand which has thus far upheld him.

SCRIPTURE TESTIMONY INDEX

279

In a vision, Ned is brought before the judgement seat of God where he's found guilty of sin. So vivid was this vision that Ned finally surrendered his life to the Lord.

The very night Ned became a new man in Christ Jesus, his heart of stone towards his children was replaced with a tender heart, full of love and compassion. No longer would he be a reckless father, he vowed instead to henceforth act the part of a Christian parent.

On the night Ned and his wife became Christians, they received a very timely visitor in the person of a Christian man who was able to encourage, direct and strengthen them in their newfound faith.

Ned had no food to feed his family and was tempted to provide for them "either by fair means or foul." But he resisted the devil even in this desperation and turned to God for help. Within an hour after praying, God answered and provided for the family.

Smoking was one demon Edward Wright struggled to defeat, even after his conversion. While not expressly forbidden in the Scriptures, his wife feared it could lead him back into worse habits. One night as he sat in his garden to smoke, his apprehensive wife went to God in prayer on his behalf. That night her prayers were answered. Ned never smoked again.

Ned found "grace to help in time of need" when he was enabled by God, to resist the devil's offer to make dishonest gain at a vulnerable period in his life. Not only did he overcome, but he was blessed to receive the exact sum he had refused to receive via dishonest means.

Ned was regarded as the last person in the world to turn from his drinking habits. Yet, having found the Lord Jesus, this same Ned was now preaching to his old companions. He was now truly a new man for old things—like his drinking habit—were gone for good.

Abused daily by foul language and malicious acts, Ned was so provoked one day that he grabbed the offender and almost threw him off the dock. But at that moment, God came to mind and Ned relented and repented. But while he was sure God had forgiven him, he had no peace until he returned and asked the unpleasant man to forgive him.

Ned's simple faith in the power of prayer was greatly strengthened when he was unexpectedly left alone to pilot a giant barge through a narrow bridge opening. He prayed specifically, telling the Lord his trouble. His heavily laden barge safely passed through, without any human assistance.

Delicate in health since his birth, Ned's young son Teddy showed an unusual spiritual sensitivity which led him to share the love of Jesus with others, and to sweetly prepare him for an early death.

Ned was preaching one night and quoted Proverbs 15:3, 'The eyes of the Lord are in every place, beholding the evil and the good,' at the very moment a thief had his hand in the pocket of his potential victim. The Holy Spirit used this text to powerfully convict, and then to convert, the would-be criminal.

Ned Wright recounts how a detective, clever but unable to apprehend him before his conversion, was deeply moved by the message of Christ during an open-air Bible reading. Later, as the detective lay on his deathbed, tormented by the weight of his own sins, Ned was able to share the love of Christ and His power to cleanse from all sin, leading the dying man to find peace and salvation.

In the bustling streets of Stamford and Trinity, a chance encounter with Ned Wright led a young man burdened by the weight of his sins to the foot of the Cross, where he discovered for himself that Jesus casts away no one who comes to Him.

Ned seized every chance, be it rain or shine, in season or out, as an occasion to preach Jesus. His unwavering commitment to casting bread upon the waters bore fruit, bringing forth a rich harvest of souls for his Master.

In a remarkable testament to the transformative power of salvation, Ned Wright, formerly a source of fear in a neighbourhood, returned years later. This time he came not as a burglar, but as a messenger of the gospel, reaching out to men, women, and children with the message that had rescued him from a life of thievery.

Throughout his preaching ministry Ned encountered frequent opposition, yet he was undaunted. His great patience, even in the face of repeated provocation, ultimately led to the conversion of a disruptive drunkard.

Looking within, Ned had the best evidence of what the gospel could accomplish, and thus he was unshaken in his faith. This made him feel that no devil-beguiled creature was out of the reach of Divine mercy. Through his own testimony he was able to help the most hardened sinners come to Jesus.

When H——, a wild and reckless individual since his teenage years, listened to Ned's account of his terrible past and the transformative power of God's salvation, he found hope that a similar change could occur in his own life. He was right, as the same love of God that rescued Ned reached H——, turning him into a new man.

A heartfelt letter written to Ned Wright recounts the writer's tumultuous journey from the streets of London to redemption. The profound declaration of God's love for all sinners as captured in John 3:16 was the turning point for this wanderer, who today, despite hardships and temptations, remains faithful to His Lord and Saviour.

Ned resolved to live dependent upon whatever the goodness of the Lord might supply him. In confirmation he received a timely gift and an invitation to preach. From that time onward he lived by faith and never made his needs known except to God.

Inspired to preach to poor thieves-his former friends, Ned secured a house for his mission, trusting that God would provide the £60 rent. Within weeks donations poured in, enabling the transformation of the place into a venue where hundreds of lives were changed.

Ned was facing a £10 shortfall to pay the hall rent and turned to prayer with fellow believers. The next day, at the very last moment, as he started to his meeting with the landlord, a mysterious letter arrived containing a £10 note wrapped in a blank sheet of paper.

After tearing his beloved top-coat, Ned and his simple-hearted wife prayed for a new one. An anonymous letter arrived the very next morning, directing him to a prestigious outfitter, where he found a perfect replacement for his overcoat.

Ned and his companion, on a foggy journey from Dublin to Liverpool, seized a divine opportunity to preach the gospel to a crowded boat of Irish laborers bound for the English harvest. In the thick darkness Ned's voice pierced through proclaiming salvation, and as the fog lifted, it was clear that the light of the gospel had illuminated not just the physical surroundings but also the hearts of those who listened, bringing joy and transformation.

With a heart full of compassion for men trapped in sin, much like he was before finding redemption, Ned Wright held soup suppers. These gatherings went beyond sharing the word of God, they became havens offering temporary housing, support, and employment opportunities to many who were marginalized.

A jeering crowd of six hundred at a Flint-street schoolroom meeting was silenced when Ned abruptly knelt on the platform in prayer. This preemptive approach exceeded even Ned's expectations, leading to the redemption of thirty souls.

Upon discovering the Lord and repenting of his sins, the transformation in a man's life became unmistakable to all. His nine-year-old daughter, curious about the sudden shift from a wicked father to a virtuous one, pondered whether the prospect of dying was to blame for his remarkable change. But through her father, she too found new life in Jesus.

A man, burdened by guilt and the weight of his past transgressions, resolved to lead a better life on in the new year. But the resolution was a mere "castle in the sky." The Holy Spirit fire of conviction continued to burn in his heart until he saw that even the most undeserving can find salvation, but only through the free grace of the merciful Savior.

Tom's rebellious path as a shoe shiner took an unexpected turn when he encountered a steadfast Christian coworker. Despite facing persecution, from Tom and others, this quiet and industrious believer only responded with kindness and prayers for those who persecuted him.

Mr. Wright's earnest prayer, calling upon the power of Christ for forgiveness and healing, became the conduit for God's intervention, miraculously curing a woman plagued by fits.

Believers suffer for Christ, not common crime
1 Peter 4:12-19

*Matthew 10:34-39 · Matthew 12:48-50 · Luke 8:19-21 · Luke 9:59 ·
Luke 12:49-53*

After she surrendered to the Lord Jesus and became a Christian, a woman became the object of her husband's drunken persecution. He verbally abused her, threatened her life, and otherwise opposed her newfound faith.

Salvation transforms
2 Corinthians 5:16-17 · Galatians 6:15

1 Timothy 5:8

When a lazy vagabond found the Lord and became a new creation, the change in his life was visible for all to see. He became known for cheerfulness, industry, and cleanliness, and he worked hard to support his mother.

John 3:16

In a letter to Edward Wright, a brother told the story of his conversion, which started with his bold decision to leave his unwilling friends and to attend a service alone. Ned preached about God's love and the offer of life to all who would believe in Jesus, this brother believed and was converted.

Romans 5:1-2

In a brief but no less profound letter, a grateful man wrote to Edward Wright, thanking him for kindly sharing with him the gospel of Jesus. The man blessed the Lord for the happy change the Gospel brought to his previously miserable life.

For God so loved the world that He gave His only Son
John 3:16

1 Corinthians 15:33

Spurred on by bad friends, a young man had taken up theft in order to support his gambling habit for which he was twice imprisoned. His resolutions to change his ways failed. But one day while walking along a road, he heard a preacher declare, "Sinner! God loves you!" That statement, along with the rest of John 3:16, led him into the saving arms of Jesus.

Be reconciled to your brother before going to the altar.............271
Matthew 5:23-24

Two boys in Folkestone had a quarrel and went on to fight with the defeated one vowing to exact revenge on the other. That same evening, they met at a townhall where Ned Wright was preaching and were both convicted of their sins. They apologized to each other and reconciled one to another.

No one can serve two masters...272
Matthew 6:20-24 · Luke 12:22-34

In a public-house Ned Wright knelt and prayed for an opium-smoker. He opened his eyes to find the pub owner and his wife kneeling beside him. All three persons confessed Jesus as Lord. The next day, the pub owner puts his place up for sale, saying that he could not serve two masters and so he meant to quit the business altogether.

At the right time, Christ came and died for sinners...................274
Romans 5:6

Ned met a woman at a night refuge and took her home to his wife. Together they provided this woman with food and shelter for weeks. The woman had significant Biblical knowledge but was rebelling against God over the prevailing doctrine of predestination. But Ned was able to share the simple gospel with her, helping her to see that Jesus died for all sinners and not just a select few.

Walking Together Press is a non-profit publishing company devoted to supporting grassroots libraries in Africa through global book sales and through providing free library editions.

To read our story, to see our catalog, and to learn more about how you can help us in our mission, visit our website at:

https://walkingtogether.press